THE
MUMMY
CONGRESS

THE
MUMMY
CONGRESS

SCIENCE, OBSESSION,
AND THE EVERLASTING DEAD

HEATHER PRINGLE

NEW YORK

LIBRARY OF CONGRESS CATALOGING-IN-PUBLICATION DATA

Pringle, Heather Anne.
    The mummy congress : science, obsession, and the
everlasting dead / Heather Pringle.—1st ed.
        p.   cm.
    Includes bibliographical references.
    ISBN 0-7868-6551-2
    1. Mummies.   2. Human remains (Archaeology).
3. Forensic anthropology.   4. Physical anthropology.
5. Body, Human—Social aspects.   I. Title.

GN293 .P75 2001
393'.3—dc21
                                            00-054487

Book design by Richard Oriolo

FIRST EDITION

10 9 8 7 6 5 4 3 2 1

FOR ALEX SENIOR,
WHOSE LOVE AND WISDOM SURPASS
EVEN HIS SKILL ON THE ICE

I will have more to say when I am dead.
—E. A. ROBINSON

CONTENTS

THE
MUMMY
CONGRESS

THE
CONGRESS

~

I N   T H E   G R A N D   S C H E M E   O F scientific meetings, the
Mummy Congress is a small, intimate affair, long on singular personalities and surreal slide shows and short on
sophistication, hype, and ballyhoo. There are, after all, far
larger scientific meetings, gatherings where thousands of
name-tagged delegates in identical conference bags swarm
city streets like ants, taking over every cab, restaurant, and
bar in sight. There are also far more sophisticated events,
where the world watches through simultaneous Webcasts
and where handlers manage large, jaded crowds of reporters.
And there are certainly far more lavish affairs where atten-

dees dine in gilded French châteaux or toss back glasses of chianti in Tuscan vinyards, all paid for by generous corporate sponsors. But the Mummy Congress is none of these things. It is not large. It is not savvy. And it certainly is not deluxe. What makes the Mummy Congress so memorable—some might say gloriously eccentric—is something a good deal rarer and far more interesting. It is the odd, lonely passion of its delegates. With few exceptions, those attending the congress love mummies. And they relish being around others who feel the same way.

This strange shared passion colors nearly every aspect of the congress. But it makes itself particularly known in the organizers' choice of a host city. During three years of planning, those responsible for the Third World Congress on Mummy Studies, as it was officially known, paid little attention to the amenities that preoccupy most other conference organizers—an abundance of fine five-star hotels and good restaurants, the existence of colorful nightlife and sightseeing opportunities, the availability of good airline connections and cheap fares. Indeed, they ignored all obvious places to host such a conference—grand cities like Cairo, New York, and London—and found a spot much more to their tastes. They chose Arica, population 180,000, a tiny dot on the map of northern Chile. Nearly a thousand miles north of Santiago, Arica perches on the frontier of a vast, almost lifeless desert, the Atacama. Arica's claims to fame are modest at best: it possesses a very good port on the Pacific and a large fish-meal plant. It also boasts a church and customs house designed by Alexandre Gustave Eiffel, the famous French engineer, after a tidal wave had washed away part of the town.

Over the years, local tourism officials have tried very hard to lure visitors to Arica. They dubbed Arica the "City of Eternal Spring," an epithet that rather glossed over its dry, brittle climate, and they encouraged Chilean families to holiday along the spectacular beaches that lined the waterfront. But Arica never really took off as a tourist town. The ocean, cooled by the frigid Peru current, is simply too chilly for anyone to contemplate leisurely swims. Only a few hardy surfers in head-to-toe wet suits dare brave its whitecaps for long. And hardly anyone is interested in roaming the barren Atacama: it is too vast, too intimidating, too fierce. As a result, Arica remains dusty and rather insular. To fly there, many delegates to the Mummy Congress spent twenty-four hours or more jackknifed in airline seats and nodding off to sleep in a series of ever smaller departure lounges. Indeed, one determined researcher hauled herself off and on eleven successive flights from Beirut.

But Arica had one sterling qualification in the eyes of the Mummy Congress organizers, and that single attraction more than compensated for all its many shortcomings as an international conference center. For Arica, unknown to most of the world, is blessed with almost perfect conditions for the long-term preservation of the human body. Bordering what is likely the driest place on earth, the Atacama Desert, it receives just three one-hundredths of an inch of rain in an average year. In bad years, it receives none at all. This relentless, inescapable aridity is precisely what is needed to dry a human corpse to the texture of shoe leather and to keep it that way. Arica abounds in mummies. It is a mummy expert's Mecca. To see these remarkable treasures and to catch up on the latest mummy news, scientists had converged on the little Chilean port from what seemed the far ends of the earth.

On the night before the congress opened, a certain euphoria infused the parched desert air in the lobby of the Hotel Arica, a sprawling beachfront resort complete with shady palm trees and nonstop Andean panpipe music. By the check-in desk, an impromptu one-man welcoming committee, Larry Cartmell, boisterously greeted arrivals. A pathologist in his early fifties from Ada, Oklahoma, Cartmell had taken the same flight from Santiago that I had; we had sat together on the school bus that picked up Mummy Congress researchers at the airport. He was very entertaining. For the last few hours, he had scarcely stopped talking and enthusing and cracking jokes, all in a booming southern drawl. Cartmell, I discovered, loved Arica and the desert that lay just beyond, where hundreds and hundreds of mummies had been found over the years. He loved analyzing little plastic bags full of mummy hair, which is his particular speciality. He loved the Chileans, although he seemed slightly less partial to those nostalgic for the old Socialist government of Salvador Allende. He even loved his colleagues' favorite local hangout, the Restaurant of the Dead, a dining establishment that would never find its way into any tourist brochure but which was located just across the street from a local cemetery and a stone's throw from an important collection of Chilean mummies. The menu was no great shakes, with its sandwiches and roast chicken, but who could resist the name? For Cartmell, who got his start in the mummy business in Arica, the little Chilean town was a piece of heaven.

"This whole place," he told me, beaming ear to ear, "is *built on mummies.*"

As Cartmell and I waited for a few of his colleagues to join us, he kept a sharp lookout for all new arrivals. An infectious extrovert, he had an ulterior motive. He was dying to see if anyone had a copy of the congress program, which would tell him exactly when organizers had slated his session, the one he had painstakingly organized on mummy hair. It seemed that time slots were everything at the Mummy Congress, as they are in television. Cartmell prayed he had been given prime time. So as soon as he spied someone he knew, he roared out a name and charged over for a chat, shaking hands, hoping like hell that the new arrival had an advance copy of the conference program. From the look of it, Cartmell knew just about every one of the 180 or so mummy experts who had flocked to the congress from all over North America, Europe, South America, and the Middle East. And nearly everyone seemed to know him. As the knot of people expanded around us, Cartmell disappeared to find a table big enough for everyone in the hotel restaurant. Before long I found myself squeezed into a noisy, shrieking, hooting group of mummy experts. To my eyes, the congress was quickly taking on the air of a house party. Indeed, I'd just seen more people hugging warmly in the hotel lobby than I ever had in an airport arrivals gate. "I love these congresses," rhapsodized Karl Reinhard, who was sitting on my left. "I get to see so many of my friends here."

Lean and fit-looking in his mid-forties, with a bushy black beard and a Brazilian good-luck charm wrapped around his wrist hippie-style, Reinhard teaches anthropology and palynology, the study of pollen, in Lincoln, Nebraska. But his real passion, it transpired, is for parasites, specifically the types that inhabit the bodies of mummified people. Reinhard had just flown in with his wife, Debbie Meier, a museum conservator, to chair a session before heading down to Brazil, his favorite place for studying all manner of weird parasites in mummies. Fortunately for a guy whose speciality doesn't make appetizing dinner conversation, Reinhard likes to keep it light. He gives his papers playful titles like "Exploding Worms and the Consequences of Close Human-Parasite Evolution." He is full of trivia on all kinds of unexpected stuff, such as how the creators of the movie *Alien* got their ideas for the monster. According to Reinhard, they relied extensively on his speciality, parasitology. The alien's egg, he said, was a fluke egg. "The molt was based on a tick. Its body structure was like a thorny-headed worm and the lifestyle was based on a parasitic spider. Sigourney Weaver would be *nothing* without worms."

Reaching for his beer, Reinhard surveyed the room. Out of the corner of his eye, he spied Bob Brier, a cadaverously thin philosophy professor from Long Island whose popular books include *The Encyclopedia of Mummies* and whose controversial new tome on the murder of Tutankhamen had just landed on the bestseller list in England. Nearby was the spry, white-haired form of Minnesota pathologist Art Aufderheide, one of the grand old men of mummy research and a leading authority on ancient disease in mummies. In the doorway, the young Peruvian physician Guido Lombardi, who had just spent months tracking down two long-lost Egyptian mummies in New Orleans, scanned the room for a colleague who specialized in human sacrifice in South America. "It's a very small world here," Reinhard said, laughing.

It was also, as I swiftly realized, a world where nearly everyone was gainfully employed doing something other than studying mummies. The immense public interest in mummies has never translated into real research money. There are few salaried jobs and very few full-time mummy experts. Most delegates are professionals—anthropologists, archaeologists, or pathologists—who dip into their own pockets to cover their field expenses and who spend their summer holidays, Christmas vacations, or retirement years flying to Egypt, the Canary Islands, and Peru to work on mummies. More than a few had exhausted the patience of their bewildered spouses. Some had ended up marrying each other. Most had paid their own fares to Arica, and they were squirreled away in half a dozen budget hotels scattered around town. At seventy dollars a night, the Hotel Arica was simply too rich for most of the crowd.

No one seemed to mind, however. Most were just enormously happy to be in attendance at the world's largest regular gathering of mummy experts and eagerly awaited what lay ahead over the next five days. The South Americans, explained Reinhard, didn't believe in wasting time. Sessions on subjects as diverse as ancient human disease, animal mummies, ancient DNA in mummies, Mexican mummies, high-altitude human sacrifices, and mummy conservation would begin each morning at 8:30 A.M. and end eleven or twelve hours later. In between, papers in two languages— English and Spanish—were scheduled every fifteen minutes.

Moreover, the organizers planned to keep the congress dead simple: there would be no concurrent sessions. To ensure that every delegate could hear every paper, the sessions were scheduled consecutively in one large room. To ensure that everyone could understand everyone else, the organizers had flown in a team of interpreters from Santiago. Attendees would be issued headphones.

It sounded perfect, but not everyone was happy. At the far end of the table, a howl of protest rose as Cartmell flipped through a faxed program of scheduled papers he'd managed to find. "I can't believe it," he moaned, betrayal stamped all over his face. He looked as if he'd just lost his best friend. His session on mummified hair had been scheduled from 4:25 to 6:20 P.M. the day after tomorrow. It was just about the time the overheated brains of delegates would require a serious soaking at the hotel bar. It was one of the worst time slots of the conference.

⌒

THE MUMMY CONGRESS is held every three years, and, in between, it is the subject of much fond talk and anticipation among mummy experts. But the Congress is not well known outside the small circle of delegates. For nearly twenty years, I had made my living as a science journalist covering the arcane world of archaeology and during that time I had met and talked to hundreds of archaeologists. I had spent countless hours sitting in conference halls, slouching in train stations, and excavating side by side with archaeologists. I had subscribed to archaeological journals, pored over archaeological Web sites, and joined archaeological news groups. I had never heard so much as a whisper of the Mummy Congress and I am quite sure I would not have been the wiser even now were it not for a rambling conversation that I had with a Canadian mummy expert.

At the time, I was casting around for a mummy story. My editor at *Discover* magazine had asked me to keep an eye open for new research on the preserved dead: stories about mummies are very popular with readers. So I began making phone calls. Despite the line of work I am in, I had encountered few mummy experts. In Canada, where I live, and in the United States, archaeologists seldom investigate the ancient human remains they happen upon: strong sentiments prevail against such studies. The reasons are religious, social, and political, and they are rooted in history. For many decades, anthropologists and archaeologists had plundered native cemeteries to gather up collections of skulls, skeletons, and mummies for study in universities and museums. Outraged by this desecration of their dead, native activists had fervently demanded the pillaged bodies back. As the outcry reached a crescendo in 1990, American legislators passed a sweeping law, the Native American Graves Protection and Repatriation Act, protecting native graves and ordering many museums to return bones and mummies to native bands. This righted some old wrongs, but the bitter controversy had left an unfortunate scientific legacy: the study of North America's ancient dead had become virtually taboo.

As a result, I didn't encounter many researchers who openly professed an interest in mummies. But a few years back, I had interviewed a loquacious paleopathologist from Canada, Patrick Horne. Horne was a bona fide mummy person. Like others of his ilk, he considered a mummy to be any ancient cadaver whose soft tissues had partially or wholly resisted decay. He had studied many of them. During the 1980s, he had examined the spectacular frozen body of an ancient Inca boy, known today as the Prince of El Plomo, who had been recovered by climbers atop a mountain peak in Chile. During the 1990s, Horne had worked with Egyptologists in the Valley of the Nobles, identifying parasites in the dessicated tissue of Egyptian mummies. The day I called him, we chatted for almost an hour about the latest mummy research. Finally, just as we were about to hang up, Horne mentioned, as an afterthought, an upcoming conference that he dearly hoped to attend. It was the Mummy Congress in Arica.

Just from the note of longing in his voice as he described it, I knew I had to go. I had no idea what to expect, but I was sure it would be worth the trouble it would take to get there. I wanted to know, after all, who these people were who studied the bodies of the ancient dead so unabashedly. And I wanted very much to see what I had been missing in all my years of writing about the distant past. I had described and recounted at length many of the clever things that archaeologists had deduced from the humblest of clues—tiny bits of broken pottery and stone, scatterings of ancient fishbones around a hearth, imprints of nets in Ice Age clay. I had gleaned as much as I could from the things that humans had left behind on their long twisting journey through time. Now I wanted to see their ancient faces. I wanted to know what they had looked like, how they had frowned, squinted, arranged their hair, tattooed their skin, draped their tunics, shaped their fingernails, and tied their shoes. I began scrambling to find a way to get to Arica.

BY LUNCH THE first day of the congress, I had begun surfacing from a bad case of jet lag. For four hours that morning, I had perched on one of the posh brocade-covered chairs provided by the Hotel Arica, taking in the first session on human paleopathology, the study of ancient disease processes and injury. Framed between two huge maroon-colored conference posters—each featuring the cracked and crumbling mummy of a child unearthed just behind the hotel—the speakers had wasted little time in getting down to business. An Italian researcher had described a new immunological technique for diagnosing malaria in an ancient mummy. A Canary Island physician had clicked through several slides of grimacing, half-decayed Guanche mummies exhumed from the holiday island of Tenerife, then launched into a brief account of their demographics. An American neurologist had prefaced his talk by describing how the great sixteenth-century Flemish painter Peter Paul Rubens once employed a withered Egyptian mummy as a model for his drawings. Then he proceeded to describe all the ailments—from diabetes to inflammatory bowel disease—that modern researchers could track through time, thanks to the ancient blood clots and wizened nerves of mummies.

It was a broad, eclectic collection of papers, and this, I quickly discovered, was a hallmark of the congress. Session topics served more as rough guidelines than real defined categories. Moreover, one never knew for sure what was coming next; speakers continually vanished from the program without much explanation, while others unaccountably materialized. Indeed I had the distinct impression that if someone just walked off the plane in Arica with a good paper in hand, he or she would be swept up instantly and scheduled in wherever a spot could be found. All that seemed to matter was that a researcher had something interesting and new to contribute on the subject of mummies. The audience was very accommodating. It was also very attentive; some delegates were even jotting down notes. After four hours of papers, they seemed reluctant to break for lunch. Small groups milled at the back of the room, chatting quietly.

In the front row, Bob Brier grinned as he held a small impromptu press conference. Curious, I slid into a chair beside the international press corps. This consisted of just one reporter, a Londoner named Steve Connor, who had stumbled as I had upon the congress and claimed that he'd managed to wangle a ticket to Chile by promising his editors a true story on mummies that came back to life. Connor was good company—wry, hardworking, and sociable. But I was rather amazed: I had expected to find a noisy mob of television and newspaper reporters running riot in Arica. Neither I nor Connor missed them, however; there was a relaxed, unguarded air to the delegates that would never have survived a prolonged media scrum.

Brier, for example, was clearly enjoying himself as he answered a few questions. A self-taught Egyptologist who had learned to read hieroglyphs while recovering from a serious sports injury, Brier joked about the documentary that he and colleague Ronn Wade had made as they were

experimentally embalming a modern corpse by the methods
of ancient Egyptian embalmers. The pair had succeeded
admirably—their modern mummy would soon be exhibited
alongside ancient corpses in a museum in San Diego. The
resulting documentary had made Brier quite famous.
"*National Geographic,* called the program 'Mr. Mummy,' " he
grinned, "and I was never sure if the title was referring to me
or the mummy."

In recognition of this fame, Brier had opened the
congress, giving a brief measured report on Queen Weret,
recently discovered in a dark tomb sixty-six feet underground in Egypt. Weret, it seemed, had lived a life of pam-
pered sloth. Her bones were so slender and underdeveloped,
observed Brier, that she had probably enjoyed an existence
"virtually free of labor." She had seldom walked, likely
lounging in a litter wherever she wished to go. But what
excited Brier most was the fact that her shriveled brain still
clung to the curve of her crania: he could see it there when
he looked into a hole at the base of her head. It surprised the
hell out of him. Most Egyptian morticians had tossed out
such gray matter while mummifying the dead. Brier hoped
to gather brain-tissue samples from other periods and examine them to see whether elderly Nile dwellers in the time of
the pharaohs were plagued with Alzheimer's disease. But
Brier and his colleague Michael Zimmerman had a long way
to go. So far they had found only three Egyptian brains.

As Brier hustled off for lunch, Connor and I amicably
compared notes. We were both surprised by the small number of papers from the place generally thought of as the
fount of mummy research: Egypt. Only two Egyptologists

had signed up for the congress. I had begun to discover that most scholars of ancient Egypt regarded mummies about as favorably as a gem collector does a bag stuffed with cubic zirconium. There are good reasons for this. Egyptologists spend years of expensive university training boning up on minute details of Egyptian art, history, and language. The last thing they want is to sink their trowels into a tomb of linen-wrapped dead folks: such a find would invariably bog down excavations on things nearer to their hearts—temples, houses, stelae, and stashes of papyri.

The congress did not suffer because of the lack of news from Egypt, however. It merely looked farther afield. For decades, the world's mummy experts had been recovering ancient preserved bodies in a host of unlikely places, from ghoulish-looking bog bodies submerged in Dutch fens to pristine mummies of saints exhibited in Italian churches, and from Inca children sacrificed on Andean mountain peaks to Buddhist monks venerated in Japanese temples. Indeed, every continent on earth, it seemed, had once possessed a trove of mummies. Even Antarctica could boast of a few: the frozen bodies of the failed polar explorer Sir Robert Falcon Scott and his men still lie entombed beyond human reach under the creeping glacial ice.

During the morning session on the first day, Guita Hourani, a slim, vivacious Lebanese historian, had described in glowing detail a previously unknown trove of medieval Christian mummies from the Crusades in the Middle East. Exhumed from a cave floor in the Valley of the Saints in northern Lebanon, these thirteenth-century mummies, she explained, were victims of a brutal seven-month siege by invading forces. Exquisitely dressed in embroidered silk and cotton clothing and interred with coins, manuscripts, necklaces, combs, house keys, and other goods, the defeated Christians had outlasted their foes. Hourani's slide of a four-month-old infant, preserved down to the tiny wisps of hair caught between her toes, brought a sigh from the audience. The hairs, Hourani explained, likely came from the grieving mother. Hourani had seen many women pull out their own tresses as they tearfully kissed the bodies of their dead children.

But the Crusades mummies were not the only sensation. Just a few papers after Hourani's, delegates had gasped at slides of the mysterious bodies from the northwestern corner of China. Sporting blond and ginger-colored hair, beards, fair skin, and prominent noses, these mummies appeared far more European than Asian. Indeed, one willowy woman sported what seemed to be a tall black witch's cap. No one knew who these people were, much less how they had gotten to China some four thousand years ago. And delegates were similarly enrapt by a video of dozens of ancient mummies recently recovered from the humid cloud forests of the Peruvian Amazon. Dating to the time of the Inca, they were wonders of ancient mummy making. "Even in that humidity," marveled researcher Federico Kauffman Doig, "you get almost perfect preservation. Even the genitals and eyeballs are preserved."

BY DAY THREE of the congress, I had begun to notice some of the invisible lines that divided the delegates. As united as they were in their grand passion for mummies and their singular dedication to their studies, the world's mummy experts did not coexist easily as a big extended family. They were, on the whole, too stubborn, too wayward, too headstrong, too intense, too in love with the ancient dead—and this had led on occasion to bitter professional disputes. The most notorious of these battles had taken on all the trappings of venomous personal combat as researchers fought tooth and nail for the right to investigate important new troves of mummies.

For the sake of appearance, the combatants tried to ignore one another in the halls and corridors of the Hotel Arica. They kept to different sides of the conference hall and studiously avoided one another in the small hotel restaurant, but these seemed awkward truces. All the senior mummy experts knew exactly what was going on—it was their business to know, after all—and I began hearing stories of the ugly mudslinging matches that had taken place in private and in public in the past. One expert, I was told, had even gone so far as to accuse an opponent of sleeping with a high-ranking cultural official in order to obtain control over a major mummy find.

It sounded bizarre, this unseemly feuding over dead bodies, but in the small impecunious world of mummy experts, it made perfect, if unhappy, sense. Most mummy experts yearn to take charge of a find as wondrous and rare as the bodies of the Peruvian cloud forest: the scientific possibilities are dazzling and the public announcement invariably attracts world attention. Within weeks, offers begin flowing in from television producers, magazine editors, book publishers, lecture tour organizers. After toiling for years on their own savings, few mummy experts can resist. A major book contract, after all, can subsidize much valuable new research. (During the early 1990s, the German publishing house Bertelsmann paid a $400,000 advance to publish the story of Europe's famous frozen mummy, the Iceman, as told by the research team's principal investigator, Konrad Spindler.) A vitriolic battle is almost inevitable after every major find, as researchers jockey for control and clash over the extent of media access.

Acrimonious as these rivalries can be, they were not the only flash points in Arica. An even more divisive controversy effectively separated the congress into two politely warring camps. On the surface, the debate hinged on the rightness or wrongness of something that mummy experts had once taken for granted: mummy autopsies or dissections. Such invasive procedures, undertaken to glean medical data, pose a difficult ethical question: Does science have the right to destroy an ancient human body in its quest for knowledge for the living? Or should researchers respect a human's inherent dignity, even after death, conserving and protecting ancient flesh?

Nearly everyone at the congress had a strong, carefully reasoned opinion on the matter. The opponents of dissection seemed to far outnumber the advocates, and each group spoke a rather different scientific language. The dissection-ists consisted mainly of medical people, primarily patholo-gists, with a few physical anthropologists thrown in for good measure. They included several of the most senior mummy researchers in the field. The conservationists, on the other hand, were mainly archaeologists, cultural anthropologists, and museum curators. As a whole, they were a far younger group: indeed, they struck me as the wave of the future.

Before arriving in Arica, I had never heard of a mummy autopsy, and the idea sounded rather antique and barbaric. Like most other people, I shied away at the thought of someone laying a knife to the recently dead, even in the service of science. And my qualms grew stronger still at the thought of subjecting ancient cadavers to such procedures. After hundreds or thousands of years, the everlasting dead had been granted a rare dispensation. They had escaped unscathed from all the regular forms of destruction—the nibbling of maggots, the blistering of bacteria, the gnawing of dogs, the ransacking of grave robbers. So it seemed hideously callous to subject them to the scalpel, carving open ancient flesh to bare all secrets. It also seemed terribly unwise. Exquisitely preserved mummies are becoming increasingly rare as looters continue to plunder ancient tombs indiscriminately, destroying fragile mummies in the frantic search for gold and jewels.

Conservationists abhor the idea of cutting up mummies and refuse even to unwrap them. Most collaborate with medical-imaging specialists who peer into coffins and ancient mummy bundles with three-dimensional computer-aided tomography (CT) scans or with tiny fiber-optic tubes, techniques that offer little if any insult to the ancient dead. They see mummies as frail elders deserving of protection. "The mummies," explained one Chilean archaeologist, "were actual people. They lived their lives, they died, they suffered, they ate, they made love, as people do today. What we want is for people to keep this in perspective. We are dealing with human beings and not with samples."

The dissectionists view matters very differently. As medical people mostly, they owe their loyalties to the living. They see the world's mummies as an immensely valuable repository of scientific data on matters as diverse as ancient mummification methods, ancient parasites, ancient diseases. To glean such data, they regularly dissect the ancient dead, examining their organs and gathering tissue samples for testing. These surgeries are often extremely destructive, however, something that increasingly distresses cultural officials around the world. As a result, dissections are becoming rare. Some medical people at the congress made open pitches at the end of their papers, asking for tiny scraps of ancient tissue for their studies. Others were more discreet, schmoozing behind the scenes for bits of shriveled intestines, nerves, and lungs.

BY THE CLOSING banquet on Thursday night, delegates were ready for some serious unwinding. The final session of the congress, a series of papers on Mexican mummies, had stretched on so long that the team of interpreters had been forced to rush out in the middle of it in order to catch their plane back to Santiago. Undeterred, discussants had pressed on for another hour or so, seemingly oblivious to the fact that half the audience was unable to understand a word that was said. But now everyone seemed primed for a good time. In the hotel banquet room, a local band played an eclectic but infectious mixture of tangos, sambas, rumbas, bossa novas, and old Beatles standards. At the evening's end, the dance floor was jammed with bodies; there was hardly a person left sitting at the tables.

I hated to see the congress come to an end. After five

days in Arica, I had become immersed in the bizarre world of mummies and mummy science. I was strangely reluctant to return to the grayer realm of the living. The people I had met at the congress were fascinating and, in listening to their stories, I had begun to see how much a part of our lives the preserved dead are. The deep, almost primal fascination we feel at the sight of such bodies is almost inescapable. Humanity, after all, has always regarded mummies, with their gaunt cheeks and their slender limbs, their long thin hands and their soft tresses, as something separate and distinct from the scraps of bone that constitute other human remains. Still recognizable as individuals, even after hundreds or thousands of years, mummies call to our imaginations, and we readily impart something of ourselves to them. We give them stories, histories, names, moments in time. We marvel at their immortality and we dream of sharing it. We explain how it was that they came to be the way they are and we connect with them on visceral, emotional, and intellectual levels. We see each one of them as one of us.

I was keen to explore this intimate relationship between the living and the everlasting dead and to do so through the lens of science and the research of some of the world's most accomplished, dedicated, and unheralded mummy experts. So I set out to learn how mummies came to be and how the capriciousness of nature and the adroitness of ancient mummy makers bestowed this strange form of immortality on something as frail as the cells of our soft tissues. And as I did so, I tried to pick out the still intelligible voices of the dead from the din of the living, to hear what they have to tell us about ourselves.

THE
DISSECTOR'S
KNIFE

~

F OR MONTHS AFTER I RETURNED from Arica, I
kept recalling strange snippets of things I'd heard and
seen at the congress. Even as I slipped back into the world
of the living in Vancouver, the mummies and all those
obsessed researchers continued to haunt my imagination.
I'd be standing in a line at Starbucks watching a mother
gently tuck her fretting infant into the canvas seat of a
stroller and I'd suddenly remember the photo of the wizened baby mummy from the time of the Crusades with its
chubby, bowed baby legs and its tiny clenched fists. Or I'd
be alone planting nasturtiums in a common garden I some-

times helped to tend, when a strangely famous story about the British philosopher Jeremy Bentham would pop unbidden into my mind.

Bentham was a strong proponent of utilitarianism. He believed, among other things, that the goal of human life should be to do the greatest good for the greatest number of people. In keeping with this philosophy, he willed his body after death to a prominent London anatomist, though that was not the end of Bentham. To spare admirers the expense of commissioning a stone sculpture of him, he asked that his body be preserved and displayed. After a public dissection of his remains in 1832, his body was skeletonized and his head mummified with a pair of glass eyes. The result was so grim, however, that his friends swiftly arranged to have a wax head made. This they placed atop his reconstructed skeleton. Then they dressed Bentham in his old topcoat and breeches, arranged him comfortably in a chair with his walking stick and put him on display in a glass case at University College London. As a finishing touch, they laid his mummified head between his feet. For decades after, admirers reportedly trundled Bentham to college council meetings, making note of his presence in the minutes. Even today, the curious can still gaze at these bizarre remains in their case at University College, though Bentham's mummified head has been discreetly removed. Students had been in the habit of stealing it for pranks.

Such tales from the congress had incredible staying power, playing as they did on some deep chord in my imagination. I didn't mind so much being possessed by them; they seemed more quirky and eccentric than disturbing. But as I reflected on the congress I realized that something much more powerful had also lodged itself deeply in my brain. It was a strange new hunger, a desire really, for the fleeting but intense feeling that had flashed in the darkened conference room each time someone produced a new slide showing an exquisitely preserved mummy. There were many of these photos at the congress. Sometimes the photographer had zoomed in on a telling detail, such as a startlingly lifelike hand with its blunt calloused fingers and ragged fingernails. Or sometimes he or she had stepped back, taking a loving head-to-toe picture of a four-thousand-year-old person with tousled ginger-colored braids and felt-covered toes. Yet the response in the room was always the same. There was a sharp intake of breath, an audible gasp. Then a deep, primeval kind of thrill, almost something orgasmic, passed through the room. I think everyone felt it. It was the shock and wonder of glimpsing—even briefly and even secondhand through the camera's eye—immortality.

Mummy experts don't always like to admit to this fascination: it seems terribly unscientific and unprofessional. To make it more presentable, researchers have developed code words for exceptional preservation. It took me a while to realize what they were actually talking about. Sometimes they referred only to the presence of dermal ridges on a mummy. These are the tiny grooves and elevations on human fingertips that yield police fingerprints. An exceptionally well-preserved mummy still has them. Or they pointed to the existence of fine down on a child's upper lip or a fringe of eyelashes on an adult. Occasionally, they spoke in more abstract terms. They boasted about the number of DNA base pairs that their team had succeeded in retrieving from a mummy tissue sample. Among mummy experts, it seemed generally understood that the greater the number of base pairs, the finer the preservation and the more closely the mummy resembled a living human being. As I learned later, this has never been proven.

But although preservation was never far from anyone's mind at the congress, few people made any mention of how this wondrous transformation had taken place. To my frustration, none of the books I read about mummies came close to answering my questions. I was intensely curious about the grim laws of death and decay, and how they combined to strip someone in the bloom of life to bare bones. What normally happened to a body in the first few hours after death? What exactly took place in the days that followed? How had nature and ancient human embalmers subverted these laws? Egypt, I reasoned, would be the best place to search out the answers: it had a long, celebrated history of preserving the human body. And the dead, I realized, were bound to be the most eloquent sources. I considered all the possibilities. In the end, I decided to head off to a small makeshift morgue in the middle of the Sahara Desert. I suspected the mummies there could answer my questions.

◦—

ON AN EARLY December morning in the ancient Egyptian town of Kellis, Art Aufderheide contemplated his next move. Outside, along the abandoned streets, bitter gusts blasted fallen columns and forgotten temple walls, reducing everything to sand and dune and desert. But Aufderheide paid little heed to the cold fury that surrounded him. Taking a swig from a smudged water bottle in his small morgue, he studied the body of a man lying on a plank. The dead man's face looked hard and smooth, as if cast in molten metal, copper perhaps. His features, all sunken hollows and sculpted cheekbones, possessed a strange unyielding strength. Aufderheide pored over the corpse, then reached for a red Swiss Army knife. Sharpening it with long strokes on a whetstone, he tested its edge against his thumb. He turned back to his subject, sliding the gleaming blade into the crook beneath the man's chin. Then he commenced sawing. It was quick, easy, bloodless work, decapitating an ancient Egyptian mummy.

At eighty years of age, Aufderheide is one of the world's foremost experts on ancient preserved bodies. He knows more about the arcane science of outwitting natural human decay than just about anyone else alive. Aufderheide had come to Kellis to study preservation in a little-known trove of two-thousand-year-old mummies. But for the elderly pathologist, there was a deep irony in this work. Understanding immutability in the ancient dead often meant slicing them into pieces. Propped up beside the corpse were some of the fruits of his morning labors—dozens of clear plastic bags of various sizes. Inside were a miscellany of body parts—two dessicated human ears; ten fingertips complete with fingernails; ten toes complete with toenails; one penis; numerous samples of muscle tissue; and bits of lung tissue, heart tissue, and a thin scrap of liver. All this withered flesh belonged to the man on the table, or at least it once had. Aufderheide had claimed it for science.

In pursuit of mummies, the aging pathologist had journeyed restlessly from one desert to another—arctic deserts, tropical deserts, island deserts. He had traveled from Alaska to Italy, the Canary Islands to Chile, and by his own estimate had dissected nearly eight hundred ancient preserved bodies. He took this work very seriously. With fellow researcher Conrado Rodriguez Martin, he had written the bible of his trade, *The Cambridge Encyclopedia of Paleopathology*, and he continued to publish diligently. Still spry, with a pair of alert blue eyes framed by thick horn-rimmed glasses and a thatch of unruly white hair, he is the first expert most people call when they stumble on a new mummy trove. If there were a Kevin Bacon game in mummy studies, Aufderheide would be Kevin Bacon. He has worked with just about everyone and has the inside track on most major recent mummy discoveries. "Ask Aufderheide if you have a question," said

Bob Brier at the mummy congress. "He knows everything. He does."

Until fairly recently, however, Aufderheide had never worked in Egypt. No Egyptologist had ever invited him, perhaps because so few were terribly interested in mummies. But in the early 1990s archaeologists working in Dahkleh Oasis, some five hundred miles southwest of Cairo, came upon a series of ancient tombs cut into the cliffs behind Kellis. The chambers were small and dark and stuffy. They reeked of the sickly sweet smell of decay. Inside team members discovered snaking piles of linen bandages on the floor. Tangled within were human bones and smashed bits of gilded mummy masks. These were the leftovers of grave robbers. But in a few tombs, the team found mummified heads, arms, torsos, and occasionally whole mummies, only partially unwrapped and still finely preserved. They called Aufderheide at the University of Minnesota in Duluth, where he heads his own paleobiology laboratory. They asked if he would like to study them before looters caught wind of the discovery.

Aufderheide didn't have to think about the proposition for long. Others had studied mummies in Egypt. Before engineers began raising the level of the Aswan Dam in 1907, for example, the Australian anatomist Grafton Elliott Smith and his associates examined and autopsied eight thousand ancient bodies. But Smith's studies were relatively simple by current scientific standards. The researchers who followed him concentrated mainly on the mummies of kings and queens and nobles, giving short shrift to the ancient cadavers of ordinary folks. They also

devoted their energies to tombs lining the Nile Valley, paying little heed to those dotting the rest of Egypt. Aufderheide knew there was a lot left to be done. He wanted to see
how embalmers carried out their work among the forgotten
lower classes. He also wanted to take tissue samples for
future medical studies. The Egyptian government rarely
permitted such exports, but it was prepared to do so for
Aufderheide. So the pathologist booked his ticket to Dahkleh Oasis and paid for it himself, as was his practice. He
didn't like to go cap in hand to the funding agencies. He'd
discovered years ago that they didn't really understand
mummy research. As a result, he and his wife, Mary, lived in
the smallest physician-owned house in Duluth.

Aufderheide liked Dahkleh very much. A tiny shred of
green life in desert so barren that the ancient Egyptians
believed it a land of the dead, Dahkleh had long struggled
against invading sands. But some two thousand years ago,
when the Romans plucked Egypt from its Greek pharaohs
and added it to their own sprawling empire, they introduced
a new form of irrigation. In Dahkleh, the town of Kellis
enjoyed a brief fling with prosperity. It had a painted temple
dedicated to a local god. It had estate agents literate enough
to leave their accounts in what might be the world's oldest
book. It had two-story houses and Egyptian inhabitants with
fashionable Roman names like Hilaria, Matrona, and
Valerius. It had fields that produced wheat and olives and
vineyards that made a popular wine. And, of course, it had
mummies. Just because a Roman emperor ruled Egypt
didn't mean the Egyptians were about to give up something
as dear to their hearts as mummification.

In Dahkleh, Auderheide rose each morning at 5:30. He grabbed a quick breakfast of Egyptian flatbread, jam, and eggs in the field camp dining room, then clambered into the back of a dusty panel truck that shuttled him and other crew members to Kellis. A good thirty years older than most of the archaeologists, anthropologists, and Egyptologists at Dahkleh, Aufderheide was clearly the grand old man of the camp. But he refused to trade on his age in any way. He asked for no special treatment—no shorter workday, no softer seats in the cab of the truck—and he received none. For this, the crew greatly admired him, although it soon became apparent that no one, with the exception of the camp physician, was keen on hanging out with him in his makeshift morgue. Even around the boisterous dinner table at night, Aufderheide seemed enveloped in solitude, an isolation imposed not only by his dissections, which disturbed people, but by the deafness that had begun to plague him. It was becoming an effort for him to converse with others.

He stood out in other ways too. Unlike most of the members of the team at Dahkleh who had donned some form of convenient Arabic clothing, pulling on long *djellabas* or wrapping Palestinian scarfs around their faces to keep out the sand during the frequent sandstorms, Aufderheide conceded not an inch to local custom. He was dressed, as he had been since he arrived a week earlier, in a cotton Tilley hat, a blue cotton bandanna, an immaculately clean pair of beige work pants, and a similarly immaculate beige work shirt. The pocket bulged with a small black notebook labeled "Egypt 1993 1999" in handwritten letters. Aufderheide looked like an aging car mechanic, or perhaps a retired Maytag repairman sent out on a call to the middle of the Sahara. All that was missing was the bow tie and the name "Art" embroidered on his pocket. He was astonishingly dapper in that dusty place. Everyone else looked grotty by comparison. Perhaps he felt he owed it to Dahkleh's dead to keep up professional appearances.

On the second day I was in Dahkleh, the panel truck deposited us on the outskirts of Kellis, near the ruins of what must have once been an elegant stone mausoleum. Aufderheide dropped his knapsack at the morgue, then hustled off to a small roofless magazine. Inside were half a dozen or so tattered linen bundles. They looked like giant cocoons. He gently nudged first one, then another with the toe of his boot. He didn't say so, but he was clearly thinking of snakes, specifically sleeping cobras and vipers. Standing beside him, I thought of all the dead people inside these bundles. I couldn't see their faces, but somehow that anonymity made them seem all the more doleful. Aufderheide hunted around, trying to find the best preserved one to show me. When he finally spied it, he waded gingerly into the tangle of tea-colored shrouds and lifted the bundle into his arms. He looked like a man cradling a load of firewood.

We set off briskly for his makeshift lab. The sun was beginning to rise over the eastern horizon by then and Kellis looked spectacular, like a giant stone Lego set scattered over the tan-colored desert. There were bits of ruined houses and lines of stone walls in the sand, vivid testaments to the fleeting nature of human ambition. There were painted reliefs crumbling to dust on temple walls. Aufderheide said that one of the things he liked best about working at Kellis was being able to gaze out at the ruined streets where the people on his autopsy table once strolled. I didn't doubt it: for all his brisk clinical manner, Aufderheide had a streak of romanticism in him.

When we reached the morgue, Aufderheide laid the mummy on a wooden plank supported by two sawhorses. On a low bench at the back of the morgue, two mummified heads rested companionably against the wall. One, dusty rust-red in color, was a boy with long silky eyelashes. The other was a man with a permanent scowl and a mass of tiny perfect auburn curls. "I saw him in the tomb and he had such a pretty hairdo, I decided I wasn't going to dissect him," remarked Aufderheide. "I was just going to take him out and photograph him."

But these were definitely the exceptions. Over in a corner was a mound of nearly two dozen large Glad bags. Each was carefully labeled with its own number and each held the remains of a dissected mummy, or rather, the parts that Aufderheide had not chosen for his samples. It was not easy to stuff the rigid body of an adult mummy into a standard green garbage bag. It took some cutting of limbs and folding of torsos, and even then there were awkward moments of cramming brittle flesh down so the bag could be closed with a twist tie. But Aufderheide had managed. In some of the bulbous green bags, the jutting angle of a shoulder or the jagged edge of a knee pressed outward against the green. But Aufderheide didn't pay them much attention. Eventually, he explained, archaeologists would re-inter all of them in the nearby tombs.

Shrugging at this, he began rooting around in his knapsack. It was filled with all the tools of his itinerant trade—a wrinkled sheet of black velvet; a camera; various lenses; a selection of plastic Whirl-pak bags that dairies generally used to collect milk samples for testing; two Swiss Army knives; a set of scales; and a Home Depot–style whetstone, chisel, and hacksaw. In the absence of electricity at Kellis, he explained, he had to keep his gear simple. Turning to one side he set a dusty bottle of water on a ledge. A week earlier, he had worked all day without stopping for as much as a drink of water. Between dehydration and jet lag, he had keeled over right beside a mummy. When a member of the crew dropped by a few moments later, he was shocked to find Aufderheide sprawled motionless on the table. "He thought I was dead," recalled Aufderheide with a grin. This struck him as terribly funny.

Aufderheide, after all, is on intimate terms with death. The son of a small-town businessman in New Ulm, Minnesota, he had devoted his entire adult life to teasing out its secrets. As a medical student during the Second World War, he had gravitated to pathology as surely as a magnet to iron. It wasn't that he disliked living patients or that he lacked the right bedside manner. Aufderheide is far too affable to have trouble relating to patients. But as a young man he had been fascinated by the conundrums that pathology, the study of disease processes, continually posed. Other doctors rely on pathologists to make difficult diagnoses: Aufderheide loved being a doctor's doctor and after the first few dissections he performed, something strange happened. He began to see dead bodies as little more than decaying lattices of proteins. He didn't think of them as human beings anymore. He had become a death professional and some part of his mind had permanently disconnected. "I have virtually no corporeal identification," he explained. Although he had loved and admired his mother, for example, those emotions had not transferred to her corpse. "If I'd been in the same room when my mother died, I'd have autopsied her. I just view a dead body as a broken-down car."

That didn't mean he accepted death, however. He was vigilant for the least sign of its encroachment. When he was in his forties, he had detected the first traces of stagnation in himself. He had a wife, three bright kids, and a good living. But he no longer felt the familiar quickening of his pulse as he walked through the hospital door. His life was slowly taking on a gray pall. So he made a remarkable decision. He resolved to try living off the land with the Copper Inuit in the Canadian Arctic. To make contact with the Inuit, he rafted down the Mackenzie River with a few friends all the way to the Arctic Ocean, a wild thousand-mile ride. Two years later, he spent the winter living with an Inuit family on remote Bathurst Island. His hosts taught him how to hunt caribou on the tundra and harpoon seals on the sea ice. He feasted on raw meat when his companions were successful and he drank up as much as he could of what he calls "four thousand years of distilled survival method."

The experience gave him a new lease on life. At an age when many of his hospital colleagues were collecting stocks and bonds and polishing their golf game, Aufderheide began venturing farther and farther afield in the remote north. In 1967 and 1968, he skidooed to the North Pole with a small party of fellow adventurers in the Plaisted Polar Expedition.

This was the first time anyone had been insane enough to try motoring over hundreds of miles of polar ice floes and crevasses to reach the far ends of the earth.

Finally, when he'd had his fill of the great north, he returned to pathology and to his little house in Duluth. There he began scouting out intellectual pursuits that would rival his Arctic travels. He finally settled on studying mummies, something that he could do together with his personable wife, Mary. It was a good choice for a man who hated lassitude. Mummies just happened to lie in some of the most exotic and legendary real estate on earth: the Sahara, the Gobi, the Taklamakhan, the Atacama deserts. There was no better place for an adventurer.

CLIMBING UP A stepladder, camera in hand, Aufderheide clicked away at the tightly wrapped mummy. Then he was ready to get down to business. He brought the bundle back inside and slipped the blade of his Swiss Army knife under the first few layers of bandages covering the mummy's chest. Lifting up, he ripped the ancient cloth, showering the table with particles of ancient linen. He dug in a little deeper and ripped again. Then he tried yanking the severed edges of the upper layers apart. It was hard, dirty, scrabbling work, nothing at all like the smooth unraveling one might expect. The undersides of the mummy bandages were smeared with an oily black resin that had hardened like cement and fused onto the linen. Aufderheide's fingers and shirt cuffs were soon filthy.

During his first visit to Dahkleh some years ago, he explained, he had taken detailed notes on the way in which each mummy was wrapped. As time passed, he discovered that the packaging seldom varied. As a rule, the wrappers began by slopping resin onto the back of the cadaver and lying two or three long sheets down the back of the corpse, folding them over the head to cover the face. Then they wrapped the neck, arms, torso, and legs in horizontal bands, using whatever scrap linen they had at hand, including patched and worn-out clothing. So uniform was this method of wrapping at Dahkleh that Aufderheide now checked it only by glancing at the layers revealed by an incision. As he cut deeper into the bandages, he tossed aside the linen strips, stuffing them in yet more plastic garbage bags. He hoped a textile expert might arrive one day to study them.

As I stood back, watching him huff over the bundled body, I felt strangely divided. One half of my brain reeled at seeing something so old and beautiful so roughly treated. Each rip echoed terribly. At the congress I had agreed with the conservationists: it seemed so clear that unwrapping and carving up an ancient human being in the search for knowledge was a kind of sacrilege, like smashing a Ming vase in order to discover exactly how it was made. Moreover, I couldn't help but worry about what might be lost. At one point, Aufderheide tossed aside a large square bandage on the heap of linen beneath the table. A few minutes later, camp physician Peter Sheldrick popped in for a visit. Idly, Sheldrick picked up the square bandage, then shook it out with growing excitement. It was a patched man's shirt. An Egyptologist in camp later said it was one of the few pieces of ordinary Egyptian clothing ever recovered from the Roman era.

But my sense of horror at watching this rude unveiling was attenuated by something else: an insistent, overriding sense of curiosity. I could barely look away from what Aufderheide was doing. I desperately wanted to see who lay swaddled in so many layers of cloth. It was not just the anticipation of seeing something forbidden nor a simple fascination with death. Nor was it the tantalizing thought of finally laying eyes on the face of someone long hidden away, although this certainly added piquancy to my desire. This curiosity was altogether far more visceral and urgent. It was an innate craving to connect with the long dead, to pass through some kind of portal of time. It was a desire to go beyond history and the dry, bloodless words on the page and make contact with someone who had lived in an alien world, who had worshipped strange gods and bowed to the power of the pharaohs, who had worn faience and kohl and striped linen tunics, and who had spoken the languages of the papyri. A mummy is eminently, recognizably, a person, an individual. That he or she would look at me with unseeing eyes did not matter. I wanted to slip under the barrier of time and step over the edge of a lost world.

That was the desire. But the reality, half an hour later, fell a good deal short of this. On the table sprawled the naked body of a young man in the prime of life. Stripped of the tightly wound cloth and resin that had protected him like a placenta for two thousand years, he looked strangely frail and vulnerable, a lesser being than he had been only an hour before. I felt ashamed that his eternity had been sacrificed for our selfish pursuit of knowledge. It seemed an act of cruelty. But I remembered that the Egyptians themselves had been pragmatists. More than two millennia ago, Egyptian physicians had conducted autopsies on the dead for the benefit of science and medicine, just as Aufderheide was doing at Dahkleh.

I was still intensely curious. I wondered who this young man had been. His fingers were long and slender, his nails neatly manicured. His dark brown hair was curled and slicked to his scalp with resin. His features, fine and delicate, seemed almost pretty but for one thing. Those who wrapped the bandages about his face wound them so tightly they broke his nose. Viewed from the side he looked like a boxer who had taken a wicked jab.

In the midmorning heat, a pungent fragrance like fenugreek wafted up from the discarded linen on the sand. It smelled both acrid and smoky. As Aufderheide took a break from his exertions, I asked him if he knew what the fragrance was. He shook his head ruefully. "You would know better than I," he observed. "I have almost no sense of smell. In fact, people accuse me of going into this field because of that."

LEFT TO ITS own devices, death shows scant respect for the human body. Almost from the moment it winks out breath, stills the heart, and glazes the eye, it begins inflicting a million small cruelties. Within hours, it stiffens all the major muscles—first the eyelids, then the jaw, neck, and shoulders, until all the body is racked with rigor mortis. Within days, decay transforms a familiar face into something nightmarish. Within weeks, it corrodes skin, dissolves tissue, and pares away flesh, leaving only hard white bone. But for all this mayhem, death goes about its work with a certain fastidious orderliness, inflicting injuries in a roughly prescribed pattern. The ancient Greeks believed that this systematic insult was the work of stone coffins, which they dubbed *sarcophagi*, literally "flesh eaters." But the truth, as Aufderheide explained, is rather more insidious. Almost all of these injuries are perpetrated by death's principal henchmen, protein molecules known as enzymes, which are invisible to the naked eye.

The word *enzyme* itself comes from the Greek word *enzumos*, meaning "leavened," and this gives some clue to the special properties of these molecules. Like the yeast that encourages bread to rise, enzymes are powerful catalysts that trigger key chemical reactions in the body. During life, they reside largely in our cell nuclei, where they serve as our allies, gobbling up bacteria and other harmful foreign invaders. But when death strikes, these enzymes are suddenly freed from their cellular yokes. They begin seeping out of the nuclei like drops of acid, digesting everything in sight. In the days following death, hardly a cell in the body escapes disfigurement.

Sadly, this is only the first modest wave of destruction. Bacteria in the gut are armed with enzymes, too. After death, they begin digesting the intestinal wall. Spreading out through the network of veins, the body's superhighways, these bacteria start feeding to their hearts' content. They devour connective tissue, fatty tissue, muscle tissue, nerve tissue. All the while, they belch out a foul gas that living humans instinctively find repulsive. Nothing can mask this hideous stench, which is largely due to the presence of butyric acids. "Bathe a decomposing cadaver in sweet perfumes," wrote anatomist F. Gonzalez-Crussi, "and it will smell of rotten carrion on a bed of roses."

But while putrefaction assaults the nostrils of the living, it ravages the body of the dead. Within days, the epidermis loses its waxy pallor. It turns a delicate shade of green, then purple, finally black. The face, scrotum, and vulva swell and the abdomen bloats. In some cases, the body puffs up like a balloon to three times its normal size. Then it cracks open like a cocoon. A bloody ooze trickles from the nose and mouth. Eyeballs liquefy. Blisters bubble along the skin and burst. Nails fall off and the upper layer of skin comes sliding away at the first touch. On occasion this poses problems for forensic pathologists trying to identify a partially decomposed body. They must delicately remove the shed skin of the cadaver's hand and roll it like a translucent glove over their own to ink it for fingerprints.

In the midst of all this decay, death calls in reinforcements. Long before humans can detect the first fetid traces of human rot, insects are attracted to the odor from as far as two miles away. They turn up in a predictable order. First come the carrion flies, such as the aptly named *Sarcophagidae*, or flesh flies, and *Calliphoridae*, or blowflies. They light on the body and lay tiny eggs in wounds, gaping mouths, and other available openings. These hatch within two or three days into writhing maggots that often move together as a teeming pack through the body, feeding on flesh. Then the Dermestids and other beetles appear. To liquefy flesh so that they can feed, both the carrion flies and beetles exude a battery of powerful enzymes. This is a very efficient way of dismantling a human body. Finally, when these creatures have

picked a skeleton almost clean, spiders, mites, and milli-
pedes arrive at the human dining table. In the tropics, a
cadaver completely exposed to the air and to insects will be
stripped to bone in just two to four weeks.

ANCIENT SOCIETIES WHO wished to preserve the
dead and put a stop to all this corruption, said Aufderheide,
had to find a way to break the terrible chain of decay. In
essence, that meant switching off the enzymes. There are
two main ways of doing this. The first is to deprive enzymes
of the water they need for their chemical reactions. The second is to destroy the precise chemical environment they
require. Although early societies such as the ancient Egyptians had no knowledge of the complex chemistry of
enzymes, they had a great deal of practical experience in preserving food and extending the shelf life of animal flesh.
Hunters, for example, knew that to keep the meat of a
gazelle or a brace of ducks, they had to gut the slain animals.
By this one step, they curbed the spread of enzyme-carrying
intestinal bacteria. Fishermen knew that to store their catch,
they needed to dry or salt the fillets. By these simple acts,
they deactivated enzymes.

Over time, human societies devised many ways to sabo-
tage these protein molecules. In Babylon, ancient embalmers preserved the dead by immersing them in honey, which
not only desiccated their flesh but destroyed bacteria. In
Southeast Asia, Buddhists saved the bodies of beloved monks
by coating them in a thick layer of powdered sawdust and
earth to wick away the moisture. Then they sheathed them
in silver and paint. Others resorted to alcohol. After the great

British naval hero Horatio Nelson breathed his last during the Battle of Trafalgar, his men immersed his body in a cask of brandy. But their grief did little to assuage their thirst. According to one story, the men could not survive the voyage home without their accustomed tots of brandy, so they stealthily siphoned the cask until it ran dry. This desperation produced a memorable turn of phrase still heard in the British navy today: "Tapping the admiral" is slang for pouring a drink of rum.

In ancient Egypt, a special guild of death professionals arose. Known as embalmers, these dehydration experts took the basic knowledge of preserving game and fish and gradually perfected it to create an elaborate technology of immortality. Just when this happened in Egypt and under what circumstances is still woefully unclear. What is known for certain, however, is that expert embalmers began practicing their craft along the Nile at least 4,500 years ago, preserving select members of the royal family. One early client was Queen Heteferes, whose famous son, Khufu, built the Great Pyramid at Giza.

So enamored were Khufu's successors with mummification that they tried to reserve the privilege for themselves and their families. As pharoahs, they were assumed to be living gods, and perhaps they wished to keep up appearances for as long as possible. A ruling king could not easily claim divinity as his birthright, after all, if it became known that his father and ancestors were simply moldering piles of bones like the kin of everyone else. But the pharoahs could not maintain their monopoly on immortality for long. Some four thousand years ago, Egypt's nobles usurped the right, and from then on mummification percolated downward through Egyptian society. As the demand grew, Egypt's embalmers thrived, setting up special workshops along the outskirts of towns, near tanneries and other such businesses. The "industrial park" location was probably no accident: the ancient Egyptian word for embalmer includes a hieroglyph commonly tacked on to words that denote smelly things.

The Egyptians did not sneer at these early death professionals, far from it. The embalming workshop was euphemistically referred to as "the pure place" or "the beautiful place." The embalmers themselves were deemed priests and as they worked they chanted magic spells. This was because the Egyptians viewed embalming as a deeply religious act. Every living human being, they believed, possessed a spiritual force and a life force, as well as a body. At death, the bond between these three elements was shattered. To be reborn and to live forever in a land where everyone remained lithe and young and beautiful—surely a notion of paradise with universal appeal—a person's spiritual and life forces had to recognize his body and re-unite with it. The sweet hereafter depended on the skill of an embalmer, who alone could maintain the body in recognizable form.

As priests, Egypt's embalmers were not in the habit of discussing their practices with the uninitiated. As businessmen, they guarded their trade secrets zealously, passing down the knowledge in their families, from father to son. Consequently, we have only a few brief contemporary accounts of mummification, and most of these were penned by foreign travelers, such as Herodotus, who were forced to glean their information where they could. But these out-lines, together with detailed anatomical studies and experi-ments conducted over the past century, form the basis of what we know today about Egyptian mummification.

For their wealthiest and most powerful clients, Egyp-tian embalmers used every trick of their trade. They likely began their operations by piercing the cranial vault of the corpse. Threading a metal tool—most probably some form of cylindrical tube—through one of the nostrils, they punc-tured the tiny porous ethmoid bone between the eye sockets and either drew or poured out the gray viscous folds of brain. Then, with an obsidian knife, they made a small, fist-sized incision on the left side of the abdomen. They reached inside the abdominal cavity and began slicing the sticky webs of connective tissue. Blindly hauling out fistfuls of ropy intestines, they excised the slippery spleen and moved on to other organs until they had removed most of the rapidly decaying viscera. The heart they generally left, and they often refrained from cleaning out the kidneys and pelvic structures.

With the evisceration done, they began stuffing the abdominal and chest cavities with dozens of small linen bags. Each contained a substance deemed divine by the Egyptians: natron. A naturally occurring compound of sodium carbonate and sodium bicarbonate that was often riddled with salt, natron was a superb desiccant. Egyptian embalmers were very fond of it. After packing the abdominal and chest cavities, they poured jar after jar of natron over the body to cover it. The amount needed was staggering. When American researchers Bob Brier and Ronn Wade tried replicating the ancient methods on a modern cadaver in 1994, they used 550 pounds of natron on the body and ran out before they could properly cover the feet. These they tucked into natron-filled booties. Then the pair locked the corpse in a storeroom set to the temperature of an average Egyptian summer day, 104 degrees Fahrenheit. When they opened the door five weeks later, the room smelled like sea air. Only a trace of a spicy, pepperlike odor lingered on the body itself as they removed the upper natron crust—suggesting exactly why the Egyptians considered natron divine.

For ancient embalmers, however, there was still much to do. They washed the desiccated flesh with sterilizing alcohol, thereby killing remaining bacteria, and rubbed the body with fragrant imported spices, such as cassia, a type of cinnamon from Asia, and myrrh, a tree resin from the Horn of Africa and southern Arabia. Then they painted the cadaver with a thick liquid coat of something that researchers generally call resin today, although this gives little sense of the diverse substances Egyptians used and their sometimes wondrous complexity. Not surprisingly, Egyptologists have argued for decades about the exact nature of this substance, and in the 1970s, a team of scientists led by an American epidemiologist, Aidan Cockburn, tried hard to answer this question by dissecting an Egyptian mummy from the Pennsylvania University Museum.

As part of the project, Cockburn and his colleagues took samples of the resin coating the mummy's skin. They subjected these samples to X-ray diffraction tests to separate out the main ingredients and managed, with great difficulty, to detect three compounds: myrrh, oil from the camphor tree, and oil from a member of the juniper family. But what struck Cockburn's team was the way these ingredients had naturally melded and polymerized to form "a vast and continuously molecular form," as they noted in one of their reports. It looked very much as if the mummy were preserved in amberlike layers of organic glass. This fascinated Cockburn and his colleagues. "Embedded in glass, as it were," they noted, "there is no reason why the body, as long as it is kept in a warm, dry, or cold place, should not survive until the end of time."

The Egyptian recipe for resin was never hard and fast, however. Over three thousand years of mummification, embalmers had a lot of time for tinkering and tweaking and depleting key ingredients. In the 1990s, an Israeli researcher, Arie Nissenbaum, ran molecular tests on resin from four Egyptian mummies. The results startled many Egyptologists. The Israeli researcher detected asphalt in the resin on all three bodies from Greek and Roman times. Further studies showed that the asphalt came from the Dead Sea, the salty lake that straddles the border of present-day Israel and Jordan. Huge blocks of the tarry substance still occasionally float to the surface of this lake from subterranean faults.

Aufderheide suspected that the resins at Dahkleh also contained asphalt. Some of his radiocarbon test results had revealed the presence of hydrocarbons, and to study this further, Aufderheide had dispatched samples to Nissenbaum. In his makeshift morgue, Aufderheide conjectured that later Egyptian embalmers had been forced to resort to asphalt. Tree resins would have been far preferable as an ointment: they smelled sweet and would have bathed the dead in a beautiful golden amber. But after millennia of mummification, he suggested, Egyptian embalmers could have depleted the junipers and other conifers that produced such resins. This shortfall likely caught them at a bad time. The dehydration business was booming in Greek and Roman times. Egypt's embalmers serviced not only native Egyptians, but also Europeans living in places like Alexandria. The embalmers had also begun preserving children, a practice unknown in earlier periods, attracting many new customers. "By this time," observed Aufderheide, "mummies had become an industry and there were only so many trees to go around." So embalmers had stretched and diluted the resins with small amounts of asphalt. The black stuff reeked, but it effectively waterproofed the mummy, ensuring that desiccated tissues would remain so for a very long time.

Intriguingly, this simple change in the resin formula may have exacerbated political tensions in the Middle East. To acquire asphalt, Egyptian traders journeyed to the Dead Sea, where they bartered for supplies from the local Arab merchants. Before long, news of the Egyptian gold to be made from Dead Sea tar circulated in the Middle East. Listening enviously to this, the king of Syria dispatched a military expedition to seize control of the lucrative Palestinian trade. This enraged the Egyptians. Worried that the Syrians were about to jack up the price of asphalt, or, even worse, turn off the tap, they responded by sending troops of their own in 312 B.C. According to Nissenbaum, the ensuing battle was likely the world's first oil war. Be that as it may, the Egyptians trounced the Syrians soundly, and from then on asphalt again flowed freely to the Nile.

* * *

IN THE MIDMORNING light, Aufderheide pushed aside the mound of tangled bandages at his feet. Picking up a large paintbrush, he began gently brushing off the body on the table, sending small clouds of fine linen dust aloft. Satisfied, he studied the ancient cadaver. Often, he explained, it was difficult to sex a mummy merely by looking at it. If the body had not dried properly, the genitalia rapidly rotted away, and mummification was hard on breast tissue. It was a simple fact of chemistry. After death, all the fat in this tissue turned into fatty acids. These acids were soluble, so they quickly evaporated with the body's stores of water. Frequently all that remained of a once generous bosom after dehydration was a miserly fold of skin, easily confused with wrinkles caused by overzealous wrapping. Sometimes, researchers could make an educated guess at gender based on the size of the nipples, a woman's areola being larger than that of a man's. But this was a judgment call—in less than half of all females could sex be established on the basis of breasts.

There was little question, however, about the body on the table. Nestled between the thighs was a perfectly preserved penis. It was clearly circumcised. Aufderheide jotted down the sex on a lengthy form he filled out for every mummy. He had devised this document himself and, like nearly everything that he put his hand to, it was meticulously organized and very thorough. It had a myriad of little boxes to check off and complex charts to fill in, complete with places for recording the presence or absence of mummy tattoos, beards, pierced ears, pubic hair, tumors, fungal growths, abcesses, bone fractures, rectal prolapses, umbilical cords on infants, and foreign bodies in mouths. There were also spaces for marking off one of forty-three different hairstyles and dental charts for recording tartar, lost teeth, and caries. Aufderheide was not one for missed opportunities. At home in Duluth, he was compiling a biomedical database of the mummies he had autopsied.

Putting down the pen and clipboard, he moved on. He cut a large oblong-shaped hatch on the man's chest and pried it open like a lid on a manhole. He peered inside. A dark, oily, crumpled mass of linen rags and chunks of crystallized black resin filled the abdomen. Aufderheide tried to pick out some of the largest pieces with his Swiss Army knife, but it was almost impossible. The linen stuffing had fused to the walls of the man's abdomen. Aufderheide shook his head, clearly disappointed. The embalmers, he said, had scooped out all the organs, even the heart that ancient Egyptians believed they needed for the final judgment.

Wiping off his hands, he jotted down the findings. Then he began severing the head. In Aufderheide's view, modern imaging techniques, developed for diagnosing ailments in living patients, could not hold a candle to the knife for obtaining medical information from mummies. CT scans, for example, recorded the minutiae of internal organs in living patients by detecting tiny differences in tissue density. They were much less capable of picking up minor variances in mummified organs. "Once you take the water out of tissues, they're all about the same density." The resulting uniformity obscures the delicate signatures of many diseases. Moreover endoscopy is little better. It gathers images by threading a small flexible fiber-optic tube into various body cavities and collecting tissue samples with tiny metal jaws. But the internal architecture of a mummy bears little resemblance to that of a living person. Often the dessicated visceral and pleural tissues have collapsed, leaving no space to insert even a small tube. And even if one could position the endoscope properly, it is extremely difficult to interpret its close-up images. "You've lost color, you've lost texture, and you can only identify something based on its location." Moreover, the metal jaws frequently crush brittle samples.

Turning back to the work at hand, Aufderheide started peeling off brittle patches of the scalp with its dark curls attached. This made a hideous ripping sound, a little like fingernails on a chalkboard. But Aufderheide quietly ignored it. Individual hairs, he explained, could be tested for the presence of ancient drugs or analyzed isotopically for clues to ancient diet. They were valuable samples. So too were fingernails and toenails. Made of keratin, the same substance as hair, they could also be tested for trace molecules of drugs. Aufderheide slipped the knife beneath the free edge of the man's right thumbnail and tried popping it loose, but it wouldn't budge. Neither would the nail on the next finger. So he took a hacksaw to these fingertips. They sounded like marbles as they hit the plank.

Next came the ears. Almost transparently thin, they dried swiftly after death, and this meant that they often retained the outermost layer of skin, the epidermis. Aufderheide bagged them in a single Whirl-pak. Then he began matter-of-factly severing the penis. The sight of this reminded me uncomfortably of a story I'd heard about Grafton Elliott Smith, the Australian anatomist who conducted thousands of mummy autopsies, including those on the bodies displaced by the Aswan Dam work in 1907. Smith had apparently taken an unusual interest in mummified genitalia. He had sketched them in his notebooks and amassed a large personal collection of private parts. His obsession seemed to have greatly disturbed his family. After Smith's death, someone tried destroying all records of it. This bowdlerizer ripped out the sketches from the notebooks and destroyed Smith's drawerfuls of shriveled penises. But the destruction wasn't complete. The bowdlerizer hadn't read the facing pages in the notebooks: these described in Smith's own handwriting the genitalia that had fascinated him.

Working away, Aufderheide explained his own reasons for this dissection. The penis, he observed, was the best place to find residues of ancient blood. "It has very little tissue other than vascular channels. That's all that's there. So it isn't subject to the enzymatic decay process to the same degree as the heart is. It's much more apt to survive intact." Aufderheide wanted samples of ancient blood in order to test for blood-borne infections and the like.

Satisfied that he had collected all he could, Aufderheide began sawing off the top of the skull. Inside, a skim of black resin coated the interior. At the base, a few rust-red maggots curled, themselves perfectly mummified. The cadaver, it seemed, had already begun rotting before an embalmer went to work on it. Then Aufderheide plucked a splinter from the wooden plank. He eased it gently into the nostril, probing until he found the small hole that the embalmers made to extract the brain. "Most people think the Egyptians used a hooked rod to pull the brain out," he observed, "but a normal brain is the consistency of a half-set gel. Those of us who have done forensic work and who've had the experience of working on a body that has sat in a summer room for three or four days know that you can just open the skull up and pour the brain out. So I suspect that's all they did."

When the elderly pathologist had finished, the cadaver on the table was a headless, ragged mass of bone, torn tendons, shorn muscles, and oily resinous rags. It scarcely looked human anymore. What two thousand years of nature, with all its insect hosts and its invisible armies of bacteria, had failed to accomplish, Aufderheide had managed in the space of just a few hours. The young man with the broken boxer's nose was now well on his way to joining the rest of humanity, turning first to carrion, then to whitened bone, and finally to a sad handful of dust. Eyeing all this devastation, I felt a deep sense of regret. The table looked like a miniature battlefield.

People who dissect mummies have different ways of justifying what they do. For the most part, however, they are pragmatic researchers who firmly believe that the pursuit of knowledge among the living takes precedence over the faith, beliefs, and hopes of the dead. They go about their work quietly, in out-of-the-way places, and choose their subjects carefully. They seldom dissect the most spectacularly preserved mummies, for these are often claimed by museums, institutions that have vowed to protect their collections. Nor do they often dissect the mummies of royalty or nobility, for these are now treasured too dearly to be subjected to the dissector's knife. Instead, they largely confine their autopsies, as Aufderheide does, to the mummies of ordinary people that have turned up by chance in recent excavations.

Aufderheide sincerely believes that such procedures

make the best of an impossible situation. A developing country like Egypt, he noted, could not possibly find sufficient funds to preserve Kellis's linen-wrapped mummies indefinitely. To purchase just one climate-controlled mummy case would set back the Egyptians somewhere between ten thousand and fifteen thousand dollars. Moreover, an Egyptian museum would then have to spend several thousand dollars more to put the case into operation. To properly house all the fifty or so mummies that Aufderheide had autopsied at Kellis would run to nearly three-quarters of a million dollars. "There's not a museum in the world, not even the Smithsonian Institute in Washington, that could deal with that situation if you drove up with a truck full of mummies," he noted.

Nor was it likely that the mummies could enjoy eternity undisturbed in their tombs. Grave robbers in Egypt and in many other parts of the world frequently tear apart such ancient bodies in search of gold, jewelry, and amulets. "The international ancient art market is insatiable," observed Aufderheide sadly. He had seen this for himself in Chile, when a peddler turned up at his hotel door one night with a box of antiquities. "When I examined his items closely, I was astonished to find that, while we were excavating a cemetery during the day, this man was looting it at night." The only solution, he concluded, was for archaeologists to stake out a cemetery and dig it quickly, recovering everything possible. Excavators could then set aside a few mummies for long-term preservation and rebury the rest, once a medical researcher had autopsied a small number. This was exactly what had happened at Dahkleh.

Aufderheide made a good case for dissection, but it occurred to me later that there was another, even more fundamental issue raised by such autopsies. Such destruction was only tolerable if it had the potential to benefit many others in some significant way. To take apart and ruin the body of a person who believed that all eternity depended on a whole, intact, preserved body was no small ethical problem. Indeed, such a radical act seemed impossible to justify for the sake of mere scientific curiosity about matters such as mummification techniques. But if, by this destruction, one could achieve something for the clear benefit of all humanity—if, say, one could find a cure for some cruel, wasting illness that had no cure— then perhaps all this cutting and ripping and savaging was not too high a price to pay. Aufderheide hoped to do just that.

He brushed the powdered linen from his shirt and pulled out a green garbage bag. It was nearly two o'clock. The panel truck would be back soon. It was time to wrap things up.

HOSTS

～

THE THOUGHT OF ALL THOSE plastic bags that Aufderheide had filled with brittle flesh remained with me when I left Dahkleh. I wondered just what would come of them. In our conversations in the desert, Aufderheide had frequently talked about the scientific value of such tissue samples, and I believed him. Mummified human tissue, even just a few fractions of an ounce, was becoming a scarce commodity for medical researchers. In some parts of the world, museum curators had taken to refusing all requests from aspiring researchers for scraps of ancient flesh, complaining bitterly about the deluge of letters of solicitation. At the rate things were going, they said, there soon would be nothing left of the preserved bodies in their care, not even a lock of hair.

The situation reminded me uncomfortably of stories I'd read of the infamous Resurrection Men. During the eighteenth and early nineteenth centuries, British and American anatomists faced a serious shortfall of something essential to their profession: human cadavers. As researchers, they needed fresh bodies in order to investigate the intricate arrangements of human muscles, tendons, sinews, bones, and internal organs. As teachers, they required corpses for their students to dissect. Without such firsthand experience of anatomy, young doctors and surgeons risked grave malpractice. In one notorious case, described in *The Lancet* in 1823, a confused British physician mistook a dislocated shoulder for a sprained muscle. His ignorance was not terribly surprising: there were simply not enough corpses to go around in anatomy classes. According to the British laws of the day, medical schools could only dissect the bodies of executed criminals, and the gallows could scarcely keep up with demand. In 1826, 701 English medical students had to make do with fewer than 600 cadavers.

But what the law prohibited, the spade and shovel nimbly provided. Professional body-snatchers stole into city cemeteries at night, digging up recently buried coffins by the light of a shaded lantern. Sliding the bodies into burlap sacks and tea chests, these Resurrection Men, as they were known, sold their ill-gotten merchandise by the inch to anatomists. News of this practice scandalized England. To save their kin from dissectionists, wealthy citizens began burying their relatives in costly guarded cemeteries. Middle-class families kept bodies until putrefaction clearly set in; no self-respecting Resurrectionist wanted such spoiled goods. Eventually, European and American legislators came to their senses, relaxing laws governing the dissection of cadavers. But as a result of this grim history, many people came to view medicine's hunger for human bodies and tissues with considerable distrust.

Such misgivings linger even today and extend to ancient bodies and ancient flesh. I certainly share these qualms. But those researchers who collect mummified tissue for their studies do their best to set these doubts to rest. They have very high hopes for their work. Aufderheide and a small group of his colleagues are struggling to advance scientific knowledge of some of the world's most serious plagues by tracing their history and origins through distant time. Reflecting on this, I wondered how much we could expect from such investigations. Could the flesh of mummies supply us with clues to cures or drug treatments for an ancient scourge? Could it help researchers develop something as complex as a vaccine? Could the ancient dead somehow reach out from the stillness of their tombs and give life to the living? The answers, I discovered, lay in places such as the Chihuahuan Desert of North America and along the lush Nile Valley of Egypt, with hundreds of mummies ravaged by tiny, microscopic parasites.

◦‿

RESEARCHERS HAVE DISCOVERED more than one hundred kinds of creatures that parasitize human beings, quite apart from bacteria, fungi, and viruses. Most of these organisms dwell in tropical parts of the planet, where they assume a stunning variety of shapes and forms, from simple-looking protozoa to more fantastic life-forms, such as the tiny cactuslike organisms known as thorny-headed worms. Some of their invasions produce nothing worse than a bad case of itching or a fleeting bout of intestinal cramps. But at the more serious end of the spectrum, their incursions lead to mutilation and hideous disfigurement, chronic illness and death. The microscopic protozoan *Leishmania brasiliensis*, for example, so ulcerates human mucous membranes in the mouth and throat that it corrodes away the lower half of the face, turning its victims into mute ghouls, while the tiny tapeworm *Echinococcus granulosus* so entrenches itself in the brain and other human organs that it forms immense growing cysts of poisonous fluid: the slightest rupture can bring rapid death. By such means, obscure parasites spread misery, infecting an estimated 4.5 billion people.

To protect human beings from these creatures, medical researchers have long sought to learn more about them.

As early as the turn of the last century, this quest for knowledge led science to mummified human tissue. In 1909, Marc Armand Ruffer, the son of a French baron and a former student of Louis Pasteur, detected dozens of minute calcified eggs, each equipped with a tiny spine, in the kidney tissue of Egyptian mummies. Ruffer had gone to Egypt to convalesce from a nearly fatal bout of diphtheria that he had contracted in London. He found Egypt to his liking and he stayed, taking a post as professor of bacteriology at the Cairo Medical School. When surveyors began turning up mummies by the cartload during preparations for raising the Aswan Dam in 1907, Ruffer recognized the value of these finds for medical science. He took tissue samples and began scouring them for traces of infectious disease. The three-thousand-year-old calcified eggs he detected belonged to a parasitic worm, *Schistosoma haematobium*, that damaged its victims' bladders and kidneys to such a degree that their urine turned bright bloody red.

Other researchers followed this lead, eventually identifying dozens of serious parasites in the withered organs of the ancient dead. But it wasn't until the late 1990s that mummy researchers began to envision something grander and more ambitious. At the mummy congress in Arica, they talked about ways of charting the waxing and waning of devastating parasites in ancient populations over hundreds or thousands of years. They were eager to study the epidemiology of the ancient past. An infectious disease, after all, is a delicate minuet danced over time by three parties: a parasite, the environment, and human behavior. Changes affecting any one of these dance partners can trigger or quell an epidemic. When the Aswan High Dam was built in Egypt during the 1960s, for example, economists hoped that construction would bring a new prosperity for farmers along the Nile. The dam would help irrigate more desert lands and, with a perennial source of water, farmers could sow four crops a year. The future looked very bright. What the economists did not take into account, however, was the parasitic worm *S. haematobium*. All the new, perennially filled water canals created prime habitat for snails that harbored *S. haematobium* during part of its life cycle. Four years after the dam was built, the incidence of schistosomiasis, the debilitating and often fatal disease caused by the parasite, rose sevenfold among farmers from Aswan to Cairo.

Aufderheide and a small group of other mummy experts were intent on examining the rise and fall of such parasites in the distant past. This was not an academic exercise. With a clearer understanding of these ancient scourges, they hoped to discern clues to new weapons against the most serious parasites. Medicine was desperate for treatments, vaccines, and cures. Aufderheide and his colleagues didn't want to waste time. So they turned their attention to three of the world's most destructive parasites. The first was a protozoan known as *Trypanosoma cruzi*, which causes Chagas' disease. More widespread in Latin America than HIV, *T. cruzi* infects an estimated 16 to 18 million people. It kills 43,000 of them annually.

KARL REINHARD DOESN'T look like someone who has spent most of his career squinting over the dregs of human intestines. He is an energetic and enthusiastic man with a passion for all things Brazilian. In his mid-forties, he has a beard, curly black hair and a thinning pate, and looks extremely fit, the consequence of a passion for both cycling and running. When he isn't teaching or lecturing, he favors wraparound sunglasses, T-shirts, and bicycle shorts and wears a Brazilian good-luck charm—a thin, faded-blue piece of cotton printed with the word *Bahia*—tied to his wrist. He has a teenager's breezy, casual way of talking and it makes him sound decades younger than he is. He still calls his wife, Debbie, of nearly twenty years "his bride" and uses expressions like "kind of groovy" to describe human organs that resist putrefaction. Instead of saying good-bye on the phone to friends, he often closes with, "See you on the flip side."

With interests scattered all over the scientific map, Reinhard has variously taught physical anthropology, palynology, and parasitology at the University of Nebraska in Lincoln. He is also on call to identify the bones of local murder victims, work he loathes. Lincoln, it seems, is still a small town at times: on one occasion, he was called in to piece together the remains of one of his own students who had been murdered. But Reinhard has a striking gift at times for turning sows' ears into silk purses. At the morgue, he infused a local forensic pathologist with his enthusiasm for studying disease in mummies. After that, the friendly Nigerian helped him get CT-scan time and collaborated with him on papers. "We became very good friends over red wine and dead bodies," observed Reinhard with a grin. "Not necessarily together."

Reinhard's speciality, however, is the study of ancient parasites. There are not many people in this esoteric field;

Reinhard has the only accredited paleoparasitology lab in North America, work that he gravitated to naturally. His father was an epidemiologist who studied disease in remote Inuit communities in Alaska, his mother a nurse. At universities in Arizona and later at Texas A&M University, Reinhard combined archaeology with parasitology, becoming an expert on the strange parasitic worms that colonize the human gastrointestinal tract. This entailed becoming an expert on everything that came out of this tract—parasite eggs, parasite larvae, bits of adult worms, pollen, partly digested food, and other wastes. He is an expert in the poop end of things, as some of his mummy colleagues like to put it.

It is a great discipline for someone who likes attention and who remains an overgrown kid. Reinhard is fond of livening up lectures by describing in plain language the grotesque biology of the creatures he studies, such as the female pinworm, which slithers out of the anus of an infected human at night and explodes shortly after, showering her eggs into the darkness like a cloud of spores. Audiences, he knows, love the graphic details. Moreover, Reinhard is constantly astonished by his subjects' endless hunger for life. "I once watched hookworms mate in a petri dish after we had removed them from puppy intestines," he recalled. "The puppies had been dead for eight hours, but the parasites were still alive and happy as can be, to the point of copulating blindly in a petri dish after we had taken them out. They just didn't care."

Reinhard came across his first case of ancient Chagas' disease in 1986 while visiting a rancher along the Texas-Mexico border. The man possessed a mummy that his father had casually exhumed during a Sunday afternoon outing in 1937. The preserved bodies of ancient Native Americans were once relatively common in caves overlooking the Rio Grande and its tributaries. Indeed, archaeologists had discovered several hundred of them in the remote region, which lay along the northern fringes of the Chihuahuan Desert. These mummies were the work of nature. Dry sand in the cave floors had wicked moisture away from their bodies, naturally dessicating their flesh.

When the rancher first uncovered the mummy, it wore a rabbit-fur robe and bore a painted red deer-hide strap about its waist. The rancher brought the body home and laid it out on the spare bed in his son's room. He and his son treated it like a family member, even building a special shed to house it. As Reinhard looked at it for the first time, he asked one of his companions, a prominent Texas archaeologist, what she thought the likely cause of death was. She pointed to a badly abcessed tooth. Reinhard, however, had his doubts. The skin and tissue covering the abdomen had rotted away. Inside, the large intestine was clearly visible. It was so packed with food that it literally filled the entire pelvic girdle. It looked as if its owner hadn't relieved himself for months before his death. "That mass of food haunted me for years after," said Reinhard. "I couldn't put it out of my mind."

Reinhard knew that Aufderheide and another American pathologist, Marvin Allison, had found several mummies in Chile with similarly distended intestines. In a paper Allison published on the subject, he suggested that these ancient Chileans had perished from Chagas' disease. Now

Reinhard had turned up a similar-looking case along the Texas-Mexico border, five thousand miles to the north. If the unfortunate man in the rancher's house had died from Chagas', the case raised some interesting questions. Where had the ancient plague begun and how quickly had it spread across Latin America? Reinhard decided to go back to the Rio Grande in the spring of 1998 to take a better look. He got permission from the ranch owner and headed south.

He spent several days photographing, measuring, and visually examining the mummy, meticulously studying the various organs exposed by decay. He couldn't get over the state of the body. An average mummified human has a large intestine just a bit over an inch in diameter. It generally holds about an ounce of fecal matter. The Rio Grande mummy had a terribly distended intestine. It was four inches wide and bulged with thirty-eight ounces of food. This included half-digested fish, rodents, bats, grasshoppers, plant fibers, seeds, and grass pollen. All this food occupied nearly a cubic foot of space. "The volume was so incredible I calculated it three times to make sure," said Reinhard. Crammed with food, the intestine crowded out the kidneys and the bladder and jammed up against the spine. "There was actually an indentation in the colon from the bones of the spine. And this man must not have been able to urinate, either, at the end. He had no body functions. What an awful way to die."

Medical researchers have a polite name for this condition: megacolon. There are two main causes. Children can inherit megacolon as part of a rare congenital disorder,

Hirschsprung's disease, which affects the nerves in the large intestine. Without any form of treatment they die. Adults, on the other hand, develop megacolon as a result of a massive infection from a tiny flagellate protozoan, *T. cruzi*.

T. CRUZI LOOKS A little like a microscopic wisp of egg white in water. It has a pointed posterior and a long whip behind that propels it. Stretched out end to end, *T. cruzi* measures no more than the width of two red blood cells. Its tiny size, however, is no measure of its destructive capability. It has a great affinity for mammalian muscle and nerve cells, particularly those in the intestines, esophagus, and heart. "When it attacks the nerves of the colon," observed Reinhard, "what happens is that peristalsis, the normal contractions of the intestines, becomes disrupted and after a while it stops. Then the intestine fills with food. The muscles of the intestinal wall lose their tone and the intestine becomes incredibly enlarged." The colon ends up looking like a knee sock that has wearily sprung its elastic. "The individual who is infected eventually dies, usually of blood poisoning, after several months of not being able to defecate."

In the Rio Grande Valley that separates Mexico from Texas, there is no shortage of suitable vectors for the disease. *T. cruzi* is carried by several different insect species that all belong to the *Reduviidae* family. Collectively known as assassin bugs or kissing bugs in English, or *vinchuchas* in Spanish, the reduviids are nocturnal winged creatures that vary in color from a dark brown to an ugly, viscous-looking amber. They range from Patagonia in South America to the northern forests of Canada. They are relatively small creatures, measuring about half an inch in length, and they suck blood with a long conelike beak. There is nothing pretty about them, and they are not the kind of company humans like to have around. But in poor communities in Latin America, families seldom have much choice.

Most assassin bugs live in the wild, hiding out by day in prickly pear thickets or under the bark of mesquite trees. But a few species—the worst kind, from a human point of view— prefer the walls of thatched mud-brick houses. Often families are blissfully unaware of the extent of the infestation in their homes because assassin bugs have the eerie trick of melting away during daylight into tiny cracks around windows and doors. Even entomologists have a hard time trapping them. To gauge their numbers in poor South American houses, researchers have experimentally taken apart buildings mud brick by mud brick. In one small house, they gathered up nearly ten thousand assassin bugs.

At night, the insects emerge from their hiding places like an army of tiny vampires. What they crave is a blood meal, a prerequisite for molting. Almost any mammal will do, from guinea pigs and dogs to humans. Lured by the carbon dioxide in exhaled breath, they crawl onto sleepers' faces and quench their thirst, defecating as they drink. If the insects are infected with $T.$ $cruzi$, they excrete the miniature parasites along with their wastes, and humans who absently scratch or rub a bite risk sweeping the protozoa into their mouths or eyes. Once inside the human body, $T.$ $cruzi$ gravitates swiftly to local lymph nodes and begins multiplying. This often triggers an acute infection, which can be lethal in young children. The most serious trouble, however, generally follows much later. Two decades or more can pass before an infected person realizes something is seriously wrong. By then the tiny invaders have stormed nerve cells in the central and peripheral nervous systems and muscle cells throughout the body. Nearly one in four of the infected develop severe and often fatal cardiac problems. One in seventeen present more gruesome symptoms—megacolon or megaesophagus.

The rancher's mummy, a man in his late thirties or early forties, had been just that unlucky 1,100 years ago. In all likelihood, said Reinhard, he was sleeping in a cave when he picked up *T. cruzi* from an assassin bug. Archaeologists in the region have found ancient grass beds in caves, which show that the early desert dwellers slept there. Such beds would have been ideal homes for vegetation-loving species of assassin bugs. But the infected man did not know this. Nor would he have known that anything was seriously wrong with him for a very long time, until one day he lost the ability to defecate and his abdomen began growing. Before long, he would have found it painful to move about, which is why he wrapped the deer-hide strap around his abdomen. This helped brace the ponderous mass of food. But it gave only temporary relief. With every meal he ate, his abdomen grew larger and harder until finally it could expand no more. His death was a misery. His intestines likely ruptured, spilling bacteria and partially decayed food into his bloodstream.

IN MANY WAYS, Reinhard had been very lucky. Researchers didn't often encounter such textbook cases of advanced Chagas' in mummies—for two good reasons. First of all, the ancient inhabitants of Latin America seldom lived to a ripe middle age. Most perished of malnutrition, pneumonia, diarrheal diseases, abcessed teeth, infestations of intestinal worms, complications from childbirth, swimming and hunting accidents, and the like before they ever reached their forties. This meant that many ancient Americans infected with *T. cruzi* succumbed to other things before the wispy protozoa could wipe out a major organ. The second problem related to the visibility of the disease. Three out of every four people infected with *T. cruzi* failed to develop any obvious anatomical signs of the disease. Their organs looked perfectly normal to the naked eye.

Both problems have long stood in the way of researchers interested in tracing the ancient epidemiology of *T. cruzi*. They bothered Art Aufderheide. As a pathologist, he had spent decades helping physician colleagues make difficult diagnoses and, through his studies of mummies, he had seen for himself the suffering that *T. cruzi* caused. So Aufderheide decided to apply all of his medical experience to solving the problem of detecting the microscopic parasite in mummies. The best way to find the minute protozoa in hundreds or even thousands of ancient bodies, he realized, would be to look for them on a molecular level. The best target would be the distinctive pattern of proteins that made up the DNA of *T. cruzi*. "If we could find the DNA of the bug," he explained, sitting in his Duluth laboratory one early spring morning after his return from Egypt, "then we'd be able to identify Chagas' even if there were no anatomical marks at all."

Aufderheide knew that this approach could work. A few

years earlier he and a biochemist colleague had spearheaded similar research on a test for *Mycobacterium tuberculosis* in mummies. But he also knew the work would be complicated. Human geneticists were accustomed to analyzing tissue samples taken from living or recently dead human beings. Their tests targeted relatively long strands of DNA that had undergone little or no decay at all. "The problem with ancient DNA," said Aufderheide, "is that it's usually broken up into smaller pieces. Most people would never bother trying to chase down DNA unless it was more than two hundred base-pairs long." With mummified tissue, Aufderheide didn't have that luxury. The double helix strands in the cells of an ancient cadaver often look as if they had been run through an office shredding machine.

For assistance, Aufderheide contacted Felipe Guhl, a Colombian biologist he had met at the mummy congress in Cartagena. Guhl was the head of a DNA lab in Colombia and had a strong interest in Chagas'. Intrigued by the project, Guhl agreed to start by looking for longer segments of ancient *T. cruzi* DNA, just to see if it could be done. Aufderheide sent the Colombian researcher a small box containing tiny bits of heart, esophagus, colon, rectum, ileum, and lung tissue he'd collected over the years from his dissections of South American mummies. The two researchers worked together closely. By the spring of 1997, they registered their first success. They identified a small but telltale segment of *T. cruzi* DNA in one-third of the heart samples and in all of the esophageal samples.

It was a solid beginning, but this form of testing wasn't nearly sensitive enough. It would almost certainly miss the really tiny snippets of *T. cruzi* DNA, all that remained in many mummies. Aufderheide wanted a test that could pick them up. As it happened, a medical lab at the University of Minnesota, where he worked, was experimenting with modern DNA. The lab's director offered to look for an 85-base-pairs segment of ancient *T. cruzi* DNA. After considerable trial and error, the team finally found it. Still Aufderheide wasn't satisfied—he knew the test was too cumbersome to be of much practical value. Mummy researchers needed something much simpler and swifter—a molecular probe for the tiny targeted segment. With this, they could test a batch of twenty mummy tissue samples in just a few hours. This would make an ancient epidemiological study possible.

So Aufderheide discussed the matter with biochemist Wilmar Salo, who agreed to make the probe. In his lab, Salo split a tiny targeted segment of DNA up the middle with an enzyme, creating two molecules. Repeating this reaction twenty times, he obtained a million-fold amplification of the DNA snippet, which became the probe. To test it, Salo coated a glass slide with nitrocellulose, a compound formed by the treatment of cellulose with nitric and sulphuric acids. Then he added a drop containing DNA from a mummy already diagnosed with Chagas'. The probe worked beautifully.

DOCTORS IN THE developed world usually think of *T. cruzi* as a Latin American problem, but this isn't true. During decades of civil wars, death squads, and unrelenting poverty in Latin America, millions of migrants have fled to the United States and other safe havens. Many carry *T. cruzi*. According to estimates based upon contagion rates in their countries of origin, nearly 370,000 Latin American immigrants in the United States alone are infected with the parasite. Worse still, few are aware of it. Physicians in the developed world, for example, seldom consider Chagas' as a possible diagnosis. Cardiologists rarely order blood tests for *T. cruzi* when they detect cardiac muscle degeneration in their patients. Instead they assume they are looking at coronary artery disease and other heart muscle ailments.

Moreover, migrants aren't the only infected ones. In the American South, assassin bugs also carry *T. cruzi*, occasionally transmitting it to humans. During the 1970s, researchers drew blood samples from five hundred longtime residents of the Rio Grande Valley in Texas, testing them for antibodies to *T. cruzi*. A positive result meant that the donor had come into direct contact with the protozoan. One in every forty of the Texans tested positive. Since then, health authorities in Texas have recorded nearly half a dozen home-grown cases of Chagas'. Some researchers now worry that this represents only a small fraction of the real number of infections in the region. They also suspect that the incidence of the disease is silently growing. Among new transient communities, known as *colonias*, just north of the Mexico border, houses are simple and assassin bugs are free to nestle in makeshift walls riddled with cracks and crevices.

Undiagnosed, the infected pose a threat to the safety of blood banks, for *T. cruzi* is perfectly capable of inveigling its way into a transfusion bag. Latin American studies have shown that one in every six people who receive blood tainted with the protozoa becomes infected—a risk factor that American and European blood banks have been slow to recognize and screen for. Medical researchers have reported four cases of transfusion-transmitted Chagas' disease in North America. In one of these, a seventeen-year-old boy died from an inflammation of the heart muscle after receiving tainted blood.

What makes this plague even more worrisome is the fact that medicine has few ways of battling it. Physicians possess just two drugs, benznidazole and nifurtimox, for combating the parasite. Both are toxic and of dubious value for established infections. In South America, where the death toll from Chagas' is highest, health experts have pinned their hopes on schemes to break the chain of *T. cruzi* infection. Their main tactic is to wipe out the assassin bug from mud-brick and thatch homes. Since 1991, teams have sprayed more than two million rural dwellings with insecticides, but no one really knows how effective this will be in the long term. Almost a half century ago, the World Health Organization launched a similar campaign against malaria-carrying mosquitoes. Health workers sprayed houses and mosquito-breeding grounds in the tropics with DDT, wiping out most of the insects. But the few that survived bred offspring resistant to DDT and other insecticides, creating an even worse problem. Further complicating the campaign against Chagas' are sweeping changes in places such as Brazil. As settlers slash and burn the forests of the Amazon, pushing into previously uninhabited areas, they create new frontiers for assassin bugs and *T. cruzi*.

As a result, medicine urgently needs to know everything it can about the parasite. So Aufderheide and his colleagues have gone to work, testing South American mummies with their new DNA probe. The new data, they believe, will tell science a great deal about where Chagas' came from. Reinhard and others have theorized that the plague was born during an ancient agricultural revolution in the South American Andes. Some four to five thousand years ago, wandering bands in the region began sowing corn along the banks of winding rivers. To tend fields and store the harvest, families had built houses and settled in villages, raising guinea pigs for meat. All these conditions—the new houses with their cracks and crevices, the veritable shopping market of hosts—would have attracted hordes of assassin bugs infected with *T. cruzi*. Under the circumstances, it would have been only a matter of time, said Reinhard, before the parasite made its way into the human bloodstream. "I would guess that Chagas' was an almost inevitable consequence of settling the New World."

In addition to tracing the origins of Chagas', Aufderheide wants to find clues to controlling the devastating parasite. By charting the prevalence of *T. cruzi* infections over time and space, he and others hope to study the ancient waxing and waning of the epidemic. A sharp decline in infection rates in some part of *T. cruzi*'s range could point to a previously unrecognized biological, chemical, or environmental agent effective against the protozoa, something that medical researchers could develop into a weapon.

It would not be the first time, noted Aufderheide, that ancient epidemiology had supplied clues to a new vaccine. English researcher Keith Manchester had turned up something important while investigating the ancient relationship between two parasitic diseases, leprosy and tuberculosis.

Through written records from the Middle Ages and the Renaissance, Manchester had charted prevalence rates of the two diseases over time. What he discovered was a neat inverse relationship. Leprosy sharply declined in England in the fifteenth century just as tuberculosis began to rage. It turned out that the human immune response to tuberculosis had a suppressive effect on leprosy, reducing infection rates in a community. Earlier researchers had suspected this, but Manchester demonstrated the relationship superbly. And as a result of this, physicians in India and elsewhere are now employing a weakened strain of tuberculosis as a dual weapon against tuberculosis and leprosy. "So that was the payoff," concluded Aufderheide. "Once we recognized what caused the changes in the relative frequencies in these diseases, we found a way to exploit that by modern methods."

Aufderheide has only begun testing the mummified tissues in his private collection, but he firmly believes that such ancient samples might hold similar revelations. He is not alone in this conviction. At the Mummy Congress in Arica, I had met another leading researcher tracking ancient disease. With a team of American and Egyptian medical researchers, Rosalie David is testing the tissues of Egyptian mummies for residues of two other deadly parasites, *Schistosoma haematobium* and *Schistosoma mansoni*. David seemed excited about the research. She gave me her card and encouraged me to call. Curious to learn more, I decided to take her up on the offer.

IN A SMALL restaurant on the University of Manchester campus, David briskly brushed the crumbs from her suit, irritation mounting. After weeks of unanswered e-mails and unreturned phone calls, I had finally succeeded in arranging a meeting with the prominent Egyptologist and had flown to Manchester with a notebook full of questions. But once she had speedily downed lunch and a dish of sticky toffee pudding, her favorite dessert, David had begun wrapping things up, pleading other engagements. I had, it seemed, just crossed an entire continent and the Atlantic Ocean for a one-hour lunch. It was maddening, but then David's brush-offs were well known to some of her colleagues. Desperate to stretch out lunch another five minutes, I offered the harried waitress a credit card for the bill. David wasn't amused. Across the table, her pale-blue eyes followed the waitress's every movement. She looked like a fox ready to pounce.

David is the keeper of Egyptology at the Manchester Museum and director of the famous Manchester Egyptian Mummy Research Project. Less officially, however, she is the grande dame of mummy studies in England and like grande dames everywhere, she doesn't seem to care much what others think of her. She favors sensible floral frocks and sturdy navy suits and wears her long graying brown hair in a bun on the top of her head, a style she hasn't changed a whit in almost thirty years. She wears no makeup. She sports no jewelry, other than a wedding ring. She seldom smiles or laughs. In all likelihood, she wouldn't draw a second look in a crowd.

But this seeming ordinariness camouflages one of the shrewdest minds in Egyptology. The author of more than twenty books on ancient Egypt and its mummies, David first recognized her calling at the age of six, when a teacher held up a photograph of the famous line of pyramids at Abu Sir. At home, David devoured books on Egypt, and eventually she applied to the prestigious Egyptology program at University College London. The university took only one student in Egyptology every few years, and in the 1960s they picked David, the daughter of a sea captain from South Wales, as their student. Delighted, David immersed herself in the study of hieroglyphics and Egyptian history.

When a position for an Egyptologist finally came open at the Manchester Museum, David took it. With its dour gray stone and Gothic atmosphere, the museum looks more like a set for the *Addams Family* than a serious research institution, but its galleries hold a superb collection of Egyptian antiquities. David decided to study its mummies. One of her heroes, Margaret Murray, had autopsied two mummies from the museum in 1908, aided by an interdisciplinary scientific team. Since then, few English researchers had been daring enough to bring science into the shuttered confines of Egyptology. David thought it time to try again. She picked a team of medical specialists and chose a mummy from the Manchester collections. The autopsy she conducted on it in 1975 became a media frenzy, something that appalled many of her colleagues. "They thought I was just trying to get on television," huffed David. She ignored the gibes, however, and the new data she gleaned from that autopsy and from later explorations of mummies through medical imaging and endoscopic sampling convinced many of her colleagues to take up similar projects.

Since then, David has published widely on mummies and, six years ago, she came in contact with George Contis.

Contis is the president of Medical Service Corporation International, an American health services firm that helps governments in developing countries control their deadliest parasites. At the time, Contis had an idea for a new project. His firm had just completed an epidemiological study of schistosomiasis in Egypt, and he wanted to extend investigations of S. *haematobium* and S. *mansoni* into the distant past there. The schistosomes are the source of much human suffering, infecting nearly 200 million people globally and killing 20,000 annually. Contis was keen on seeing the past geographical range of S. *haematobium* and S. *mansoni* and studying the differences in infection rates between men and women and adults and children. Such studies could give clues to a new vaccine.

David was fascinated. She loved the idea that research on the ancient Egyptian dead could yield tangible benefits for the living. "It was one way our studies could help the modern day, apart from being extremely interesting," she said. She was also keen to see whether parasitic infections such as schistosomiasis, also known as bilharzia, increased during periods of turmoil in ancient Egyptian history. Moreover, she suspected there would be sound financial benefits to combining Egyptology with medicine. Public enthusiasm for mummies rarely translates into funding for research. Medical studies do.

David was optimistic that ancient mummies along the Nile could reveal much about schistosomiasis, for the Egyptians themselves had frequently recorded its symptoms. In the famous Ebers papyrus, ancient physicans described a condition that turned men's urine red, one of the principal early symptoms of schistosomiasis. So common was this condition that many Egyptians believed that boys came of age when blood appeared in their urine, rather like a woman's menstruation. It was not until the modern era that parasitologists in Egypt managed to tease out the real cause. In 1851, a young researcher at Cairo's Kasr-el Aini hospital, Theodore Bilharz, found a strange white worm in the blood of the portal vein of a human cadaver. It was the first time that science had taken note of S. *haematobium* and Bilharz was enthralled. As he pored over his find, he observed its peculiar biology, describing it in wonderfully detailed letters to his mentor, the famed German zoologist Karl Theodor von Siebold. The pale worm, it transpired, was not one creature but two. The long flat-bodied organism was the male of the species; the female was a gray thread that lay in a groove bisecting the length of his body. From this strange quirk of biology came the name *schistosome*, or split body.

Modern studies have revealed much about the destructive lives of the schistosomes. As the males copulate with their respective females, they migrate into smaller and smaller veins in the human intestine or bladder. Raising and lowering their posterior suckers, the females release a cloud of tiny eggs at each stop along the way, laying as many as two thousand a day over a five-year period. Nearly half these eggs are swept into the gut or the bladder, where they are safely shed into the outside world, but the others are trapped. They lodge in gut and bladder walls by the thousands and calcify, causing serious damage. Schistosome eggs in the urinary system can trigger bladder cancer, kidney disease, or liver failure. Those embedded in the intestines can lead to lethal complications of the liver and spleen.

Infected humans who seek out irrigation canals and

rivers as toilets release the eggs into water. In this new medium, the schistosomes hatch into juveniles and immediately begin searching for their next hosts, freshwater snails from three different genera. Inside the bodies of the snails, the schistosomes undergo further development. Each produces as many as four thousand more juveniles, and a month later this parasitic armada takes to the water again, this time in pursuit of mammalian hosts. Humans who bathe, swim, fish, or work in contaminated waters are prime targets. Schistosomes are attracted to humans by the secretions on their skin, and the microscopic worms creep about the hair follicles until they are finally able to penetrate the epidermis. Shedding their tails, they worm their way to the nearest vein, where they are swept into the liver, launching the whole cycle again.

After decades of concerted effort, medical researchers have found few effective defenses against the schistosomes. There is no safe effective vaccine and no cure. The most effective treatment is chemotherapy with a drug called praziquantel, but it seldom gives long-term relief. When patients return to working on irrigation canals or fishing boats, they often become reinfected. Moreover, physicians have recently noticed something alarming: the schistosomes are beginning to develop resistance to the chemotherapy. "So if we could see what had actually happened to the parasite over a long period of time," observed David, "it might be possible to see where it was going in the future, or what it was likely to do, because it's a very clever parasite. You've got to try to find methods to treat it while it's changing and developing."

An important first step was to devise a sensitive and

cheap technique for detecting the parasites in mummified human tissue. David's medical collaborators chose to home in on the chemistry of the ancient human immune system. When schistosomes invade the human bloodstream they produce distinctive proteins known as antigens, which circulate freely in the blood and produce an immune response. By developing a kind of litmus test for these antigens, team members could check any type of ancient tissue available— whether skin, brain, or lung—rather than just the urinary or intestinal tracts where the parasites thrived. "You don't have to have the parasite, because the reaction against it will be present throughout the body," observed David.

At the Mummy Congress in Arica, David had described the team's first major success. After months of work, her colleagues had finally succeeded in detecting schistosome antigens in the ancient Egyptian mummies they had tested. One of the most encouraging results came from the liver sample from a four-thousand-year-old mummy. "It's the first time, as far as I'm aware, that this technique has been developed for this purpose," observed David with pride in her voice. But before the team could proceed with wide-scale testing for the parasite, they needed something enormously difficult to obtain: tissue samples, thousands of them, from mummies of every time period in ancient Egypt.

For nearly anyone other than England's doyenne of mummy research, this would have been a tall order. But David and colleague Patricia Lambert-Zazulak had devised a sound plan. They had compiled lists of all the world's collections of Egyptian mummies. Then Lambert-Zazulak canvassed each by letter, asking curators and private collectors to donate tiny bits of ancient tissues. Such donations, obtained by careful endoscopy and gleaned from already exposed organs, would be housed in a new tissue bank at the University of Manchester and shared by researchers worldwide. "The point of taking the samples," observed David, "is that you only have to do it once, so you're not having to go back and intrude on the mummies time and time again. The sample is there for future study."

David was pleased with the replies the team had received. "Many of the major Egyptian collections have responded favorably, and I think we'll end up with several hundred institutions and multiple samples from each one. So we'll probably have in the region of several thousand samples." With such a tissue bank at the University of Manchester, David believes that she and her colleagues will be able to trace the ancient history of the schistosomes back nearly five thousand years in Egypt, a record that will help answer many of the questions that Contis had first posed to her. Further down the road, David said, similar studies could explore many other diseases. She is personally very interested in charting the ancient history of malaria, the world's most devastating tropical disease. Each year, malaria kills one million people, and with global warming many experts fear that this toll will rise.

As I later thought about our conversation, I began to see the stunning range of possibilities that people like David and Aufderheide envisioned. In years to come, medical researchers struggling to outwit all manner of deadly parasites—from viruses to bacteria, rickettsia to amoeba, fungi to protozoa—could turn to the mummified dead in search of new weapons. Sealed in their preserved cells is an astonishing molecular archive of disease, a record of misery and malady far more ancient and far more complete than any noted on rice paper, papyri, clay tablets, or stone. Humanity, after all, discovered its knack for writing just five thousand years ago, and the written history of disease is woefully incomplete.

In decades to come, as we remake our world with technology, as we log entire rain forests, drain seas, dump our wastes in rivers and oceans, and warm the world with our greenhouse gases, we will have great need of such an archive. Transforming the world beyond recognition, we will blindly tip the balance of disease, freeing ancient parasites held in check for millennia, and we will succumb to a host of their new plagues. That is the essence of life and parasites hungry for life. Their diseases are inevitable. And the more the world around us changes and evolves, the more help we will need from the mummified dead who lie unchanged in their tombs.

Drug

Barons

⌒

U NTIL I BEGAN THINKING AND writing about
mummies, I had never seen any of Hollywood's
famous mummy movies. Like most other North American
teenagers in the sixties, I had loved horror films, the
cheesier the better, and rarely passed up a chance to watch
the mayhem wreaked by werewolves, vampires, and cat-
women. But though I loved the gothic gloom of these
movies, so at odds with my own sunny suburban upbring-
ing, I had never had the pleasure of seeing Boris Karloff or
Lon Chaney Jr. rise from the dead and trudge wearily across
the screen in something suspiciously resembling torn bed-

sheets. One day, I happened to mention this to my neighbor Neil, who is an artist and a film buff, and he quickly offered to remedy my ignorance. Neil collects old horror movies. So every second night or so for two weeks, I curled up on my sofa and watched mummy movies.

For the most part, the old Universal Picture films were entertaining, although to my more jaded adult eyes, they were rather lacking in real horror. But what struck me most while watching them was the curious way in which Hollywood screenwriters had chosen to flesh out the Mummy's character. For all his extraordinary powers—his lethal hugs and his bizarre ability to chase down and corner far more agile victims—the Mummy was a creature trapped in the machinations of the living, a superhuman who was pathetically vulnerable. His Achilles' heel was a chemical one. Larger than life though he was, the Mummy was mad for an invention of Hollywood's screenwriters: tana leaves. The bandaged monster needed three of these leaves to keep his heart beating, nine to animate the rest of his body, and even the slightest whiff of the stuff seemed to send him reeling for more. On the silver screen, the Mummy was a junkie.

His insatiable hunger for tana was a simple plot device, but it reminded me of a new branch of mummy research. For many decades, anthropologists had wondered about when human beings first began consuming potent narcotic plants and the circumstances under which this had occurred. Had Mediterranean farmers first dabbled with opium for its medicinal powers, or had they smoked it as a drowsy pleasure? Had Inca rulers reserved coca leaves for themselves, or had they distributed them freely to their subjects in order to work them harder? Was drug addiction an affliction only of the modern world or was it also a social problem in the past? These were fascinating questions, but no one really knew how to get at the answers. The only existing evidence was circumstantial. Archaeologists in Greece, for example, had unearthed ancient jars shaped like the pods of the opium poppy, while Egyptologists had discovered wall paintings of Egyptian nobles clasping bouquets of narcotic plants. Even Tutankhamen, the famous boy king with the sleepy eyes, had been depicted holding opium poppies and mandrake, a source of the narcotic scopolamine. Impressed by this, one Spanish researcher theorized that Tutankhamen was an addled addict held in thrall by his pusher, the ambitious prime minister who sought control of Egypt.

Wall paintings and pottery styles are clearly open to interpretation. The early potters who worked clay into poppy shapes may have merely meant to copy one of nature's more beautiful designs, nothing more. The Egyptian artists who decorated tomb walls with paintings of narcotic plants may have been innocently unaware of their powers. What archaeologists and Egyptologists needed was hard proof of ancient drug use, something irrefutable, something that they could even have taken to court, if they had chosen to do so. What they eventually turned to was something that had long lain under their eyes in museums around the world: the fine hair of mummies.

～

IN THE EARLY 1950s, a team of American dermatologists stumbled across something unexpected while studying the side effects of phenobarbital. A popular sedative and depressant that acted indiscriminantly upon the central nervous system, phenobarbital was frequently prescribed to quell and control the seizures of severe epileptics. But the drug had several worrying drawbacks. It was highly addictive. It could induce hallucinations and extreme agitation. And it sometimes painfully affected the skin, producing patchworks of scaly rashes. While examining these latter effects in guinea pigs, the dermatologists noticed that trace amounts of the phenobarbital they injected into the rodents ended up in the animals' hair. As blood from the circulatory system flowed around the living roots of hair, minute quantities of phenobarbital permeated the shafts. When the hair grew outward and died, the shaft trapped the drug molecules like insects in fossil amber. Each hair became a tiny, complete document of drug use over time.

The team published their findings, but in the polite bobby-sox era of the 1950s the paper passed without much notice. A quarter century later, however, after the "Electric Kool-Aid acid test," Woodstock, and the war on drugs, chemists were mesmerized by the implications. Law enforcement agencies and Fortune 500 companies were clamoring for ways of screening job applicants and checking employees for pot smoking, cocaine addiction, and heroin injection. Hair promised to be revealing: a two-inch-long strand could potentially chart five months of personal drug history. A vial of urine, on the other hand, could reveal only what had taken place in the previous few days. So toxicologists began working on protocols for testing strands of hair. By 1999, hair testing had become big business. Parole officers were testing parolees, hospitals were checking staff, banks were examining guards, and vice squads were running samples from suspects. Indeed, hair helped convict Marion Barry, the former mayor of Washington, D.C., of cocaine possession. "The drug test is moving from the bathroom to the barber shop," trumpeted *U.S. News and World Report*.

Such high-profile drug busts seemed a world away from the closeted discipline of Egyptology. But in the early 1990s, an energetic young physical anthropologist at the University of Munich got very interested in testing the ancient dead for drugs. Franz Parsche had spent several years hovering over bodies exhumed from a Roman-era cemetery in the eastern Nile Delta, investigating everything from their mummification methods to the trace elements that resided in the hardened plaque on their teeth. While baring these intimate secrets, he had become intensely curious about ancient drug use. Under the reign of the pharaohs, Egyptian traders had bartered avidly for seeds of *Cannabis sativa*. Their Asian neighbors prized the plant for its hempen fibers, and the Egyptians seem to have taken a similar interest. They retted the stems and twisted the fibers into sturdy ropes and ground the plant to make a soothing eyewash, a treatment they recorded in medical papyri. But the Egyptians made little mention of other parts of *C. sativa*—the flowering tops and leaves that yielded marijuana or the dark resins that produced hashish.

Parsche wondered about all of this. While studying Egyptian mummies in Munich with colleague Wolfgang Pirsig, he began casting around for ways of giving the ancient dead drug tests, an inquiry that led him to hair testing. Hair, after all, is one of the body's most enduring tissues. Few bacteria possess the enzymes needed to break down its primary protein, alpha-carotene. As a result, many mummies are crowned in curls, braids, or neatly combed hair; even skeletons occasionally sport a few grotesque locks, a melancholy reminder that whitened bone had once been sheathed in flesh and blood. But finding drugs in modern hair was no guarantee of success with ancient strands. Parsche wondered whether chemicals like tetrahydrocannabinol (THC), the primary alkaloid in marijuana and hashish, could survive in the hair shaft for centuries, even millennia. So he and Pirsig contacted one of Germany's foremost specialists in hair testing, Svetlana Balabanova.

A toxicologist and endocrinologist at the Institute of Forensic Medicine in Ulm, Germany, Balabanova had worked closely with German police forces, publishing widely on her successes in detecting hashish, cocaine, methadone, caffeine, and nicotine in human hair. Moreover, she had research interests far beyond her own narrow speciality. Possessed of immense self-confidence, she relished social history and anthropology and was in the midst of writing a popular book on the cultural significance of human hair, from the carved coiffeurs of the famous Venus figurines of Paleolithic Europe to the gelled spikes of punk rockers in EU times. Solid and thickset in her early sixties, with a long oval face, high Slavic cheekbones, soft hazel eyes, and dark chestnut brown hair pulled back from her face, Balabanova, a Bulgarian refugee, is no ordinary scientist.

She didn't know whether drug molecules could survive for millennia in human hair, but she thought it possible. A few years earlier, an American colleague had discerned traces of an opiate in a hair snipped from the famous nineteenth-century Romantic poet John Keats. Keats had been an opium eater. But it was one thing for an opiate to linger in a tress preserved with loving care by an admirer for a century and a half. It was quite another for a narcotic or stimulant to persist in locks exposed to the elements in a desert tomb for millennia. Balabanova was game, however, to try testing for them. She has a restless, inquiring mind and an appetite for scientific adventures. "To find something new," she explained to me, "is always tempting."

Thus encouraged, Parsche and Pirsig began collecting mummy hair. With permission from Munich museum authorities, they obtained locks from more than eighty Egyptian and Peruvian mummies, which ranged in age from five hundred to three thousand years old. Parsche and Balabanova agreed that they would test all the samples for three drugs: THC, cocaine, and nicotine. These seemed logical choices. Both tobacco and coca were New World plants that the ancient Peruvians had known well; mourners often tucked bags of tobacco and coca leaves into shrouds as gifts for the next world. Tests for tobacco might also shed light on an earlier brouhaha. In 1975, French scientists had recovered bits of brown leaves that looked suspiciously like tobacco from the abdomen of one of Egypt's greatest pharoahs, Ramses II. Under the microscope, the cells closely resembled those of tobacco, and chemical tests revealed molecules of three drugs, one of which was nicotine. Intriguingly, the French team also found tiny beetle carapaces in the linen bandages. They belonged to *Lasioderma serricorne*, the aptly named cigarette beetle, which dines on stored tobacco leaves and other dried plant materials. Egyptologists had dismissed these finds, however, suggesting that early pipe-smoking excavators and museum curators had merely spilled tobacco from their pouches on the body.

So to be thorough, Balabanova decided to test all of the Munich mummy samples for each of these drugs. Washing the samples with distilled water and ethanol, she pulverized the hairs with a steel ball and chemically released the molecules remaining in their shafts. Then she added antibodies, tagged with a telltale isotope, to the solution, in a technique known as radioimmunoassay. Antibodies are molecules that the human immune system makes to neutralize and disarm potentially harmful foreign substances in the body. They are a specific system of defense. A cocaine antibody, for example, will only target and react with cocaine molecules, seeking them out with eerie accuracy. To determine whether the antibodies had locked on to their targets in the hair samples, Balabanova measured the isotopes with an instrument resembling a Geiger counter.

She tallied the number of positives for each drug. Then, to be certain of the results, she ran a different test on each sample. Known as gas chromatography/mass spectrometry, this type of analysis is often used to identify components in an unknown mixture. To run the procedure, Balabanova once again pulverized tiny samples of the hair and chemically released the molecules within them. Then she injected the resulting fluid by syringe into a long narrow tube in an ovenlike instrument. As the temperature rose inside, the components in the fluid each vaporized according to their own level of volatility, and this created a distinctive fingerprint for the solution. Balabanova then compared these fingerprints to those known for cocaine, nicotine, and THC.

She was deeply puzzled by the results. The Egyptian hair contained not only THC, but also cocaine and nicotine. The Peruvian hair disclosed cocaine, nicotine, and minute traces of THC. This seemed all wrong, for how could the Egyptians and the ancient Peruvians, separated by thousands of miles of uncharted ocean, obtain drugs from one another so far back in the distant past? The youngest Egyptian mummy had died 1,600 years ago, a millennium before Christopher Columbus sailed from Spain to the West Indies, thus charting the first trade routes across the Atlantic. Admittedly, there were a few researchers, such as the Norwegian adventurer Thor Heyderdahl, who had speculated about earlier ocean crossings, but on the whole the scientific community considered these theorists to be cranks and loose cannons.

Balabanova ran the samples again. "I retested the positives three to four times." Each time she expected to turn up some mistake, some source of contamination, but she didn't. Thinking that the problem could lay with the samples themselves, she acquired hair from natural mummies recently excavated from the Sayala region of northern Sudan, which had once been part of Roman Egypt. Nearly 80 percent of these bodies scored positive for cocaine and nicotine. No matter what Balabanova did, it seemed, the results were still the same.

Other researchers would have been strongly tempted to file away such data, in the interests of their scientific reputation. But Balabanova refused. She was convinced she was onto something important and she loathed the thought of suppressing a truth. When she was a child in Sofia, her father, a writer whom she admired deeply, had stood up and repeatedly criticized the Communist Party. When the Communists rode to power after the Second World War, he was arrested and imprisoned. Destitute, her family fled to Czechoslovakia, and when Soviet tanks rolled into Prague in 1968, Balabanova packed her bags once again and fled to Germany. She couldn't and wouldn't stay in Czechoslovakia. "I was raised to say the truth," she recalled. "It's a question of life philosophy, I suppose. There are people who just follow and there are people who choose their own paths, irrespective of the criticism."

So she and Parsche published the findings. But they kept strictly to the facts in their papers. In their letter to the editor in *The Lancet*, for example, they offered no explanation for how these drugs had come to be where they were, nor did they so much as allude to an ancient transcontinental trade. But readers of *The Lancet* had little trouble connecting the dots. They could see all too clearly where the work was heading. "Was Thor Heyerdahl right about Egyptians going to South America," wrote one exuberant reader, "and did they come back bearing tobacco and coca? Was there already an international trade in drugs, with hashish exchanged for cocaine and tobacco? Were there already drug barons?"

Newspaper and magazine editors rubbed their hands with glee, writing riveting headlines such as "Toke like an Egyptian" and assigning illustrations of mummies smoking joints and shooting up. At Channel Four in England, producers began hastily researching a new documentary, *The Mystery of the Cocaine Mummies*. But in cooler scientific and scholarly circles, there was little but disbelief. "It is very unlikely that tobacco has an alternative history, because I think we would have heard about it," observed Sandra Knapp, a botanist at the Natural History Museum in London, in front of TV cameras. "Drugs like tobacco rarely disappear or are kept secret for long." Oxford University Egyptologist John Baines was similarly incredulous when approached by the Channel Four crew. "The idea that the Egyptians were traveling to America is, overall, absurd. I don't know of anyone who is professionally employed as an Egyptologist, anthropologist, or archaeologist who seriously believes in any of these possibilities."

I FIRST CAUGHT wind of the controversy at the Mummy Congress. I had missed both the Channel Four documentary, which portrayed Balabanova's findings in a favorable light, and the sensational articles, but I heard a great deal about them over cocktails in Arica. No one knew exactly what to think about Balabanova's findings or how she had come by such results, and this confusion was exacerbated by her absence. The German chemist had yet to attend a Mummy Congress to present her controversial findings. Despite all the gossip, however, I decided to keep an open mind. I knew the ancient Egyptians were not the nautical incompetents that many made them out to be. A few years earlier, while writing about the ancient frankincense trade in the Middle East, I had discovered how intrepid the builders of the pyramids could be when they hankered for luxuries.

Some 3,900 years ago, for example, the Egyptian pharoah Sesostris I conceived a magnificent plan for a sailing expedition to obtain the precious golden-yellow resin, frankincense. Sesostris's subjects were in love with frankincense. They burned small chunks of it for incense and charred and ground it to make black kohl for eyeliner. But frankincense was frustratingly rare. The trees that yielded the tiny resinous teardrops did not grow anywhere in Sesostris's realm. Instead, the finest quality came from a region that the Egyptians called Punt, and which some leading authorities on the frankincense trade now believe is Oman, along the eastern Arabian coast. From there, the much prized resin traveled north overland, trading hand to hand to Palestine and Egypt.

Sesostris, a shrewd businessman, wanted to cut out some of the middlemen. He ordered his vizier to construct a fleet of wooden boats sturdy enough to travel the often stormy Red Sea. At the town of Koptos along the Nile, the vizier put a small army of Egyptian laborers to work, and after months of sawing and cutting and planing, they finished the new fleet, all but for the stone anchors. Then the vizier instructed his men to take the ships apart, piece by piece. When the new fleet had been reduced to tons of cedar planks, he ordered his men to prepare for a long journey to the Red Sea coast. They packed the ships in pieces across nearly seventy miles of austere desert and over mountain passes. On the coast, the vizier ordered them to reassemble the boats and find local craftsmen to carve quarter-ton blocks of local stone into anchors. This they did. Then they set sail for Arabia.

When the fleet returned, it carried frankincense and many other treasures. The vizier's representative, Ameni, ordered the men to dismantle the ships. The vessels couldn't be left behind for thieves. The stone anchors were too heavy, however, to haul back across the desert. So Ameni made a shrine of the anchors above the harbor on the Red Sea and had the walls inscribed with an account of the journey, which archaeologists found in the 1970s. Then Ameni and his men carried their ships back in pieces across the sweltering Eastern Desert, like a line of straggling ants. "So you can just imagine this spectacle with the Bedouin looking out and seeing these people marching by with boat pieces," marveled Juris Zarins, an archaeologist at the Southwest Missouri State University and a leading researcher on the ancient frankincense trade, in our conversations. "People have always been told that the Egyptians did not know how to sail. Well, that's just baloney."

But could they have voyaged all the way across the Atlantic to South America? A few enthusiasts think it possible. In his global wanderings, Thor Heyerdahl observed certain resemblances between the ancient cultures of the Americas and of the Nile. Both, noted Heyerdahl in his best-selling 1970 book *The Ra Expeditions*, had quarried stone for giant stepped pyramids, written in hieroglyphics and constructed paved roads. In all likelihood, suggested Heyderdahl, the Egyptians had brought these ideas with them when they sailed to the Americas a millennia ago in their reed boats. To test this contention, the athletic Norwegian and his colleagues built a reed boat similar to those depicted in Egyptian temple carvings and dubbed it *Ra*, after the Egyptian sun god who created both divinities and humankind. Then Heyerdahl's crew filled it with supplies and sailed it from Morocco across the Atlantic, until the craft sank just short of the West Indies.

Heyderdahl's voyage made for a thrilling adventure yarn, but stripped of its romantic appeal and adrenaline, *The Ra Expeditions* offered little proof that the Egyptians had ever undertaken such a perilous journey. It was one thing, after all, to sail in a leisurely way down the coast of the Red Sea, as Sesostris's men did in search of a known and prized commodity. It was quite another to head off across the Mediterranean and over the Atlantic to an unknown world of uncertain value. There were simply no Egyptian records of an exotic trade in coca and tobacco and no tomb or temple paintings of the plants themselves—a curious omission among a people so fond of recording the details of their triumphs. When Egyptian traders in the reign of Queen Hapshetsut returned from their voyages joyfully bearing entire myrrh trees, the jubilant monarch had images of these exotic shrubs and their bearers carved along the walls of her own temple.

Moreover, there was little trace of any ancient transatlantic voyages. Archaeologists had never turned up convincing evidence of ancient Egyptians in major ports of call along the proposed Mediterranean route, particularly in Spain, the jumping-off point across the Atlantic. Nor had they unearthed any clear signs of an Egyptian presence in the Americas. Stepped pyramids and hieroglyphical writing each had a long history of independent development in both Egypt and the Americas. The paved roads of the Inca were constructed in a different manner from those of the Egyptians. "Ancient trade between the Andes and Egypt cannot seriously be envisaged," observed Baines. "Nothing points toward it. The Roman empire, with its vastly greater resources and knowledge of geography, had no awareness of the Americas. To posit that an earlier and more distant civilization would have had it is most implausible."

But Balabanova refuses to budge from her position and her intransigence has become something of an embarrassment in anthropological and Egyptological circles. Indeed some researchers, such as Eugen Strouhal, a prominent Czech paleopathologist who works extensively in Egypt and who coauthored a paper with Balabanova, seemed ready to wash their hands of the whole matter. "I cannot say anything about reliability of the results concerning several compounds [nicotine, cocaine etc.] she found," noted Strouhal in an e-mail, "and I have no comments to her interpretations, being no specialist in the field of drugs." And Balabanova's closest colleague, Franz Parsche, was unable to rally to her defense. He died in an accident in 1995.

Balabanova's confidence is unshaken, however. Others might seek to destroy her scientific credibility, but chemistry, she reasons, has demonstrated beyond doubt that the Egyptians acquired tobacco and cocaine and that South Americans dabbled with hashish. The German toxicologist remains convinced that her findings represent an absolute truth. Others have to be mistaken. "At the beginning, when something new comes up, there's always a negative reaction," she told me, "and that's exactly what has happened. Later people will accept it more readily."

IN HIS LABORATORY in Ada, Oklahoma, Larry Cartmell was deeply puzzled by Balabanova's findings. He desperately wanted to get to the bottom of them. A pathologist at Valley View Hospital in Ada, Cartmell had been testing ancient hair since 1990. Indeed, he was the first person to detect drugs in mummies, although neither Parsche nor Balabanova were aware of this fact when they began their work. In 1991, Cartmell identified cocaine in the hair of South American mummies and immediately rushed his paper into print in a small Oklahoma medical journal. He feared— rightly, as it turned out—that someone else would beat him to the punch if he waited for acceptance by a prominent national or international journal. Since then, Cartmell has fallen in love with his brainchild: he hated to see hair testing thrown into disrepute by two *arrivistes* from Germany.

A burly man with a round florid face, sheepish grin, and the kind of brash loudness that invariably causes heads to turn, Cartmell has spent most of his life on the outside looking in. Growing up on a dusty prairie farm in Oklahoma, just a decade after half the state had blown away during the windstorms of the Depression, he had often fantasized about the glory of discovering lost cities in the South American Andes or digging gold in Troy or Mycenae. At university, he considered becoming an archaeologist, but while mopping floors in a part-time job, he ran into an unemployed archaeologist down on his luck. Cartmell had had his fill of hard times: he applied for medical school soon after. Becoming a pathologist didn't put an end to his childhood fancies, however, it just put them on ice for a while. In his forties, he began sopping up television documentaries on Stonehenge, Easter Island, and the Great Pyramids, and paying his own way to volunteer on digs during his summer holidays.

One year, he headed down to Arica with an Earthwatch group. Art Aufderheide and his wife, Mary, were there and Cartmell spent a week with them, helping to dissect mummies. When he got home, Cartmell began casting around for a way to make his own mark as a mummy expert. He hit upon hair testing. With samples that Aufderheide supplied from his collection of South American mummy tissue, Cartmell tested for cocaine. One-quarter of the samples proved positive. To be sure of the findings, he submitted his samples to hair-testing specialists in two other labs. They confirmed the findings, and South American archaeologists welcomed them. Cartmell's study supported what many Andeanists had long suspected about the widespread use of cocaine in prehistoric South America. On the strength of this work, Cartmell became a regular at mummy congresses and paleopathology meetings. With his irrepressible sense of humor, his midwestern warmth, and his hunger to be liked and accepted, he was often the life of the party. "I really enjoy working with these people," he told me. "They are the same people I would see on the Discovery Channel. And it's good to be able to get up there and give a paper with one of those guys."

When Cartmell first heard about Balabanova's results from the Egyptian mummies, he found them hard to credit. Quite apart from the issue of transatlantic travel, the pathologist was frankly skeptical about the findings from a hair-testing point of view. "She was finding levels of drugs in everything she tested, you know—hashish, cocaine, and nicotine," he observed witheringly. "Everyone must have gone around stoned. I don't see how they could ever have built the ships to have gotten over to the Americas. Do you know what would happen if I reported those kinds of findings on modern cases and tried to take that to court?"

Cartmell wanted to see if he could replicate her findings. To do so, however, he needed a stock of ancient Egyptian hair samples, preferably from the very same mummies that Balabanova had sampled. He sent a letter to the German toxicologist, suggesting that they swap hair samples. He never heard back from her. Balabanova later told me she never received the letter.

Cartmell was undeterred, however: he had another opportunity. Art Aufderheide had invited him to Egypt to collect samples there, and Cartmell happily accepted. Obtaining a box crammed with tiny plastic bags, the Oklahoma pathologist wasted little time getting down to work. On his days off, he tested the ancient hair samples for cocaine and nicotine, as well as opium—a drug that some Egyptologists suspected was part of the ancient Egyptian pharmacopeia. Like Balabanova, Cartmell searched for drugs using specially marked antibodies and by vaporizing samples to obtain their molecular fingerprints. But he also took additional steps. He rinsed each hair sample at the outset with distilled water and kept the liquid to check for contaminants.

The pathologist found no trace at all of cocaine. Nor was there any sign of opium. But nicotine was a very different matter. Nearly three-quarters of the mummies came back positive for the drug. Cartmell was stunned. He had never really expected to corroborate Balabanova's findings and he was no believer in transcontinental trade. The results bothered him enormously. Where, he wondered, had the Egyptians gotten the nicotine?

NICOTIANA TABACUM, OR common tobacco, is an emerald wonder. The largest varieties can transform fields into miniforests, with stalks up to six feet in height and leaves the size of small kites. The smallest are miniatures by comparison, boasting leaves only a little longer than the human index finger. Centuries of plant breeding have adapted *N. tabacum* to an impressive variety of climates, from Indonesia to Canada and from Yugoslavia to Cameroon. And centuries of experimentation with curing have produced flavors as diverse as the dark smoothness of a Havana cigar and the light briskness of a pack of Virginia Slims. But *N. tabacum* is not the world's only source of nicotine. Chemical studies have shown that the drug infuses the leaves of more than fifty other species in the nightshade family.

This family has its roots deep in the Americas. But a

University of Munich researcher recently uncovered a family member growing in southern Africa—*Nicotiana africana*. In our conversations, Balabanova, who is now retired, suggested that this species, or perhaps an extinct sibling, could once have grown across a much broader region of Africa. In the eighteenth century, she explained, a Swedish botanist, I. P. Forskal, catalogued the flora of Egypt. He observed how the Egyptians grew imported tobacco in their fields and described patches of wild tobacco he had seen growing from the Red Sea coast to Libya. Balabanova believed that such wild tobacco dated back to the time of the pharoahs and was employed by Egyptian embalmers as part of an unguent to preserve the bodies of the dead. Tobacco possesses antibacterial properties. Botanists such as Sandy Knapp found these ideas extremely dubious, however. The Swedish botanist Forskal made his observations two centuries after Europeans introduced tobacco to the Old World. Moreover, it seemed unlikely to her that the African species of tobacco had ever grown in Egypt. "It's a narrow endemic in Namibia—deep in the desert—and is known from only a few populations," she explained. "It does indeed have nicotine, but seems a bit of a long shot."

There was, however, another, simpler explanation, one that Cartmell eventually came across in his reading. It was very possible that the Egyptians had eaten nicotine. Contrary to what one might think, this is an easy thing to do, as researchers at the Centers for Disease Control (CDC) in the United States discovered a few years back. While conducting blood tests on a large group of Americans, the CDC team noticed that the vast majority of results came back positive for nicotine, even though many people in the study neither smoked nor associated with smokers. Perplexed, the team began checking into other possible sources for the drug. There are many. Mandrake, a narcotic and medicinal plant, possesses nicotine in spades. Moreover, tomatoes, potatoes, green peppers, and several other comestibles from the nightshade family also possess microscopic quantities. Diners who ate them accumulated the drug in minute quantities— rarely more than 2 nanograms per milligram of hair. The highest reading for the mummies of Dahkleh was 2.1 nanograms; most were considerably lower. Cartmell now believes the Egyptians consumed nicotine in this way. He has begun working with an ethnobotanist to track down all the nicotine-spiked plants that may have grown at Dahkleh.

Balabanova's cocaine findings did not lend themselves to such a simple solution, however. The two principal sources for cocaine today are *Erythroxylum coca* and *Erythroxylum novogranatense*. Both of these small evergreen shrubs are currently grown in many parts of the world, including Africa and Southeast Asia, but they originated in the moist tropical forests of the eastern Andes in Peru and Bolivia, where indigenous people long prized the leaves for their ability to allay altitude sickness, exhaustion, and hunger. Plant collectors have found other *Erythroxylum* species in the tropical forests of Madagascar, but none of these possesses leaves spiked with concentrated amounts of cocaine. Nor have ethnobotanists come across any contemporary accounts of medicinal plants in Africa that produced cocaine's telltale stimulant effects. Balabanova does not see this as a problem. "It is possible that a similar plant was growing in Africa that actually contained cocaine," she insists. "Or, since commerce also existed at that time transcontinentally, we believe that maybe the cocaine was imported into the country."

Few botanists, Egyptologists, or archaeologists share her faith, however. Some wonder openly if her results owe more to flaws in hair-testing technology than to fact. "It struck me that these days there must be a lot of convictions of people for possessing substances they had not in fact had," observed Egyptologist John Baines. Indeed, this may be the case: several recent studies show that human hair readily sops up environmental contaminants, giving false positives. Stated simply, someone who stands in a room where others are smoking a drug such as cocaine can absorb sufficient quantities to give a positive hair reading. Moreover, the tresses of African-Americans, Hispanics, and Asians sponge up more external contaminants than do those of Caucasians, leading to a pronounced racial bias. Eight African-Americans have recently filed complaints of racial discrimination after failing hair tests required for admission to the Chicago Police Academy. All eight claim to have been drug-free.

Could external contamination account for the drugs in ancient Egyptian hair? In the nineteenth century, many Egyptologists worked with tobacco pipes cupped in their hands, and a few undoubtedly dabbled in cocaine, as it was once a popular and legal drug in Europe. This may account for Balabanova's findings, but it doesn't explain Cartmell's discovery of nicotine. The Oklahoma pathologist searched deliberately for external contaminants. After rinsing the Dahkleh samples with distilled water, he tested the liquid for the presence of drugs. He detected none. Moreover, his tests turned up a specific kind of nicotine—that which had been partially broken down after undergoing metabolism in human cells.

It is certainly possible that a cocaine-smoking or -injecting researcher tainted the odd mummy, but none of the experts really believe that it happened very often. So, in the absence of any other compelling explanation, it now seems likely that Bolobanova's findings were thrown off by conditions that few other hair testers have to contend with. When Egyptian embalmers smoothed handfuls of spices, oils, and plant resins on the flesh of the dead, they anointed the body and its tresses with a complex chemical cocktail that mummy experts have yet to describe, much less fully understand. Conventional hair tests were never designed to deal with such concoctions, nor were they intended to deal with an immense, almost unfathomable span of time. Over centuries and millennia of entombment, compounds in these concoctions could have easily broken down, yielding substances that could readily pass for cocaine today.

For all the resemblance a mummy bears to a living person, for all its serene appearance of sleep, an ancient preserved body has been transformed radically by its millennia-long slumber. Appearances, as we all know, can be deceiving, and this is particularly true of mummies, perhaps because we so wish to be deceived in this way. We are desperate to stop the inevitable railway engine of time in its tracks, to dodge the inevitable unraveling of the world. And we cloak the ancient dead in our own wishes for immortality. I have to remind myself continually of this each time I look at an exquisitely preserved human being, and I do so by repeating a phrase that Aufderheide often used as he worked in the Egyptian desert. It was a kind of mantra with him. "A mummy," he said time and time again, was little more than a "half-rotten soup of protein."

CRIME
STORIES

$\backsim$

A S SERENE AS THE PRESERVED dead often
seem as they slumber under glass in the world's museums, they do not always rest there in peace. My first inkling
of this came during a pilgrimage I made to the small Danish
town of Silkeborg to see a particularly famous mummy, Tollund Man. Silkeborg lies some 250 miles northwest of
Copenhagen in a dark moody land of heaths and fens and
small thatch-roof cottages, and it was there nearly half a
century ago that the body of a 2,400-year-old man came to
light in the waters of a local bog. Eerily preserved down to
the day-old reddish stubble on his chin and the delicate

tracery of crow's feet around his eyes, Tollund Man is a marvel of nature. He possesses one of the most haunting faces of any ancient mummy ever discovered. As a result, Tollund Man has become something of a national hero in Denmark, an indelible reminder to all Danes of who they once were and where they came from.

I reached Silkeborg rather late in the day, frayed and travel-worn from an early morning flight from Amsterdam and a dawdling milk-run trip by train from Copenhagen, but I was eager to see Tollund Man. I dumped my bags at my hotel and went hurrying off down the street to the museum, a spacious eighteenth-century manor house painted bright egg-yolk yellow. I arrived just twenty minutes before closing. The staff was clearly surprised to see a foreign traveler pitching up so late in the day, but they were too polite to say so, and the woman collecting admissions hastily gave me directions to the room where Tollund Man was enshrined. With a map scrunched in my hand, I hustled down the echoing corridors. It was a memorable twenty minutes. I had become adept at bobbing and weaving around the thick crowds that inevitably form in front of mummies. This room was completely empty. I circled the glass case, paying my silent respects to Tollund Man, but as I did so, I had a strange, unsettling sensation. I felt as if someone were peering at me intently as I peered at Tollund Man.

The next morning, I returned to spend more time and to chat with the museum's amiable director. Christian Fischer had been knighted by the Danish government for his loving care of the museum's famous charge and for his scholarship on Denmark's bog bodies. As we talked in Fischer's airy office, I discovered why I had felt so uneasy the day before. No one, it turns out, is ever alone with Tollund Man. The museum has installed three video surveillance cameras around his tomb. Tollund Man himself rests in a bulletproof case. Over the years, explained Fischer sadly, wandering psychiatric patients had become greatly distressed at the sight of the dead man, and after one or two disturbing incidents, the museum had reluctantly invested in a bulletproof case for its most famous resident. As safe as Tollund Man now seemed, these measures had not entirely allayed Fischer's fears. He worried that one day his charge would be kidnapped by thieves intent on ransom. This was not some personal paranoia. When Fischer recently squired a visiting Israeli professor around the museum, his guest was startled by the security in Tollund Man's room—not that it was too much, but that it was far too lax. "Where is the gunman?" the Israeli scientist asked Fischer in astonishment. "Where is the gunman?"

What made this story all the more poignant to me was that Tollund Man had already suffered considerably at the hands of his fellow men. Indeed, during his own lifetime, the ancient Dane had been the victim of terrible violence.

Like so many of Europe's bog bodies, he had been put to death mysteriously by his contemporaries and cast away into the cold bleakness of a bog. The murder weapon in Tollund Man's case, a sturdy rope so neatly and precisely plaited that the sight of it sent chills down my back, still trails from his neck. In Denmark, there were many theories about what had happened to the ancient man and to the hundreds of other bodies that had been hauled dripping wet and trailing tendrils of peat from northern Europe's bogs. Indeed, people had mused and told stories for generations about the fates of these ancient bog people. Over time, their tales had given birth to legends of creatures from the black lagoon.

Today we take great pride in the ingenuity of criminal investigators who are able to make so much of slender clues to a murder, bringing the guilty to justice. But these specialists are accustomed to favorable conditions, examining crime scenes that are relatively undisturbed and bodies that are but a few days, months, or years old. What would they make of cases that had gone cold hundreds, if not thousands, of years ago, and committed in places that had long vanished? Could science help finger a likely perpetrator? And could the mummies themselves tell us something important about our own murderous impulses and what had long impelled us to take the lives of others? Have we always been such calculated killers?

These questions led me ultimately to the damp fens of

the northern Netherlands. There the ancient dead had been subjected to hideous indignities.

⌒

O N   A   F I N E spring day in 1897, two Dutch villagers spotted a strange corpse lying in the murky waters of a small bog in the northern Netherlands. The men had been hard at work laying in a winter's supply of fuel, dredging sodden basketfuls of peat and stacking them to dry in the sun along the shore. The northern Netherlands had many such barrens, and with few exceptions these lands had a bad reputation among local inhabitants. Treacherous underfoot, with slippery hummocks and deep pools of cold dark water, the northern bogs had claimed several lives over the years. In surrounding villages there were tales of demons in the bogs, with long arms capable of dragging the innocent to their deaths. In Yde, where the two peat cutters lived, people generally avoided these fens. But the two men did not have that luxury. A smoky peat fire was all that stood between them and bitter cold on winter nights.

So in the spring of 1897, the pair headed off to the mere to cut peat. And it was there that one of them noticed something human in the black muck of the dredge basket. It was the shriveled body of a crone. Her face was dark as a puffball and her eyes were squeezed shut, as if she hated the sight of the world. Her cavernous mouth seemed to wince, revealing a row of tiny peglike teeth that gleamed like black pearls. Down one side of her head, a thick tress of long red hair fell to her shoulder. The two men stared in disbelief. For a terrible moment, they thought they had unearthed a carmine-haired demon. They dropped their gear and fled.

Working up their courage, they later returned, dragging what they could of the wizened body from the peat. A week or so later, the mayor of Yde came by to investigate. He examined the body, which lay beneath a stack of peat, then notified the police. He also contacted the museum in nearby Assen, for the bog was known to have special powers of preservation. Investigators hurried out. Scrutinizing the nearly naked corpse, they concluded that the woman had lain in her watery tomb for a very long time: no recent body from the bog looked as leathery and shriveled as she did. They also concluded that she was no elderly crone at all, but a girl, for her feet were tiny and childlike. But the thing that most struck the investigators was the manner in which she had died. She did not seem to have drowned accidentally. A seven-foot-long band was wrapped three times around her neck. Someone had tied a slipknot in it and tightened it beneath her left ear until she could no longer breathe. It seemed a very calculated, knowing way of killing someone.

The investigators called her Yde Girl and handed her body over to the museum in Assen. There she was put on display. Decades later, when physicists had finally devised a technology for radiocarbon dating just a tiny portion of the cloth found with her, museum officials arranged to have her dated. Yde Girl was very, very old. Indeed, she had breathed her last two thousand years ago, during the dying days of the Iron Age, when empire-hungry Roman legions were beginning to push their way north. During those troubled times, loosely knit Germanic tribes had gained a reputation as fierce warriors. They battled their enemies with iron swords, dressed in fine woven woolens, pulled on gleaming bronze neck rings, warmed their houses with peat fires, drank to the health of their allies with beer, and proudly counted their wealth in cattle.

Yde Girl's survival from that remote age was an act of nature, accomplished not by human hands but by the secret alchemy of the bog. Over the years, researchers advanced many theories to explain this phenomenon. Scientific thinking today suggests that it is due to the complex chemical changes caused by the death of sphagnum moss, the chief vegetation in a bog. When sphagnum dies, it releases an unstable substance known as sphagnan, which is slowly converted by several chemical steps into humic acid. The sphagnan and its transitional compounds, as well as the humic acid, all have a strange effect on a cadaver. They extract calcium from bones, softening skeletons. Under the weight of overlying layers of peat, human bones bend, break, and warp until some corpses take on the grotesque look of melted toffee. The same chemicals also trigger a complex reaction with the nitrogen in human flesh, slowing bacterial growth and effectively tanning skin and organs like Tuscan leather. By such means, Yde Girl escaped the way of all flesh, surviving for millennia after her executioners had turned to dust.

All across northern Europe, wherever mossy bogs are to be found, turf cutters stumbled upon similar bodies. Indeed, one German researcher, Alfred Dieck, collected reports and local stories of nearly 1,900 cadavers in watery graves stretching from the meres of Ireland to the fens of

Sweden. While some scholars now dispute Dieck's figures, most agree that the ancient practice of burying certain members of society in bogs was once widespread across Europe. And they shake their heads at the terrible fates that many in the bogs met. In Denmark, someone fed Graubelle Man a gruel tainted with poisonous fungi, then slit his throat from ear to ear. In Germany, someone bound the hands of Kayhausen Boy behind his back and stabbed him in the throat. In England, someone clubbed, strangled, and beheaded Worsley Man.

Such chilling acts of violence rival anything seen today on the streets of Europe or North America, but archaeologists have long been divided in their theories about what happened. For years, many European researchers suggested the victims were homosexuals, adulteresses, and societal outcasts executed for their transgressions. Other scholars theorized that they were people chosen for human sacrifices or cast out as vengeful spirits. None could clinch the case, however, and in the 1970s, archaeologists' interest in bog bodies died. Giant excavating machines were gobbling up vast swathes of bogs for gardeners' bags of peat, blindly tearing buried bog bodies to shreds. That left only the older finds, hauled out from the meres before the invention of modern archaeological methods. Most scholars shunned such poorly documented cadavers. And there matters might have languished had it not been for a little-known Dutch researcher, Wijnand van der Sanden, whose speciality as an archaeologist was not bog bodies at all but Iron Age villages. "Wijnand really started the interest in the bog bodies again," said Torsten Capelle, a professor of archaeology at Westfalische Wilhelms-Universtität in Munster, Germany. "It slept for nearly thirty years."

Van der Sanden is a gentle man in his late forties with a shy smile and the stiff, slightly strained manner of someone who enjoys the company of books more than he does that of most people. He lives in the small village of Rolde in the northern Netherlands. I met him on a sunny Saturday morning in neighboring Assen on the first good day after a long winter. Along the street outside the restaurant, market vendors were setting up booths to hawk homemade sausages, cheese, kites, and wooden shoes. There was a decidedly festive air to the day. Van der Sanden, however, paid it little mind. Slipping into a seat in a local restaurant, he seemed every bit the serious scholar with a short, closely cropped white beard, steel-gray hair and penetrating blue eyes. After an hour or so, his wife and young son turned up to claim him for a family outing. He gently asked them for an hour's reprieve, sending them back to the market. They returned to the restaurant an hour later, then an hour after that. Each time he begged off. Finally, seeing his absorption, they set off for home without him. Van der Sanden and I talked late into the afternoon. I felt guilty for ruining his family's day, but I had the impression that these kinds of things happened fairly often. Van der Sanden couldn't help himself. "My wife hates bog bodies," he told me with a nervous laugh.

For all his obsession, however, the soft-spoken archaeologist maintains a strict scientific objectivity about his subjects. He is cool, careful, and exact in his speech. He rarely permits himself a word too many, or an adjective or phrase that is too colorful and hence unscientific. Listening to him, I wondered how such a cautious man had ever become caught up in such a strange passion. But the measured talk is just so much wallpaper. Van der Sanden is a romantic. As a teenager, he had read a book entitled *The Bog People*, which was a lyrical account of the bodies and their mysterious past. The author, P. V. Glob, was a Danish archaeologist who had been one of the first on the scene when Tollund Man was discovered. Glob had been powerfully affected by the experience. When one of the excavators perished from a heart attack while hauling the sopping body from its watery tomb, Glob saw a certain poetic justice. "The bog claimed a life for a life," wrote the Danish researcher, "or, as some may prefer to think, the old gods took a modern man in place of the man from the past." Van der Sanden was fascinated. The romance of the ancient past seemed so much more inviting than the sensible pragmatism of modern Dutch society. "That was the most impressive book I've ever read," he explained. He decided to become an archaeologist.

Specializing in the prehistoric era in the Netherlands, he applied for a job at the Drents Museum in Assen. It had one of the largest bog body exhibits in Europe. But when van der Sanden first went to work there in 1987, he noticed that most people stared blankly at Yde Girl and the other bog bodies that had come to join her over the years in the museum. Then they quickly moved away, finding it hard to see any humanity in the rags of chestnut-colored skin and hair. The few who were curious, however, peppered him with questions about what had happened to the bodies. To van der Sanden's deep regret, he wasn't able to give them many decent answers. "I'd have to say, 'Oh sorry, these things haven't been studied.'"

This troubled him greatly. He knew that science—particularly the disciplines of pathology, radiology, and physical anthropology so useful in forensic investigations—could potentially reveal a great deal about such bodies. He had been reading of just such a case. Three years earlier, English workers had made a gruesome discovery in a peat land just outside of Manchester, uncovering what they first thought was a piece of ancient wood while cutting turf at Lindow Moss. It was actually a muck-covered human calf and right foot. Soon after, a flap of human skin was discovered in the uncut bog nearby.

The Manchester police were very interested. They had begun looking into the disappearance of Malika Reyn-Bardt, a local woman who had vanished under mysterious circumstances from her home near Lindow Moss. Investigators strongly suspected that the woman's homosexual husband, Peter Reyn-Bardt, had married her as a convenience, then murdered her, chopping her body into pieces and disposing of her remains in his cottage garden. This garden perched above Lindow Moss. Reyn-Bardt had confessed to the murder to a friend who was serving time in an English prison. But the Manchester police had so far failed to unearth any sign of the woman's corpse—or rather its chopped-up pieces. They wondered whether the mucky leg belonged to the vanished woman.

Cheshire County archaeologist Rick Turner thought it unlikely. In 1983, workers at Lindow Moss had discovered a partial skull and eyeball. Subsequent studies showed they came from an Iron Age woman. Turner believed the severed leg likely belonged to her, too, or to someone else of similar vintage. He persuaded investigators to allow him to excavate the new find under police supervision. With a team of six, he cut out an entire block of peat and transported it by a peat-works railway car to a local morgue. To identify the body within, pathologists took X rays of the teeth. Not one filling could be seen, a rare state of affairs for someone living in the age of modern dentistry. Subsequent radiocarbon tests confirmed Turner's suspicions. Lindow Man, as the corpse was soon known, had perished nearly two thousand years ago.

To glean clues to the man's last moments, Turner painstakingly brushed away the peat from the body, exposing the gnarled and deformed skull and the withered abdomen. Then he mounted an investigation of his own, bringing in fifty specialists, from chemists and microbiologists to entomologists, botanists, and knot experts. Lindow Man, it transpired, died in the prime of life, in his mid-twenties. He stood five feet six inches tall, an average height for the age, and weighed about 130 pounds. On the day of his death, his body gleamed with a blue or green coppery clay pigment, similar to the dark-blue paint that Julius Caesar saw on Britons during his campaign on the island. The ancient man had dined on a charred piece of flat bread or griddle cake. He had also consumed a small quantity of mistletoe, a toxic plant often associated with Druids, the philosopher-priests said by the Romans to practice human sacrifice. And he had not died quietly. Indeed, Lindow Man suffered not one violent death, but three. He had been bludgeoned, likely with a small ax. He had been garroted with a string made of animal sinew. Then his throat had been slashed with a knife, until he bled to death.

Sifting through the evidence, researchers concluded

that Lindow Man had perished during an ancient human sacrifice. One well-known scholar, Anne Ross, was particularly fascinated by Lindow Man's consumption of mistletoe and charred cake. It reminded her of accounts of an ancient fire festival conducted in the Scottish Highlands on the first of May. Known as the Beltane Fire, the festival was celebrated atop high hills in the region as late as the eighteenth century. All fires were doused the night before, and participants gathered on a prominence to light a sacred bonfire. Then they drew bits of toasted oatmeal cakes from a bonnet. One piece had been colored black with charcoal: the person who blindly picked it was considered a sacrifice in exchange for the gods' favor. In eighteenth-century Scotland, the sacrifice was not a fatal matter: the victim was required only to leap three times through the flickering light of the bonfire. But Ross and others believed that the fire-jumping rite had at some point replaced the Druids' ritualistic execution.

Van der Sanden, however, was far from convinced. He saw Ross's theory as just an elaborate, somewhat fanciful story built on little more than a few carbonized grains and four specks of mistletoe pollen. Such minutiae, so critical to Ross's argument, could easily be explained away. Absentminded cooks were not confined to the modern era: someone could have accidentally burned the bread that Lindow Man ate. Moreover, the ancient Briton could have consumed mistletoe as a medicine. During Roman times, Pliny the Elder described how Druids prepared a tonic from mistletoe as an antidote for poison. Still, Turner's studies greatly intrigued the cautious Dutch researcher. They showed just how much of the ancient past could yet be retrieved from a few pounds of leathery flesh.

Excited by the possibilities, van der Sanden began calling up forensic, medical, and anthropological experts, asking them for their help in recovering what they could from the bog bodies in his care in Assen and in other museums in the Netherlands. He desperately wanted to glean new clues to the final chapters of their lives.

UNDER THE LOW museum lighting, van der Sanden stood among the silent litter of bodies and smiled. Far from the restaurant, the market, and other people, he was very much in his element. All around us on the second floor of the Drents Museum, ancient corpses lay like gnarled tree roots. It was a surreal scene. There was Exloermond Man, a barrel-shaped body topped only by a thin strip of scalp and wispy red hair, and there was Emmer-Erfscheidenveen Man, a paper-thin patch of torso and thighs. He resembled, although I did not say so to van der Sanden, Wile E. Coyote after a particularly disastrous fall. Then there was the Weerdinge Couple, two headless male wraiths stretched out in a tender embrace. They made a poignant pair, but for one disconcerting detail. Someone had disemboweled the taller of the two men. His withered intestines corkscrewed out in a leathery cascade.

But the star of the exhibit was unquestionably Yde Girl. Still possessed of her head and face, she seemed infinitely more human than the rest. Wrinkled and shrunken as a moldy prune, she looked as old as time itself. But even so, something of the lost girl remained. She was tiny and frail, and in van der Sanden's artful arrangement of her remains, he had managed to capture a certain demureness in her. Only her head and toes peeked out from beneath an immense reddish-brown cloak. I found it hard to take my eyes from her. I couldn't help but wonder who she had once been and how her laughter had sounded and what thoughts had traveled through her mind on the last day of her life. Staring down at the band rudely twisted about her neck, I pitied her. It seemed a particularly brutal end.

During his studies of the Dutch bodies, van der Sanden shipped off samples of her tissues to human geneticists and blood-typing specialists. He carried her by car to Groningen University for X rays and CT scans and arranged for textile experts to examine the woolen rags found with her. He brought in physical anthropologists and pathologists to study in a nondestructive fashion both the manner of her death and the diseases that she had suffered from in life. He contacted forensic experts to study the distinctive papillary lines that ridged the soles of her feet. He left no stone unturned.

For every success, however, van der Sanden ran aground with frustrating failure. The geneticists, for example, were unable to amplify any DNA from her tissue samples: the chemicals that protect soft tissue in the bog water had destroyed fragile coils of DNA. This meant researchers would never be able to track down any modern descendants of her family line or discern any hereditary diseases. But van der Sanden was very patient. Scans of her skull showed that her wisdom teeth had neither erupted nor grown roots. This meant she died as an adolescent, at about age sixteen. X rays of her spine revealed that she had suffered from a skeletal abnormality known as scoliosis, which results in a sideways S-shaped curve of the spine. Possibly an inherited trait, this curvature leads to a certain lopsidedness, a tendency to favor one side more than the other. This was confirmed by the swollenness of the big toe on her right foot and the calluses on the toe next to it. In all probability, Yde Girl walked with a slight asymmetrical gait, as her weight fell more heavily on her right foot.

Since her discoverers had accidentally destroyed much of her lower body, including her gastrointestinal tract, the research team was unable to determine the menu of her last meal. But textile experts could hazard a guess as to what she had worn for the occasion. An examination of the cloth recovered from the find spot revealed that she had been buried with a large, much-darned woolen cloak striped with pretty pale yellow, blue, and red bands. It was quite possible that the girl had been killed with cloth from another item of her attire. The woven band knotted around her neck looked like a waistband from a garment.

There was little doubt that Yde Girl had been harshly treated. The forensic examination revealed that someone had shorn the long blond hair from the right side of her head, likely with a pair of scissors, and possibly stabbed her just under her collarbone. Her killer had then wound the cloth band about her neck three times and tied a sliding knot beneath her left ear, tightening it inexorably until she asphyxiated. The marks of this cold-blooded act could be seen even two thousand years later on her body: a deep furrow creased her neck and a large depression beneath her left ear recorded the spot where the knot had extinguished her breath. But the killers were not done with her. As a parting gift, someone had arranged her facedown in the bog, for the front of her head was far better preserved than the back.

Van der Sanden was intrigued by all this, but he wanted to know more. To see her as she had once been, he contacted medical artist Richard Neave at the University of Manchester. A stylish man in his early sixties with an arch sense of humor, Neave works closely with the Manchester police, helping to identify criminals from the blurry images of closed-circuit-display camera videos and to physically reconstruct the faces of unidentifiable homicide victims. From time to time, the artist has also re-created the faces of historical figures, from Lindow Man to Phillip the II of Macedonia, the father of Alexander the Great. To van der Sanden's immense relief, Neave agreed to try his hand at Yde Girl. He asked van der Sanden to bring her body to England.

In the Stopford Building in Manchester, Neave toiled for months on the reconstruction. He first arranged for a series of CT scans to be taken of her head, clearly imaging all the bones and bone fragments. Then he contacted experts at London University College Hospital, asking for their help in digitally reassembling the fragments until at last they had a complete skull. Entering the data into a computer linked to an industrial milling machine, Neave made an exact three-dimensional plastic model. With this replica of Yde Girl's skull, he began modeling the soft tissues, inserting wooden pegs of different lengths into twenty-four key points on the skull, from the tip of the chin to the curve of the brow ridge. Each peg indicated the average thickness of soft tissue on an adolescent girl's face. This technique allowed Neave to recreate the girl's facial muscles and skin in clay. He then made a wax cast of the results.

The day van der Sanden flew back to England for the reconstructed Yde Girl was one of the most thrilling of his life. "It was like going on a blind date," he told me a bit self-consciously. But he had nothing to worry about. The young woman who awaited him in Manchester was a haunting strawberry-blond beauty, far removed from the crone that had been pulled from the waters of the northern bog. Van der Sanden was elated. Back in Assen, the Iron Age girl captivated the Dutch public, who flocked for the first time to see her in the museum. Restored to herself, the Yde Girl became celebrated by Dutch writers and poets, no longer a nightmare figure. "People have written radio plays, poems, and books about her," said van der Sanden. "They can see now that she was a real person."

THE MEDICAL TESTS and forensic examinations were turning up vital new clues, but van der Sanden realized they could never solve the mystery of Yde Girl's death. Nor could they explain the demises of the other twelve bog bodies in Dutch museums. A more complete picture was needed, and this had to include all the ancient bog bodies that had been lost, destroyed, or reburied over time in the Netherlands. In all likelihood, reasoned van der Sanden, the sum of all these homicides would be far more revealing than the details of individual killings: it could disclose a lethal pattern to a discriminating eye. So, as the forensic tests proceeded, he began amassing all the information he could on the Netherland's lost bog bodies. He wanted to know who they had been, when they had lived, and how they had died.

Others had already attempted to gather such data. The German researcher Alfred Dieck had spent nearly half a century rooting out obscure historical records of bog bodies across Europe, interviewing the turf cutters and villagers who claimed to have found them. By such means, the elderly archaeologist had penned nearly two dozen articles and produced a series of scientific tallies of Europe's bog bodies. The last of Dieck's counts, published in 1986, listed more than 1,850 bog bodies in all of Europe, although it included airmen from the Second World War and political victims of the Troubles in Ireland. According to this tally, 49 of the ancient corpses had surfaced over the centuries in the Netherlands.

Dieck was a trusting man, however. Indeed, he had often taken local folklore, tall tales, and myths at face value. When a doctor mentioned a bog maiden so perfectly preserved that even her fragile hymen could be seen, Dieck dutifully wrote the story down. When someone else described finding a body decorated with wreaths of oak leaves—materials that would never survive in the acidic waters of the bog—Dieck made credulous notes. And when an informant recalled stumbling on an entire bog body battlefield, complete with swords and crushed shields such as the world had never known before, Dieck nodded and jotted it down, never thinking to ask for any proof. He even counted place names, such as Norway's Daumannsmoor, which meant "dead man's bog," as finds.

Van der Sanden decided to look into the matter himself, searching out reliable records of bog bodies that had gone missing. He rummaged through collections of ancient textiles and human remains in Dutch universities, searching for the slightest vestige of bog body clothes or tissue. He pored over the correspondence of nineteenth- and twentieth-century archaeologists, taking note of brief mentions of lost bodies. He combed through huge stacks of old newspapers, hunting for articles about corpses found in the bogs. In the process, the Dutch archaeologist turned up something quite wonderful: a detailed newspaper story about a bog body that had eluded Dieck's attention.

Heartened by this, van der Sanden redoubled his efforts, and every so often he scored a success. While poring over the *Emmer Courant* of May 21, 1921, for example, he spied a small article. "During the digging in the peat," noted the reporter, "about twenty-five centimeters deep in the black peat, a very complete, very old human being was found, probably a male person. The entire body was intact, and the skin was tanned and the bones were dissolved and the legs and hands were in a very good state. One of the eyes was open. The local police officer took the body away."

By such dogged work, van der Sanden found records of fifty-six Dutch bog bodies. Some had been ground up in apothecaries' mortars to make a medicine popular in Europe at the time. Others had been hastily buried along the peripheries of graveyards, where suicides and unbaptized children were customarily interred. In all, forty-six had lived during the Bronze or Roman Iron Ages, judging from published accounts of clothing styles or from radiocarbon tests on surviving bodies. Most were adult males. Many were buried in the bog without a shred of clothing, stripped of all personal possessions. Most had perished in the troubled late Iron Age, when Rome was marching north, throwing the ancient Germanic world into chaos. Of the seven bodies for whom cause of death was known, all seven revealed signs of foul play, from smashed skulls to nooses about their necks.

THERE WERE THREE main schools of thought about these bog bodies. Many archaeologists believed that the ancient homicides were an Iron Age version of capital punishment. The executioners, they observed, often stripped the victims of arm rings, cloak pins, and other valuables, as warders did prisoners. They further humiliated their captives by partially shaving their heads and stripping them of their clothes. They denied them proper forms of burial and dumped their bodies in desolate wildlands. Sometimes they anchored the corpses to the bottom of bogs with wooden posts or branches, ensuring that the offenders would never again see the light of day.

All this sounded very much like the punishments that Germanic tribes had once meted out to their undesirables. In the first century A.D., a high-ranking Roman magistrate, Tacitus, penned an account of the customs and lives of these people. Likely based on information gleaned from Germanic princes and prisoners of war living in Rome, *Germania* reads suspiciously like a lecture on morality. Making much of the simple virtues of the barbarians, Tacitus pointedly described their marriage customs for his hedonistic Roman readers. The northerners, he explained, greatly esteemed marriage, dealing harshly with adulteresses. Cuckolded husbands wasted little time in punishing their wives, shaving their heads, stripping them of their clothes, and flogging them in the streets. Moreover, they exacted even greater penalties against those who broke other social codes. "Cowards, deserters, and homosexuals were drowned," observed Tacitus, "pressed down under wicker hurdles in bogs and swamps."

In nineteenth-century Germany, researchers took note of these passages. Some, such as Johanna Mestorf, a professor at Kiel University, drew explicit parallels with the circumstances of several bog bodies, and their papers attracted a large following that eventually included a prominent twentieth-century Nazi official. Heinrich Himmler was head of Nazi Germany's Schutzstaffel, or SS forces. He ran both the country's police forces and its death camps, and considered himself a student of history. Indeed, he had borrowed heavily on the mythology of ancient Germanic tribes when designing the insignia and rites of his beloved SS. By the late 1930s, Himmler viewed both war and the shedding of German blood as inevitable, and he had become obsessed with measures for the procreation of a new generation of blond-haired youth. He urged his SS officers to raise large families and to sow their seed in whatever field presented itself. At the same time, he turned his ire on German homosexuals, whom he despised and considered an unnecessary burden on the Nazi state.

During a speech to the SS in 1937, Himmler offered a chilling history lesson to the men in his command. He pointed to the executions of the bog bodies as an example of an ancient Aryan tradition deserving of revival. "Homosexuals were drowned in swamps," he said. "The worthy professors who find these bodies in peat do not realize that in ninety out of a hundred cases, they are looking at the remains of a homosexual who was drowned in a swamp along with his clothes and everything else. That was not a punishment, but simply the termination of such an abnormal life." With history seemingly on the Nazis' side, the SS brutally proceeded with the unthinkable, rousting gay men and women from their beds in the middle of the night and stuffing them into cars. In all, fifteen thousand homosexuals were dispatched to Europe's death camps, more innocent victims of Nazi hatred.

After the war, most German researchers quietly shelved the theory that the bodies had been victims of capital punishment. They were ashamed of the way the Third Reich had used the ancient dead to justify its own fanatical bigotry. It was not the first, nor sadly the last time, that politicians tried manipulating the dead, but many German anthropologists deeply regretted the part their research had played in Himmler's schemes. They cast around for new explanations of the bog bodies. Downplaying Tacitus, some turned to traditional German folklore for ideas. The tales, they discovered, were replete with Wiedergänger—ghosts of executed criminals, suicides, murder victims, and others who had perished under violent and unnatural circumstances. The Wiedergänger were restless, spiteful beings who generally made life miserable for the living. To fend off these unwelcome guests, peasants in the tales often mutilated the corpses of those who died violently—binding their hands, shaving their heads, and covering their eyes.

Neither the Wiedergänger nor the capital punishment theories, however, seemed to fit most bog bodies. It was true that someone had shorn off half of Yde Girl's hair, but there was no striping of lash marks on her body. Nor was there any indication that she had ever been staked to the bottom of a bog. Other bog bodies were equally problematic. The two Weerdinge men had indeed been found in a timeless embrace, but there was nothing to suggest they were lovers: they could as easily be brothers or comrades in arms. And there was little to indicate that they had ever been shunned as outcasts—quite the contrary; in death they had been gently arranged side by side so that they could touch one another for eternity. This seemed more an act of tenderhearted affection than the curt dismissal of an executioner or the curse of a terrified peasant.

But if the bog bodies weren't victims of capital punishment or the remains of a Wiedergänger, who were they? Outside Germany, several researchers subscribed to the view that they were human sacrifices. Such practices had been well known in northern Europe. In *Germania*, Tacitus had described such an event during a festival held to honor a Germanic goddess who reigned over the bounty of fall harvests and the fecundity of the herds. Nerthus was a powerful deity, someone not to be trifled with, so the northern tribes regularly buttered her up with a major festival. Casting aside their weapons, they gathered en masse to watch a priest carry the goddess's shrine in a chariot from her sanctuary. Days of celebration followed. When the divinity had finally tired of mortals, she instructed her slaves to haul her shrine and chariot to a near lakeshore for ritual cleansing. Then her priests sacrificed the slaves.

The choice of a lakeshore for this carnage was deliberate. Most Germanic and Celtic peoples saw their gods not as celestial beings who floated ethereally in the sky or who perched majestically like Zeus atop mountains, but as deities enthroned in the underworld. The doorway to this divine realm lay in water, the glassy sheets that covered lakes, springs, bogs, or the rippling currents of rivers. In *Germania,* Tacitus described how two Germanic tribes once fought fiercely over possession of a river. Both were desperate to win, since they believed that the river was the doorway to heaven: a man's prayers here would instantly reach the gods. Other ancient Europeans apparently saw water in a similar light. According to the classical Greek historian Strabo, Celtic tribes to the west often bestowed precious offerings of gold and silver to their gods in sacred lakes.

Archaeological discoveries have since borne this out. During Denmark's Bronze Age, prosperous tribespeople left remarkable gifts and ritual paraphernalia in the bogs— entire chariots with gleaming bronze axles, wooden war- ships, bronze axes, bronze daggers, bronze swords, gold arm rings, and magnificient bronze wind instruments known as lurer. During one memorable ceremony, someone bestowed a huge silver caldron ornamented magnificently with scenes of gods and what might be a portrayal of human sacrifice. In other parts of Europe, however, the offerings and ritual items were often more humble. In the Iron Age Netherlands, for example, people left more down-to-earth presents in the peat lands: leather shoes, wooden wheels, ploughshares, braids of hair, bronze spearheads, bronze daggers, balls of wool, bronze arm rings, bronze neck rings, woolen clothing, deer antlers, bull horns, and earthenware pots that likely held food.

In all likelihood, said van der Sanden at the end of our afternoon together, ancient Europeans had seen the life of a human being as a precious sacrifice and they had chosen the bleak bogs with great care. Two thousand years ago and more, they had glimpsed a magical waterworld charged with religious significance in the fens, not a place of desolation and abandonment. "The best evidence for that," he said, "is seeing all the objects that have been found in bogs. I find it hard to imagine that the bogs were places where punished people were just dumped to get them out of society."

But that is as much as the careful scientist will say. After all his long years of research, neither he nor anyone else really knows who Yde Girl was or exactly why she was chosen to die two thousand years ago. She may have been a slave captured from a neighboring tribe. She may have been a physical misfit selected as an offering because of her slight physical imperfection, a lopsided gait. Or it may be, as I choose to think, that she was simply an innocent child selected by village elders as the greatest gift they could imagine. Lying her face downward in the bog, they ensured that she would see for herself the splendors of the divine world she was entering. To be chosen for such a grand fate would be an honor, and in this, her homicide, however calculated, bore little resemblance to the cases that occupy police investigators today.

Our explorations of such lost worlds are limited, however, by the telescopes that science fashions for us. As riddled with flaws as the original Hubble telescope, our lenses are often crude, capricious things. Rarely showing us what we most want to see, they shed minute specks into exquisite, breathtaking focus, while smudging giant fields into an inde-cipherable blur. This is the great frustration of studying the bog bodies. Peering through the thick lenses that science has given us, we can often see only tiny patches of light—what people ate, what they wore, how they looked, how they dressed. Try as we will, struggle as hard as we can to make better lenses, we are unable to train our sight steadily on the people themselves, their thoughts, their desires, their dreams, the inner lives that make them truly human.

Science will never be able to solve the mystery of Yde Girl's death. Investigators will never have the satisfaction of closing the case or fingering the murderer. But we have not thoughtlessly abandoned Yde Girl to a forgotten grave. We have not turned a blind eye to her plight. We have done all we can to retrieve her memory and retrace her final moments. That is all the justice the ancient dead can hope for.

INVADERS
FROM THE
WEST

⌐

TAKING THE TRAIN BACK TO Amsterdam, I thought about the shriveled rags of flesh under glass in Assen. For van der Sanden and for many other mummy experts I had met, the preserved dead were envoys from a vanished world, messengers from the shadows of time. History, after all, is a story written by winners, not those who fell beneath their heels. It is colored by the prejudices, ambitions, loyalties, fears, and vanities of the writer. It is full of the littlest doings of kings and queens and maddeningly silent on the lives of the humble. It waxes on the campaigns of generals and ignores the camp life of soldiers. It dotes on city dwellers and ignores those on the frontier. It is terribly flawed. As a result, diligent historians are constantly on the prowl for some more reliable missive from the time beyond human memory, a fresh dispatch from the faded dead. Mummies promise just such missives, and the more important the mummies are deemed to be to history, the more elaborate the historians' search.

Few mummies have attracted as much investigation over the centuries as that of the renowned Macedonian king Alexander the Great. One of the greatest generals the world has ever known, Alexander died of a fever in Babylon in 323 B.C. at the age of thirty-two, after conquering the Persian empire and most of the civilizations known to the Greeks at that time. He was greatly mourned by his men, and his body, according to classical texts, was preserved in golden honey, as was the custom among the wealthy and powerful in Babylon. Alexander was then interred in a golden coffin mounted in a miniature golden temple on wheels, and a cortege of sixty-four mules, each sporting a golden crown and tinkling with the sound of a golden bell, carried his body westward for burial. The young conqueror, however, never made it home to Macedonia. As the cortege wound solemnly through Syria, one of Alexander's most trusted generals turned up with an army. Ptolemy had just become the ruler of Egypt, and he wanted to honor his old friend and remind his new subjects of his powerful Macedonian connections. So he stole the body and carried it back to

Egypt. There his descendants kept it for centuries, occasionally showing Alexander off to visiting luminaries such as Julius Caesar. After the Ptolemies lost their throne in 30 B.C., Alexander's mummy was lost to history.

There are many theories about what became of Alexander. After centuries of searching, many scholars concluded that his honeyed remains came to rest beneath the foundations of a mosque standing at the intersection of two of Alexandria's busiest thoroughfares, Tariq al-Hurriya and Sharia an-Nabi Daniel. Moslem authorities, however, have prohibited any excavation at the mosque, fearing these earthworks would irreparably damage the building. This prohibition has not entirely deterred the curious, who have tried tunneling beneath it. Others have claimed to find clues to Alexander elsewhere. In 1995, archaeologist Liana Souvaltzi thought she had discovered his concealed crypt just outside Siwa, a remote desert oasis southwest of Alexandria. She reported finding ancient stone tablets describing how Ptolemy had carried the body of the young king to the oasis. These translations were later called into question, however, and today scholars still debate the whereabouts of Alexander's body.

Unearthing the mummy of the ancient Macedonian would almost certainly spark the engines of an entire historical industry. But historians do not confine their interests to the remains of the famous and the celebrated. Those of more obscure folk, whose lives passed without so much as a mention in ancient texts, can also have this incendiary effect, particularly when they promise to illuminate a previously unsuspected chapter of history. This is exactly what happened when a prominent American sinologist stumbled upon a trove of ancient mummies in a remote province of northwest China. Belonging to a previously unknown ethnic minority, the ancient cadavers touched a nerve in both the East and West, raising troubling questions about race, racism, and the nature of history itself. The mummies were swiftly adopted as symbols of protest by minority separatists and just as swiftly designated a matter of state security in China. To my mind, they broached a fundamental issue: What happens when the ancient dead reveal a history that many prefer to bury?

UNTIL HE FIRST encountered the mummies of Xinjiang, Victor Mair was known mainly as a brilliant, if eccentric, translator of obscure Chinese texts, a fine scholar with a few funny ideas about the origins of Chinese culture, and a scathing critic prone to penning stern reviews of others' sloppy scholarship. Mair's pronouncements on the Chinese-like characters inscribed on the Dead Sea Scrolls were intensely debated by researchers. His magnum opus on the origins of Chinese writing, a work he had been toiling at for years in his office at the University of Pennsylvania, was eagerly anticipated. But in 1988, something profound happened to Mair while he was leading a group of American travelers through a small museum in Ürümchi, the provincial capital of China's remote northwesternmost province, Xinjiang. Mair had visited the museum several times before. But on this occasion a new sign pointed to a back room. "It said something like 'Mummy Exhibition,'" recalled Mair, "and I had the strangest kind of weird feeling because it was very dark and kind of cut off in the back part. There were curtains, I think. To get in, you felt like you were entering another world."

In a glass display case so poorly lit that visitors needed to dig out flashlights to get a look at the contents, Mair spied a bizarre sight. It was the outstretched body of a man just under six feet tall, dressed in an elegantly tailored wool tunic and matching pants the color of red wine. Covering the man's legs were striped leggings in riotous shades of yellow, red, and blue, attire so outrageous that it could have come straight from the pages of Dr. Seuss. But it was not so much the man's clothing that first riveted Mair's attention. It was his face. It was narrow and pale ivory in color, with high cheekbones, full lips, and a long nose. Locks of ginger-colored hair and a graying beard framed his parchmentlike skin. He looked very Caucasian; indeed, he resembled someone whom Mair knew intimately. "He looked like my brother Dave sleeping there, and that's what really got me. I just kept looking at him, looking in his eyes. I couldn't tear myself away. I went around his glass case again and again and again. I stayed in there for several hours. I was supposed to be leading our group. I just forgot about them. I sort of got lost for two or three hours."

Local archaeologists had come across the body during excavations in the Tarim Basin, an immense barren of sand and rock in southern Xinjiang. The region was not the kind of place that generally attracted well-dressed strangers. At the height of summer, temperatures in the basin soared to a scorching 125 degrees Fahrenheit, without so much as a whisper of humidity, and in winter, they frequently plunged far below freezing. The desert at the basin's heart was one of the most waterless places on Earth, and its very name, the Taklamakhan, was popularly said to mean "Go in and you won't come out." Over the years, the Chinese government had found various uses for all this bleakness. It had set aside part of it as a nuclear testing range, conducting its blasts far from prying eyes. It had also built labor camps and exiled men there, certain that no one in his right mind would try to escape.

The Taklamakhan's merciless climate had one advantage, however. It tended to preserve human bodies. The archaeologists who discovered the stranger in the striped leggings marveled at the state of his cadaver. He looked almost alive. They named him Cherchen Man, after the county in which he was found, and they set about radiocarbon dating him. They discovered that he was very, very old. Indeed, the tests showed that he had roamed the Tarim Basin as early as the eleventh century B.C. This astonished Mair, for it undermined one of the keystones of Chinese history. Scholars had long believed that the first contacts between China and the West occurred relatively late in world history—around the mid-second century B.C., when the Chinese emperor Wudi decided to send an emissary west.

According to contemporary texts, Wudi had grown tired of the marauding Huns, who were continually raiding the richest villages of his empire, stealing grain and making off with the women. So he decided to propose a military alliance with his neighbors to the far west in order to crush a common foe. He asked for a volunteer to act as his emissary, and when one of his palace attendants, Zhang Qian, stepped forward, he sent him west in 139 B.C. Zhang Qian failed to obtain the alliance his master coveted, but the route he took to Central Asia became part of the legendary Silk Road. In the years that followed, hundreds of trading caravans and Caucasians plied this route, carrying bundles of ivory, gold, pomegranates, safflowers, jade, furs, porcelain, and silk between Rome and Xi'an.

Nationalists in China are fond of this version of history. It strongly suggests that Chinese civilization, which had flowered long before Zhang Qian headed west, must have blossomed in hothouse isolation, free of European influence. And this casts early Chinese achievements in a particularly glorious light. In one popular book, *The Cradle of the East*, Chinese historian Ping-ti Ho proudly claimed that all the hallmarks of early Chinese civilization—including the chariot, bronze metallurgy, and a system of writing—were products of Chinese genius. Those living in the ancient Celestial Kingdom had never stooped to borrowing the ideas of others. Their inventive genius surpassed that of the West.

Mair, a professor of Chinese in the department of Asian and Middle Eastern Studies at the University of Pennsylvania, doubted this history. He suspected that the Chinese had encountered westerners long before Emperor Wudi dreamed up his military alliance. Several early Chinese books, for example, described tall men with green eyes and red hair that resembled the fur of rhesus monkeys. Most scholars dismissed these accounts as legendary, but Mair wasn't so sure.

He thought they were descriptions of Caucasian men. During his studies of Chinese mythology, he had found characters strikingly similar to those in early Greek and Roman tales. The parallels were too frequent to be mere coincidences. He kept stumbling across words in early Chinese texts that seem to have been borrowed from ancient languages far to the west. He kept a list of them. They included the words for dog, cow, goose, magus, grape, and wheel. There were also tantalizing bits of harder evidence, too. Tatters of Chinese silk had been recovered from tombs dating to the eleventh century B.C. in Egypt and to the sixth century B.C. in Greece and Austria. But though Mair repeatedly argued the case for early trade and contact between China and the West, no one took him very seriously. "People would laugh at me. I said that East and West were communicating back in the Bronze Age and people just said, 'Oh yeah? Interesting, but prove it.'"

He had craved vindication, but never for a moment did he expect to find the kind of flesh-and-blood proof that Cherchen Man promised. Still, he was wary of a hoax. The man's tailored woolen clothing, with all the complex textile technology it implied, was unlike anything Mair had ever seen from ancient China. The mummy itself seemed almost too perfectly preserved for credence. "I thought it was part of a wax museum or something. I thought maybe it was a ploy to get more tourists. And I felt like that for a long time, because I said, 'How could they have such advanced technology three thousand years ago?' I couldn't put it into any historical context. It didn't make any sense whatsoever."

Mair began asking around about Cherchen Man among

his Chinese colleagues. He learned that European scholars had unearthed several similar bodies in the Tarim Basin almost a century ago, but had regarded them as little more than oddities. In 1895, for example, the British-Hungarian scholar Marc Aurel Stein exhumed a few Caucasian bodies while searching for antiquities and old Central Asian texts in the Tarim Basin. "It was a strange sensation," noted Stein in his later writings, "to look down on figures, which but for the parched skin, seemed like those of men asleep." But Stein and the Europeans who followed him were far more interested in classical-era ruins than in mummified bodies: they took a few photos and made passing references to these unusual cadavers in their books, but they did not investigate.

Early Chinese archaeologists in the region also came across some of the bodies, but they were no more interested than the Europeans. They thought it likely that a few ancient foreigners had strayed into the territory by chance. But in the 1970s, Chinese archaeologists happened upon hundreds of the parched cadavers in Xinjiang while surveying along proposed routes for pipelines and rail lines. Most of these mummies were very Caucasian looking. They had blond, red, and auburn hair. They had deep-set eyes, long noses, thick beards, and tall, often gangly, frames. They wore woolens of Celtic plaid and sported strangely familiar forms of Western haberdashery: conical black witches' hats, tam-o'-shanters, and Robin Hood caps.

Some were clearly wrapped in the wealth of the Silk Road. Yingpan Man, for example, wore a mask with a golden band across his forehead and boasted a fine brocade robe with a Western-style design. "There are figures woven into the pattern of the brocade and they are classic Western figures, like Greco-Roman deities," explained Mair. "They look like cherubs although they are not cherubs." But many of the other ancient cadavers were dressed and buried more simply. Some were outfitted only in fur moccasins, woolen wraps, and feathered caps and buried with small baskets of grain. These, it transpired, were the oldest of the Caucasians. According to radiocarbon dating tests, they roamed the northwestern corner of China in the twenty-first century B.C., the height of the Bronze Age, just as Mair had long suggested.

Convinced of the authenticity of the mummies, Mair began puzzling over their meaning in his office at the University of Pennsylvania. Who were these ancient invaders, he wondered, and where on Earth had they come from?

MAIR IS A big, rugged-looking man in his mid-fifties, a shade over six foot one, with size fourteen feet. The son of an Austrian immigrant, he stands nearly a head taller than most of his Chinese colleagues, a physical advantage that he often tries to minimize or conceal in group photographs by stepping down off a curb or onto a lower step. Robust and athletic-looking, he possesses the clean-cut good looks that one often sees in former pro football players. He has short, neatly combed, straight gray hair, a large aquiline nose, observant blue eyes, and a jesting wit, which he uses to particularly good effect, laughter being the best way of bridging any awkward cultural gap. He neither smokes nor drinks, and never did, and is by his own admission a born leader. Possessed of an uncommon self-confidence, which sometimes comes across as arrogance, he is a man of many surprising quirks. He once told me, for example, that he likes to finish his dinners at home by lifting the plate to his mouth and licking it clean in order to relish the flavors of the dish longer, a sentiment that struck me at the time as something far more Eastern than Western, which is how Mair himself often comes across.

I had arranged to meet Mair in Shanghai, where he was hoping to begin a new round of DNA testing on the Tarim Basin mummies. In our early conversations on the phone, Mair had told me that he would be traveling with a geneticist who hoped to take tissue samples from the Tarim mummies stored at the Natural History Museum in Shanghai. It sounded as if everything had been arranged. But as I quickly discovered upon my arrival in Shanghai, Mair was still a long way from gathering tissue samples. Housed in a small guest house for foreign lecturers at Fudan University, he strode the hallways like a weary giant. He had just spent two full days in meetings with his Chinese colleagues, trying to hammer out a deal. But the talks were stalling. To clear his head and ease the chronic ringing in his ears, Mair invited me to join him for a walk. In the tropical downpour, I struggled to keep up with him, dodging flocks of cyclists in their shiny yellow rain slickers and black pools of nearly invisible potholes. Mair wove past them absently. Instead of a raincoat, he wore two long-sleeved plaid shirts, one inside the other. He didn't seem to care that he was getting soaked.

Nothing, he explained as we walked in the rain, was ever simple when it came to the Xinjiang mummies. Dead as they had been for thousands of years, they still managed to

stir strong feelings among the living. In China, a restive ethnic minority known as the Uyghurs had stepped forward to
claim the mummies as their own. Numbering nearly seven
million strong, the Uyghurs viewed the Tarim Basin as their
homeland. Former allies of the Chinese, the largely Moslem
Uyghurs had become a subjugated people in the late nineteenth century. During the 1930s and 1940s, their leaders
managed to found two brief republics that later fell under
Chinese control. But Uyghur guerillas continued fighting
stubbornly, until their last leader was executed in 1961.
Since then, the Chinese government has dealt harshly with
any sign of separatist sentiment. Amnesty International's
1999 report for Xinjiang made grim reading. "Scores of
Uyghurs, many of them political prisoners, have been sentenced to death and executed in the past two years," it noted.
"Others, including women, are alleged to have been killed by
the security forces in circumstances which appear to constitute extra-judicial executions."

Still the Uyghurs refused to give up, and when they
caught wind of mummies being excavated in the Tarim
Basin, they were keenly interested. Historians had long suggested that the Uyghurs were relative latecomers to the
region, migrating from the plains of western Mongolia less
than two thousand years ago. But Uyghur leaders were skeptical. They believed that their farmer ancestors had always
lived along the fertile river valleys of the Tarim, and as such
they embraced the mummies as their kin—even though
many scholars, Mair included, suspected that Uyghur
invaders had slaughtered or driven out most of the mummies' true descendants and assimilated the few that

remained. In Xinjiang, Uyghur leaders picked one of the oldest mummies as a poster girl for their cause. They named her, with some poetic license, the Beauty of Loulan and began printing posters with her picture. The fact that she was so Caucasian looking was not a problem in Uyghur eyes: some Uyghurs had Caucasian features. People in Ürümchi were captivated. Musicians began writing songs about her, subtly alluding to the separatist cause.

This sudden outburst of mummy nationalism alarmed the Chinese government. Before long, everything related to the Xinjiang mummies was considered a matter of state security. No one in government was in any hurry to authorize a genetic test on them. If the mummies' DNA revealed even a partial link to the Uyghurs—a not unlikely prospect given the Uyghurs' mixed heritage—it would further strengthen in the eyes of the world the separatists' claims to the region. This was something the Chinese wished to avoid, especially after all the international condemnation of their treatment of another ethnic minority in Tibet. Adding to the problem was the Chinese sensitivity to any matter touching on the Tarim Basin. Beneath the dusty windblown surface of the basin gleamed immense oilfields. According to Chinese geologists, nearly 18 billion tons of crude pooled there, three times as much as the proven reserves of the United States.

Chinese officials, moreover, were not the only ones worried about genetic testing. Western scholars fretted, too. Some hated the thought that Europeans could have succeeded in planting settlements in the heart of Asia thousands of years ago. Such a migration smacked of ancient colonialism, a political oppression that many historians abhorred.

"There's a lot of Western guilt about imperialism and sensitivity about dominating other people," said Mair. "It's a real deep subconscious thing, and there are a lot of people in the West who are hypersensitive about saying our culture is superior in any way or our culture gets around or extends itself. So there are people who want to make sure that we don't make mistakes in our interpretation of the past."

Certainly, the presence of ancient Europeans in China could be twisted and distorted to political ends: people with racial agendas had long been searching for just such evidence. During the 1930s, for example, Adolf Hitler and Heinrich Himmler had taken an unhealthy interest in Genghis Khan, the most famous leader of the Mongols. A clever and hideously cruel warrior, Genghis Khan had swept out of Central Asia in the thirteenth century, swiftly conquering just about every kingdom within his immense striking range. Pitying none, the Mongol leader slew almost the entire population of eastern Persia, and by the time of his death, he controlled vast stretches of Eurasia, from southern Siberia to Tibet and from Korea to the Aral Sea. In this, Hitler and Himmler, the bespectacled head of the SS, saw much to admire and emulate. "Our strength," observed Hitler in a thundering speech to the commanders of Germany's armed forces in 1939, "is in our quickness and brutality. Genghis Khan had millions of women and children killed by his own will and with a gay heart. History sees only in him a great state builder. . . ."

But Hitler's respect for the ancient Mongol presented a serious problem for a party that placed great stock in race. Genghis Khan, after all, was not Caucasian. He belonged to an Asian race that the Nazis heartily disdained as inferior. How, wondered Hitler and Himmler, could such a menial people produce such a brilliant tactician and bold statesman? It was a troublesome problem, but Himmler, who fancied himself a historian, finally came up with a solution. It was based on pure whimsy. He explained to one anthropologist that, unknown to history, Genghis Khan and his elite Mongol followers were actually Caucasians. They had descended from the citizens of Atlantis who had decamped from their mythical island home before it cataclysmically sunk beneath the waves. These Mongols, claimed Himmler, were a special kind of Caucasian: German blood flowed in their veins.

Obsessed by questions of race, Himmler must have dreamed of finding these ancient Caucasian Mongols. It's possible he asked others to look for them. One recent book suggests that Himmler went so far as to request a collection of mummies from Central Asia. In that way, his SS staff, which included archaeologists and anthropologists, could conduct racial studies. But if Himmler did place such an order, it seems to have come to naught. German scholars did mount expeditions into the Tarim Basin and other parts of Central Asia in the early twentieth century, searching for classical ruins and early Buddhist manuscripts, but they left few if any records of unearthing or collecting mummies. "In all of my reading of works emanating from these expeditions," says Mair, "I have never come across any indication that they brought such corpses back to Europe."

Even so, the bizarre racial ideas of the Nazis troubled Western scholars. They worried about where genetic testing of the Xinjiang mummies might lead and, worse still, who might ultimately try to profit from the research. Testing the mummies was like taking a stroll through a minefield: there was no telling what bombshell would explode in the traveler's face. "It would be especially bad news if any of the mummies were German," observed Mair. "They've had two world wars in which they were the perpetrators, and if any of these mummies were even remotely Germanic, forget it. People just wouldn't want to talk about it."

AS AMAZED AS Mair was by the mummies in 1988, he didn't immediately devote himself to studying them. He was in the midst of several cherished projects. He was laboriously tracking down the murky origins of the magi, a mysterious group of soothsayers and healers who were said to have divined the future and cured the sick in the courts of the early Chinese emperors. He was also editing *The Sino-Platonic Papers*, a journal that prided itself in publishing brilliant and controversial new research. And he was slaving over what he sincerely hoped would be a groundbreaking study on the origins of writing in China. He desperately wanted to finish it.

In September 1991, however, Mair picked up a newspaper and read of the discovery of the frozen, partially preserved corpse of a 5,300-year-old man in a glacier along the Austrian-Italian border. This was Europe's famous Iceman, Otzi. The news startled Mair. His own father had grown up in Pfaffenhoffen, a small Austrian village just a short distance away from where scientists had dug the Iceman from a glacier. His father's family had summered their herds in the same alpine meadows where Otzi had likely wandered. The Iceman, he realized, might well be a distant relative. He might also have had some connection to the ancestors of Cherchen Man, who looked so much like Mair's own brother. "I saw the headlines and I jerked," Mair recalls. "I thought of the Xinjiang mummies instantaneously because I thought they were the same. I looked at that Iceman and I said, 'These guys out in the Tarim are just like him. One's in ice and the others are in sand.' It didn't take half a second."

Austrian scientists planned on performing a sophisticated scientific analysis, including DNA testing, on the Iceman. It occurred to Mair that similar tests on Cherchen Man and his kin could do much to trace the ancestry of the mummies. He immediately wrote to Wang Binghua, one of the foremost archaeologists in Xinjiang, outlining the project that was forming in his mind. He also called Luigi Cavalli-Sforza, a distinguished geneticist at Stanford University who is an expert on ancient DNA. Cavalli-Sforza immediately saw the possibilities. He recommended that Mair contact one of his former students, Paolo Francalacci at the University of Sassari in Italy. Mair picked up the phone. It never really occurred to him, so confident was he in his own ability to rise to any occasion, that he lacked the scientific expertise generally needed for such a project.

Working closely with Wang, Mair requested permission for genetics testing. He spent months hammering out details of the project and assuaging Chinese fears. It was an uphill battle, but Mair's solid reputation as a scholar and translator opened doors that would have been shut to others and his sure grasp of cultural politics in China lent a calming influence to the talks. It also helped that he had several sweeteners to add to the deal. He promised to help raise Western funds for a special mummy museum in Ürümchi. He also offered to use his connections to try to get special mummy exhibit cases from the Getty Conservation Institute in California. Beijing finally gave the team a green light.

Francalacci wanted to collect samples from mummies left in the ground, as opposed to bodies already stored in museums. This would reduce the possibility of contamination with modern DNA. So in Ürümchi, he, Mair, and Wang Binghua set off cemetery hopping. At each chosen grave, the young geneticist donned a face mask and a pair of latex gloves and docked tiny pieces of muscle, skin, and bone from the mummies, often choosing tissue along the inside of the thighs or under the armpits because these regions had been less exposed to the excavators. He sealed each sample in a plastic vial. After several days, he had collected twenty-five specimens from eleven individuals, enough for a modest study. But there was little time for celebration. In a stunning about-face, Chinese authorities suddenly demanded Francalacci's samples, refusing to allow them out of the country. Mair could scarcely believe what was happening.

Then a mysterious thing happened. Just shortly before the dejected sinologist departed for home, a Chinese colleague turned up with a surreptitious gift. He slipped five of the confiscated and sealed samples into Mair's pocket. These had come from two mummies. Gratefully, Mair passed the samples on to Francalacci, who began toiling in Italy to amplify the DNA. Francalacci focused his research on the genes in the mitochondria. Once independent organisms, the mitochondria had joined forces with nucleated cells millions of years ago, supplying energy in return for the cell's protection and food. The mitochondria possessed their own DNA, but over time many of their genes had migrated to the cell nucleus, leaving only a small number behind. Each cell, however, possessed a thousand or more mitochondria. As a result, geneticists generally had far better luck recovering mitochondrial as opposed to nuclear DNA.

The Italian geneticist labored for months on the mummy samples, trying to extract enough DNA for sequencing. The nucleic acids had badly degraded, however. Still, Francalacci kept experimenting, and in 1995 he called Mair with a piece of good news. He had finally retrieved enough DNA to sequence and his preliminary results were intriguing. The two Xinjiang mummies belonged to the same genetic lineage as most modern-day Swedes, Finns, Tuscans, Corsicans, and Sardinians.

Francalacci wanted to test more mummies. But his research suggested that at least some of the bodies were of European ancestry.

THE GENETIC STUDIES were promising, but they only whetted Mair's curiosity. He wanted to know more. It was not just that Cherchen Man bore an uncanny resemblance to his own brother Dave or that he had taken to calling the ancient man Ur-David. It also had to do with Mair's own deeply rooted politics. "Everything that I've done," he explained, "even though it's been running all over the map, it's all been tied into the common man and making things accessible to the everyday guy, the worker. That's what it's all about and that's why I looked at these mummies. They were just everyday guys, not famous people."

Mair acquired this outlook at an early age. His immigrant father, whom he adored and deeply admired, was a lathe operator for a ball-bearing company in Canton, Ohio. His mother was a poet and songwriter. Growing up in a working-class family, Mair was continually reminded of the importance of ordinary people who sweated on the assembly lines or who toiled with mops and brooms at night. He tried never to lose sight of them. A bright kid who quarterbacked for his high school football team, he won a scholarship to Dartmouth, only the second time a kid from East Canton had attended an Ivy League college. At Dartmouth, he majored in literature and acquired an enduring love of Chaucer, the first English poet to write in the language of the common man. He also played on Dartmouth's freshman football team and became captain of its varsity basketball team. When graduation time rolled around, he decided to see the world. He joined the Peace Corps, which posted him to Nepal.

In a land of saffron-robed monks and prayer wheels, he discovered a fascination for Buddhism and a natural gift for languages. Back home, a professor suggested that he switch into Asian studies, a comment that clicked with Mair. He took classes in Buddhist history and began studying Buddhist literature, which meant mastering Sanskrit, Tibetan, Japanese, and Chinese, a daunting order for most westerners. But while many of his fellow students sweated to attain the necessary mastery, particularly of written Chinese, which has thousands of written characters, Mair, by all accounts, picked up these languages almost effortlessly. He then immersed himself in Chinese history and literature, first at the University of London in England and later at Harvard. Along the way, he married a Chinese-language teacher, Li-Ching Chang.

His interest in Buddhism eventually led him to Xinjiang and the neighboring province of Gansu, where Buddhist monks had stashed an enormous collection of ancient manuscripts in caves. Mair was fascinated by these texts. Many were penned in the earliest known examples of the everyday variety of Chinese writing. Others were covered in scripts written in Central Asian languages. But a few were much more mysterious. Linguistic studies disclosed that they were written in an ancient, long-extinct European language closely related to English, German, Gaelic, French, Spanish, and Greek. Scholars dubbed it Tocharian. Separated by seas, mountain ranges, and vast deserts from its closest relatives, Tocharian stood out like a sore thumb in China. Mair wondered how it had come to be spoken there. Fortunately, the Buddhist monks who penned the texts had left clues. In some caves, they had painted pictures of fair-haired, bearded, blue-eyed knights bearing gifts for Buddhist saints. These paintings dated to the sixth and seventh centuries A.D., long after the Silk Road opened.

It was often assumed that these fair-haired knights who spoke Tocharian were relatively recent arrivals in Xinjiang. But after stumbling on the Tarim mummies, Mair suspected that they were descendants of much earlier European colonists. He redoubled his efforts to trace the mummies' ancestry. In Xinjiang, a Chinese colleague had slipped him another parting gift: a swatch of blue, brown, and white cloth taken from a twelfth-century B.C. mummy. The fabric looked like a piece of Celtic plaid. Mair passed it over to Irene Good, a textile expert at the University of Pennsylvania Museum. Good examined it under an electron microscope. The style of weave, known as a "two over two" diagonal twill, was distinctive. It bore little resemblance to anything woven by Asian weavers of the day. (Indeed, it would be almost another two millennia before women in central China turned out twill cloth on their looms.) But the weave exactly matched cloth found with the bodies of thirteenth-century B.C. salt miners in Austria. Like the DNA samples, the mysterious plaid pointed straight toward a European homeland.

As he listened to Good describe her finds, Mair could see that there were other powerful ways of tracking the ancient desert dwellers of Xinjiang back through time to their homeland. DNA was just one of many paths. "I saw that Irene was talking about spins, diameters, thickness, and scalings, twill weaves—all things she saw with her electron microscope. This was pretty specific stuff, so I said, 'Let's go with that, too, as another line of evidence. Let's get as many people in here as possible and let them do their own things.' "

He organized a new expedition to Xinjiang with Good, fellow textile expert Elizabeth Barber, and her cultural anthropologist husband, Paul Barber. As the two women pored over the mummies' clothing, Barber examined the bodies themselves, studying their mummification. Mair hoped this might offer clues to the origins of the people themselves. But the ancient desert dwellers, he discovered, had not taken any of the elaborate measures favored by the Egyptians or other skilled morticians. Instead, they had employed nature and a few simple tricks. In some cases, family members had buried their dead in salt fields, where the chemistry preserved human flesh like a salted ham. Often they arranged the cadaver so that dry air flowed around the extremities, swiftly desiccating the flesh. Cherchen Man, for example, had benefited from both techniques.

Mair, too, assisted in the work. In his spare time, he translated key Chinese reports on the mummies and later published them in his own journal, *The Sino-Platonic Papers*. This gave Western archaeologists access to the scientific findings for the first time. To make the new research even better known, he penned a popular article for *Archaeology* magazine. He wanted to make the mummies the center of a lively scientific and scholarly industry, so he set about organizing a major international scientific conference on the mummies, bringing leading archaeologists, anthropologists, linguists, geneticists, geographers, sinologists, historians, ethnologists, climatologists, and metallurgists to the University of Pennsylvania to discuss their ideas. After everyone left, Mair dutifully edited and translated their papers in two large volumes, clarifying their arcane prose until everyone interested in the field could understand it. "If I get gray hair," he joked, "it is because I was sitting there slaving over this stuff."

When he was finally done, he sat down in his office with a pad of paper and a pen. He sifted through hundreds of studies on matters as diverse as linguistics, pottery styles, methods of tomb construction, and metallurgy across Eurasia over the past seven thousand years, searching for cultures whose core technologies and languages bore striking similarities to those of the ancient Caucasian cultures of Xinjiang. These he recognized as ancestral societies. Slowly, patiently, he worked his way back through time and space, tracing the territories of these ancestral groups. Eventually, after months of work, he sketched a map of what he concluded was their homeland. The territory stretched in a wide swathe across central Europe, from northern Denmark to the northwestern shore of the Black Sea. But its heart, some six thousand years ago, lay in what is now southern Germany, northeastern Austria, and the northern Czech Republic. "I really felt that that fit the archaeological evidence best," Mair told me.

When he finally showed his map—with its Germanic homeland—to some of his colleagues, they were deeply dismayed. Elizabeth Barber, one of his closest collaborators, angrily demanded that he redraw it, insisting that linguistic evidence, particularly the ancestry of ancient words for looms, pointed to a homeland much farther east. Realizing that he had gone too far for the comfort of his colleagues, he bowed to their pressure, recognizing that he had yet to find the conclusive proof he needed. He redrew the map, placing the homeland in a broad arc stretching from eastern Ukraine and southern Russia to western Kazakhstan. Then he published it in the conference proceedings. "I thought for this book, it wouldn't be too bad," he confessed, shaking his head. "I decided I wouldn't go against the flow that much, because that is a big flow with some really smart people."

Then he looked down at the map in front of him. "But in my own integrity and honesty, I'd want to put it in here." He sketched a narrow oval. Its center fell near the Austrian city of Salzburg.

BOTH STUBBORN AND self-assured, Mair was convinced he was right, and he desperately wanted to find the proof that would dispel all doubt. He believed genetics still offered the best hope of vindication, for if DNA testing was sufficient to convict men in a court of law and send them to the electric chair, it would surely be strong enough to persuade even the most skeptical of his colleagues. It was for this reason that he had come to Shanghai. He hoped to obtain samples for another, more powerful type of DNA testing, but Chinese officials were still wary of such tests, and they had upped the ante considerably. Japanese researchers had just parted with $100,000 to acquire ancient samples for DNA testing, and officials at Shanghai's Museum of Natural History now wanted a similar sum from Mair.

The sinologist didn't have it, but he hoped to find some more modestly priced compromise. After five days of talks, the Chinese still weren't biting and Mair was running out of time. Still, he remained surprisingly upbeat. During a break in the negotiations one afternoon, he invited me to follow colleague Xu Yongqing down the stairs to a basement room in Shanghai's Museum of Natural History. Slim and stoop-shouldered, with thinning strands of hair combed over his balding pate and an inordinate fondness for both poetry and rice wine, Xu is the head of the museum's anthropology department. Chatting amiably as he descended the stairs, Xu explained how his love of drink had developed from his particular line of work. "He says that he consumes so much rice wine," said Mair, smiling, "because he's always digging up corpses and opening coffins."

Unlocking the door to a small room behind the employees' bicycle racks, Xu led the way inside. Along three of the walls, mummies in glass cases reclined luxuriously on red velvet cloth. Stacked three high in spots, they looked much like passengers bedded down for the night in their train berths. Mair stood quietly, scanning the room. Then he spied what he was looking for. In one of the lower glass cases, a young woman lay stretched out on her back, stripped of her fine woolens. Her knees were pressed demurely together, her arms rested comfortably by her side, and her breasts lay round and full, as if she had perished in the midst of nursing a child.

But it was her hair that caught my attention—a long mane of wavy golden-brown, twisted down her back. Standing in that room, I felt an unexpected sense of kinship with her, surrounded as she was by strangers. And I wondered just what had prodded her ancestors to exchange the cool greenness of Europe for the scorching barrens of the Tarim Basin. It was a true mystery, one that might never be solved, but Mair had an idea that sounded plausible to me. He believed a fancy new invention had spurred her forebears to embark on this Eastern exodus: horseback riding. Some 5,700 years ago, along the eastern fringes of Europe, people had begun rounding up wild horses, and sometime later they started sliding bits into the horses mouths and swinging their bodies onto the animals' backs. By these seemingly simple acts, they conquered terrestrial space. For the first time ever, human beings were able to travel immense distances swiftly, an accomplishment so exhilarating and adrenaline-charged that they suddenly gave full rein to their wanderlust.

The sheer act of climbing atop these huge beasts likely gave their riders a sense of invincibility and freedom, something never to be repeated until the age of combustion engines and Model Ts. It almost certainly bestowed a powerful physical advantage over pedestrian societies. "I think to control the horse—it's a thousand pounds or more of meat— you have to be brave," observed Mair. "And people developed certain military skills from that platform, like being able to fire a bow and arrow from the horse. That would have been terrifying for people who didn't ride horses."

So equipped, early Europeans easily spread out across Eurasia, their brisk march recorded in the ancient campsites they left behind. Some of the invaders swept northward, becoming the Germanic tribes; others journeyed west to become the Celts of the British Isles. But the ancestors of the Xinjiang people headed east across the grassy steppes of Asia, dispensing with any who tried to bar their path, and four thousand years ago, a small group of latecomers rode into the vacant river valleys of the Tarim Basin. Finding sufficient land to earn a living there, they stayed, passing on their love of fine horses and their knowledge of them to their descendants. When mourners buried Cherchen Man, they arranged a dead horse and a saddle atop his grave, two things he would need in the next life.

In all likelihood, observed Mair, some of these European invaders rode even farther to the east and north, beyond the reach of desiccating deserts. And there they brought with them such new Western inventions as the chariot, a high-performance vehicle designed for warfare and sport, and bronze metallurgy, which made strong weapons that kept their killing edge. In all likelihood, a few of these invaders carried the secret of writing. Mair has found many hints of this in his extensive research, but one of the most tantalizing pieces of evidence emerged from the Tarim Basin mummies. While examining the hand of an ancient woman exhumed near Cherchen Man, Mair noticed row upon row of a strange tattoo along her hand. Shaped like a backward *S*, it clearly resembled the early Phoenician consonant that gave us our modern *S*. Mair has also found the identical form of *S*, along with other alphabetiform signs, on artifacts of this era from western China.

Chinese scholars, particularly those who have long reveled in the notion of China's magnificent isolation from the West, are unlikely to take much comfort in the thought of these invaders. They will not be pleased by the pivotal role these intruders may have ended up playing in ancient Chinese life. The Western inventions, after all, shaped the course of history. Fleet chariots enabled Chinese armies to vanquish their enemies, and sturdy bronze swords gave Chinese kings dreams of empires. And a secret system of writing bequeathed Chinese officials the means to govern the conquered lands effortlessly.

Today, people place great stock on invention and they take immense pride in creative minds that forge new technologies. But as historians have long known, invention is but one small part of the story. What societies make of these technological leaps forward is as important as the act of creation itself. It was foreign geniuses, after all, who unwittingly made the West strong. They gave Europe the compass that guided mariners overseas to Asia and America. They passed along the printing press that disseminated knowledge of these new lands to the masses and the gunpowder that fueled conquest. All these inventions came from Chinese inventors, for human societies have always profited from the genius of others.

In this, there are many ironies, not the least of which are those that now join East and West in the inseparable embrace of history. Savoring the ironies, Mair is now raising funds and fervently pursuing the negotiations for permission to conduct DNA tests on Xinjiang's mummies. He has received news that Chinese archaeologists have just exhumed 100 more of the strange mummies from the sands of the Taklamakhan.

MASTER
RACE

⌒

WHILE IT WAS NOT SOMETHING that Mair often talked about, one of his fondest ambitions was to bring a major exhibition of the Chinese mummies to North America and Europe. He wanted to share the thrill he felt when he first saw them, and he knew from earlier experience that Western audiences would be captivated by such an exhibit. In the mid-1990s, *Discover* magazine had decided to run an article on these ancient bodies and, while trying to illustrate the story, the editorial staff arrived at an inspired idea for photography. They contacted Jeffery Newbury, a prominent Los Angeles portrait photographer who specialized in television celebrities and temperamental rock stars. Newbury's subjects ranged from the murdered rap star Tupac Shakur to the cast of the television hit *Friends* and the media mogul Oprah Winfrey. Newbury worked in a rarefied Beverly Hills world of publicists, stylists, hairdressers, and makeup artists, but he was sufficiently intrigued by the call from *Discover* to take the assignment. He flew to Ürümchi. With an eye for the exceptional, he immediately grasped the visual essence of these mummies: their ravaged elegance and their lithe grace. This he successfully captured on film. He returned to Los Angeles with a superb shoot, and nearly everyone who saw it wanted to see these bodies in the flesh. By his art, Newbury created mummy celebrities.

When the photos finally appeared in *Discover*, they made quite a splash, and Mair began scouting out the possibilities for a major mummy exhibit. He discovered that the University Museum in Philadelphia was too small for the expected visitor hordes and that it lacked the necessary climate-control systems to conserve the bodies. So he approached the Los Angeles County Museum of Natural History, whose management leapt at the idea. To negotiate a deal, Mair and several of his colleagues made repeated trips to Beijing, while the Los Angeles museum sank nearly $300,000 into exhibit planning. But to the immense disappointment of all, China's cultural czars refused to send a single mummy—and this at a time when the Chinese government was currying favor with America in hopes of winning the coveted preferred-trading-partner status. One high-ranking Chinese official finally explained the situation to Mair. The mummies, she explained coolly, had nothing to say about the history of China.

In turning Mair away, however, these cultural arbiters spurned a rare opportunity to capture the imagination of the world. Mummies, after all, have immense public appeal. When the venerable British Museum launched its new Egyptian funerary gallery in the spring of 1999, people jostled three deep in front of the mummies, craning this way and that to get a better glimpse. Braving the crowds, visitors came to rub shoulders with immortality, to slake their thirst for the exotic, and to satisfy their taste for the macabre. And they had a very good time. The gallery was a rave hit. But experienced museologists had expected this: they were well aware of the mummy phenomena. "The first thing that people ask us when they come in the doors," confided Rosalie David, the keeper of Egyptology at the Manchester Museum, "is 'Where are the mummies and where are the dinosaurs?' "

Indeed, mummy experts have known about this strange phenomenon for nearly two hundred years. In Victorian times, for example, some entrepreneurs catered to the public fascination by holding what were quaintly called mummy unrollings. In theaters and lecture halls across Europe, they climbed up on stages and unwrapped mummies for the benefit of the paying public. By all reports, the audiences were spellbound. Such shows, it seemed, tapped deep into their psyches. Watching an ancient human emerge from thick bundles of tattered yellow cloth was, as I had discovered in Egypt, like attending a strange kind of birth. With each discarded coil of cloth, the unwrapper released someone into the world again. Delivered from the anonymity of its cloth womb, a mummy was a recognizable person again, a human being with a past, a present, and a future.

The fashionable set loved these unrollings, and everyone who could afford a ticket bought one, from countesses in their egret-feather hats to poets in their shiny black waistcoats. But not all nineteenth-century unrollers were in the simple business of serving up sensation. As mummy experts are beginning to discover, some unwrappings assumed a strangely political message in the years leading up to the Civil War in the southern United States. As a small but influential coterie of scientists bent the truth and fudged data, mummies became potent propaganda tools to battle abolitionists and to advance a cause dear to the hearts of many southerners: slavery. A century and a half later in the sultry Mississippi port of New Orleans, a young mummy expert was beginning to cast light on this strange form of political deception, illuminating just what happened when the living manipulated the dead for their own bigoted ends.

⌒

WITH ITS GRACEFUL columns and gleaming white stone, Gallier Hall aspires to the sculptured beauty of an ancient Greek temple. Harking back wistfully to a vanished, irretrievable past, it is redolent of the Old South and the Louisiana that was. Built in New Orleans at a time when sugarcane and cotton were kings, when steamboats plied the muddy channels of the Mississippi, nervously skirting the shoals, and when healthy young black men were prodded and poked, then auctioned off at the city's slave market for $1,800 or so each, Gallier Hall served for more than a century as New Orleans's city hall. But it wasn't always mired in building permits and city bylaws. During the first few years of its existence, before the Civil War broke out and before Confederate battlefields claimed so many of New Orleans's young men, Gallier Hall was a popular calling-in spot for traveling lecturers and itinerant preachers. Known then as the Lyceum Hall, it was a temple to learning and faith. And on the evening of February 28, 1852, the cream of New Orleans society swept up the stairway for a performance that promised to be the talk of the town for weeks to come—the final lecture by British Egyptologist George Gliddon.

A handsome man of forty-three, Gliddon was a familiar figure in the American South. With steamer trunks laden with Egyptian curios and Middle Eastern oddities, he had spent the better part of the past decade tramping up and down the Atlantic seaboard lecturing on the mysteries of ancient Egypt. A consummate showman, he had earned considerable fame from his performances, attracting some of the best scientific minds of his day. But Gliddon had grander ambitions still: he craved the acclaim of the crowd. So for the grand finale of his lecture series in New Orleans, he proposed to unroll a mummy, one of those he had recently acquired from the land of the pharoahs. For the first time ever, the citizens of New Orleans would be invited to gaze upon the face of an ancient Egyptian.

Dazzled by this, the audience would be more receptive than ever to his theories, or so Gliddon hoped. Through his studies of mummies, skeletons, and ancient art, he had become keenly interested in the origins of racial differences, particularly those related to the Caucasoid and Negroid races. A strong supporter of slavery and a scientific magpie who wove together odd bits of data, Gliddon argued that the "peculiar institution" of slavery had existed since the dawn of humankind, and was hence part of the natural order of things. He also suggested that God had deliberately created an inferior black race separately from a superior white race. Gliddon and his associates called this theory polygenism, and it played very well in the South, particularly among local plantation owners. They craved some kind of a divine sanction for their enslavement of black Africans, and Gliddon seemed to offer them one. "He was helping to build the framework of the southern position for the Civil War," said Guido Lombardi, as we stood together one early fall night on the gleaming steps of Gallier Hall.

Lombardi, a Peruvian mummy expert, had spent nearly three years delving into the story of Gliddon and his once famous unwrappings. All but forgotten today, the nineteenth-century Egyptologist had been relegated to a slender footnote in the history of the American South. But while studying in New Orleans five years ago, Lombardi came across an intriguing clue to Gliddon's popular shows. Piecing together, bit by tiny bit, details of Gliddon's public life, Lombardi became fascinated by the tale. He rooted through dusty archives and ransacked libraries for clues. He peppered Egyptologists from England to Egypt with questions. He dug up Gliddon's obscure books and read every word. In the end, he became an expert on Gliddon's unwrappings, but not without a cost. A gentle man, Lombardi had long dreamed of earning a Ph.D. in anthropology. But his studies of Gliddon consumed so much of his energy and finances that he finally didn't have enough of either to continue his studies at Tulane University.

Lombardi is a short, sturdy, amiable man with the rounded, hunched shoulders of someone who spends a lot of time at his desk. A medical doctor by training, he has a large jutting jaw and a pronounced overbite and wears dark wire-rimmed glasses. Excitable and enthusiastic by nature, he frequently claps his hands together when he is making a particularly good point in conversation, which is often. He possesses a kind of genial Old World politeness rarely seen in North America these days, particularly in anyone under sixty. Lombardi is thirty-five. And he is very organized. When I paid him a visit in New Orleans, he shook my hand the first night, then immediately handed me a detailed printed itinerary of how we would spend our time together, scheduled down to the last hour.

When I first visited him in New Orleans, Lombardi lived in a small apartment near the Tulane University campus. During one of our early conversations, he confided that he missed his family's rambling house in Lima with its swimming pool and garden of rare cacti that he had helped collect. In Peru, he explained, young men traditionally lived with their parents until they married. Lombardi had yet to take that step and he had been rather lonely in New Orleans. Few people there seemed to share his enthusiasm for mummy unwrappings, and he constantly felt as though he had to explain himself to the people he met. "People say, 'How can you be a doctor and then after that become a student again? You must be crazy.' Because the image of a doctor here in America is to become rich." Lombardi, however, seemed the antithesis of an American doctor. He took buses and walked wherever he went. He carried a nylon backpack over his shoulder and watched every nickel and dime he spent. He loved his studies with a kind of monkish fervor. "I just don't have the approach that the largest satisfaction in life is to make a lot of money."

One of Lombardi's largest satisfactions in life is to find and study mummies, particularly those forgotten or lost to scholarship. He never expected that this solitary pursuit would lead him to someone like Gliddon. But that was exactly what happened. He was chatting one afternoon with a fellow doctor at Tulane University, Antonio D'Alessandro, who specializes in tropical medicine. By chance, D'Allesandro recalled hearing of two Egyptian mummies on display in the university's medical school. Lombardi picked up on this at once. The idea of finding a pair of Egyptian mummies stashed away in some forgotten attic was incredibly appealing to the young scholar.

Lombardi asked around at the anthropology department and recounted the story to the archivists and librarians he had cultivated since arriving in New Orleans. Two or three remembered something about the mummies, but they had no idea what had happened to them. Lombardi dug out a slender file on the mummies at the archives. To his disappointment, it did little more than confirm their existence, so he started asking everyone he met for leads to the whereabouts of the bodies. People just looked at him and shook their heads. Finally, he confided the story to a classmate, Sharon Halton, who had worked as a secretary in the medical faculty. Halton offered to make some phone calls. A few months later, she contacted him. One of the retired doctors she talked to remembered something about the Egyptian mummies. In the late seventies, he told her, the university had rescued two Egyptian mummies from a room under the bleachers of Tulane Stadium, where the two corpses had inadvertently attended three Super Bowls. In a brief flurry of interest, the medical school had exhibited the finds, then stowed them in the basement of the Howard-Tilton Library. No one had seen or heard of them since. Lombardi hung up in a fever of excitement. "I don't know if you believe in destiny," he said. "I don't believe in it, but when things like this happen, it makes you wonder."

He didn't think any of this story sounded at all strange. He was accustomed to finding mummies in weird places. At the age of ten, he had come across a mummy while attending a birthday party for a friend, the son of a high-ranking Peruvian navy official, on an island naval base. "Part of the tour we were given was to walk around part of the island, and I still remember, someone said, 'Look, what's there?'" Lombardi turned to where the man pointed and saw a mummified body with bits of orange feathers sticking out from the sand. He learned later that an entire Dutch fleet had taken ill offshore with cholera in 1624. Racked by diarrhea, many of the men had perished, and since they were already badly dehydrated from the disease, they had swiftly mummified. The body in the sand was one of those men; the feathered hat suggested he was a senior officer. "I think the one I saw was a Dutch admiral," said Lombardi.

So he didn't for a moment doubt the story about the mummies at the Super Bowl. He hustled over to the library and spoke to several of the librarians. They dug out some keys. In a small basement stairwell, where students sometimes sneaked away to have a smoke and a private flip through skin magazines, Lombardi found a glass display case covered by a plywood lid. He called a friend to help him lift the lid. His heart was pounding as he heaved it off. Inside were the bodies of two Egyptian mummies. One, nearly ebony in color, was exquisitely preserved. "I could hardly believe it," Lombardi recalled, "and at the same time, I was thinking, 'Oh God, thank you for this miracle that has happened.' "

Whoever stowed the bodies in the basement had also left a clue to the story behind them. A small cardboard sign written in India ink lay beside one of the bodies. It read: "The mummy was obtained from the Werda, Thebes, about 1844–45. Presented to the Tulane University in 1851 by Geo. Gliddon & Prof. J. C. Nott."

THERE WERE FEW mysteries that tugged so strongly at the scientific imagination in the early nineteenth century as that of the ancient Egyptians. Researchers knew frustratingly little about the architects of the pyramids and the sculptors of the Sphinx, and science seemed to have little help to offer. Antiquarians had yet to learn how to extract valuable information about the past from the ground, for archaeology was in its infancy and linguists had yet to crack the seemingly impenetrable code of Egyptian hieroglyphical writing. It was only in 1822 that a young French scholar, Jean-François Champollion, found the key to reading the strange bird- and human-studded script on the Rosetta stone. Even after Champollion's prodigious feat, answers about the Egyptians were slow in coming. Scholars had yet to decipher fully the hieroglyphics and work their way through thousands of papyri, pottery fragments, and temple walls.

In the absence of evidence, European intellectuals speculated wildly about who the ancient Egyptians were. Modern Egypt, after all, boasted a rich commingling of peoples. Which of these—if any—was responsible for the ancient glories of the Nile? Scholars were divided. During explorations of ancient Egyptian temples, some had noticed painted and sculpted scenes that reminded them of a nineteenth-century slave raid, with Caucasian-like men wielding clubs over black captives. From these scenes, they concluded that ancient Egypt was inhabited by a ruling white class and an army of black slaves. But others were not so sure. They pointed to fleeting passages in the texts of classical writers. The Greek historian Herodotus, for example, described the Egyptians as "black in complexion and wooly headed." From such passages, some intellectuals concluded that the wonders of the Nile were the products of black genius.

Without physical evidence, however, it was impossible to settle the matter. The only obvious way to tease out the truth, reasoned scholars such as England's Samuel Johnson, was to examine the ancient Egyptians themselves. But this was not nearly as simple as it sounded. Most Egyptian mummies were so slathered with embalmers' resins and so altered by time and mummification, that it was difficult to reconstruct their faces or glimpse their original skin color. If researchers wanted to identify race, they had to devise another way of doing it. As it happened, a young German physiologist and comparative anatomist, Johann Friedrich Blumenbach, had come up with a new method for doing so in the late eighteenth century.

Like other thinkers of his age, Blumenbach was intensely curious about the origins of human differences. He wondered whether people as physically diverse as the Hottentots of Africa and the Mongols of Asia were truly members of the same species. To examine the question, he collected human skulls from around the world and took careful measurements of them to see whether they shared common characteristics that set them apart from other primates. He also made note of what he considered any defining facial feature, such as the broad flat nose of some black Africans. After years of diligent work, Blumenbach, who is often considered a father of physical anthropology, concluded that all human beings belonged to just one species. But he observed that there were significant physical differences in the human family. In his classic work, *On the Natural Variety of Mankind*, published in 1776, he proposed dividing *Homo sapiens* systematically into four distinct races—Caucasian, Mongolian, Amerindian, and Black African. Only later, in 1795, did he add a fifth race, the Malayan.

Blumenbach thought that these races had likely evolved as a consequence of different environmental conditions. But he was puzzled. Which was the original stock? He decided to search for the answer among Egyptian mummies. Like most other intellectuals of his time, Blumenbach believed that the world began just centuries before the dawn of civilization along the Nile: the Old Testament provided evidence for as much. So it seemed likely to the German anatomist that the ancient Egyptians would closely resemble primeval humans. Blumenbach began searching for some of their bodies to study. He traveled to England, contacting among others the British Museum, which obligingly gave him permission to unwrap three of its mummies, the only time in its venerable history that it has ever sanctioned such a procedure. Blumenbach happily went to work. He unraveled the bandages, took notes on his subjects' facial features, and measured their crania. Then he compared these measurements to those he had obtained for each modern race. He concluded that the ancient Egyptians he'd examined were Caucasians. Such research confirmed his suspicions about the primacy of the white European. "The Caucasian must, on every physiological principle," he observed in 1825, "be considered the primary or intermediate of these five principal races. The two extremes into which it has deviated, are on the one hand the Mongolian, on the other the Ethiopian [Black African]."

But this was just a small study. To generalize and to answer many other scientific questions, anatomists needed to examine more mummies. Inevitably this meant more unrollings. Before too many years had passed, these events assumed the peculiar trappings of a university anatomy lesson: that is to say, they became very public. In Europe, anatomists had long been accustomed to subsidizing their work by selling tickets to their dissections. Anyone could attend and the performances were carefully staged. As one of the instructors read aloud from an anatomy text, another cut open the cadaver with a surgical knife. A third person, known as the ostensor, gestured toward the organ or structure being described. The best anatomists attracted large, festive audiences. In France, for example, the local nobility swanned in wearing masks and sipped at glasses of fine wine as they watched the demonstrator carve up a fresh cadaver.

Early mummy experts took due note, modeling their unrollings after these lessons, and it wasn't long before shrewd minds realized that handsome profits could be made from such performances. In 1837, the year Queen Victoria ascended to the throne, a prominent Egyptian antiquities dealer, Giovanni D'Athanasi, decided to stage a major mummy unrolling in London. D'Athanasi had surmised that nothing would advertise the forthcoming public sale of his collection of Egyptian sculptures and papyri better than such an event. So he asked a famous English mummy expert, Thomas Pettigrew, to conduct the affair and rented space at Exeter Hall, a new building on the Strand devoted to educational, religious, and philanthropic gatherings. To publicize it all, D'Athanasi printed handbills boldly announcing that "The Most Interesting Mummy that has as yet been discovered in Egypt will be unrolled in the large room at Exeter Hall, Strand." The tickets cost six shillings for a reserved seat next to the operating table, four shillings for one on the balcony or a platform seat, and two shillings sixpence for those situated elsewhere in the hall.

On the evening of April 10, 1837, nearly five hundred people squeezed into Exeter Hall. Society hostesses, gadabouts, members of Parliament, artists, and diplomats took their seats next to antiquarians and Egyptologists. As Pettigrew crossed the stage and gestured toward the recumbent figure of the mummy, the expectant crowd fell silent. It was not, however, the show they had hoped for. Though Pettigrew easily stripped off the outer bandages, he could not pry loose the hardened resin that encased the body like ebony cement. He tried hammers, knives, and chisels. Finally he gave up in frustration. "Finding it impossible to make greater way in removing the obstacles interposed by the preparation," noted the reporter from London's *Literary Gazette* dryly, "it was announced that the task would be carefully completed elsewhere, and the results submitted to the view of the public."

Embarrassing as this debacle was for Pettigrew, a serious scientist, it did not deter other unrollers—far from it. Mummy unwrappings became all the vogue in the fashionable set. In the late spring of 1850, for example, Lord Londesborough sent out dozens of invitations to his friends for an afternoon get-together at his city home. Nicely engraved with a line drawing of an Egyptian mummy, the invitations politely announced the feature attraction: "A mummy from Thebes to be unrolled at half-past two." Other curiosity-seekers followed suit, unwrapping mummies in stately homes and city museums across England. "If you look in the local archives," observed John Taylor, an Egyptologist at the British Museum, "everyone who had a mummy in some far-flung place did a similar thing. They unwrapped it with a little audience and a brass band playing a tune."

Few, however, paid much mind to science. Some barely bothered to unveil the entire body: it was enough for spectators to gaze at the face. They had no way of knowing, after all, who it was wrapped in all those yards of tattered linen: the mystery gave free rein to their imaginations. The mummy could have been someone famous, the Queen of Sheba, perhaps, or the Egyptian princess who rescued baby Moses from a watery death on the Nile. The audience yearned for some hint. Was the face young and beautiful looking? Bedizened in jewels? Modestly coiffed? They had to see for themselves. An unwrapping mingled the spiritual and the carnal, the morbid and the melancholy, the fantastic with flesh and blood, scientific investigation with chamber of horrors. It was a potent blend.

But by the 1850s, public and scientific enthusiasm for these spectacles was beginning to wane in England. Scholars were beginning to translate the hieroglyphical texts, revealing much more of ancient Egyptian life than could be gleaned from a quick unrolling. The accurate translation of sarcophagi inscriptions had stripped away the mystery of the mummies' identities. The bodies belonged to ordinary Egyptians—priests, singers, artisans, and the like—not the fabled figures of the Old Testament. The immense public appetite for all things ancient Egyptian had become sated for the time being in Europe. It would not rage again until Howard Carter broke the seals on Tutankhamen's tomb.

Across the Atlantic, however, Americans were still caught in the thrall of Egyptomania. There, a handsome young Englishman, George Gliddon, had begun unrolling Egypt's ancient dead in the guise of science.

"BY NOW," LOMBARDI said over dinner one evening, "I am well acquainted with George Gliddon because he is like a living person to me." Gliddon, he explained, had all the right credentials for a lecturer on Egyptology. The son of an English merchant, he had spent much of his childhood in Alexandria, where his father served as British consul. At the family dinner table, the Gliddons had introduced their precocious son to some of the most famous men in nineteenth-century archaeology—from Sir John Gardner Wilkinson, the founder of British Egyptology, to John Lloyd Stephens, an American writer and explorer who was the first to recognize the stone temples of Central America as the ruins of the ancient Maya.

The young Gliddon proved an apt student with an eye for personal advancement. He sopped up details of the antiquities trade and read as much as he could on Egyptology. He helped his father arrange for the export of archaeological finds from Egypt. When a post for an American vice-consul opened in Cairo in 1832, the twenty-three-year-old landed the job. And it was there, while attending to visas and customs documents, that he came to the attention of the viceroy, Muhammad Ali, Egypt's mercurial sovereign. The powerful ruler took a shine to the ambitious young scholar. "One of the ideas Muhammad Ali had at the time was to industrialize Egypt's production of cotton," observed Lombardi, "so he sent George Gliddon to the United States to gather information and purchase machinery."

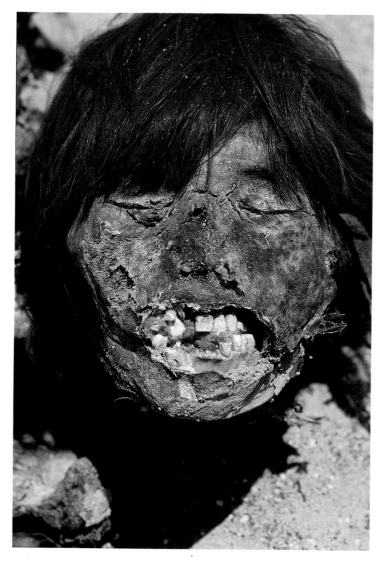

A TWO-THOUSAND-YEAR-OLD mummy grimaces in South America's Atacama Desert. Perhaps the most arid place on earth, the Atacama is littered with the ancient preserved dead—a superb setting for a mummy congress.

COURTESY PETER BENNETT.

A DEEP THRILL INVARIABLY PASSED through the
audience at the Mummy Congress whenever someone
showed a slide of an exquisitely preserved mummy. The
most lifelike bodies still possessed their eyelashes and the
wrinkled skin of their soles millennia after death.

COURTESY PETER BENNETT.

A GILDED MUMMY MASK IS all that remains of one tomb's valuables after looting at ancient Kellis, Egypt. For mummy experts, however, the real treasure lies in the mummies themselves and what they have to tell us about ourselves.

THE HEADS OF TWO ANCIENT Egyptians rest companionably in Art Aufderheide's windswept morgue at Kellis. Aufderheide thought them too pretty to dissect.

WITH A LIGHT TOUCH, PATHOLOGIST Art Aufderheide
prepares to photograph, then autopsy a mummy at Kellis.
One of the world's foremost mummy experts, Aufderheide
collects ancient tissue for leading-edge research on parasites,
infectious diseases, and mummification methods.

DEATH GENERALLY DISMANTLES A CORPSE with grim
precision. Blisters burst on the skin. Fingernails fall off. The
epidermis sloughs away. But Egyptian embalmers learned how
to break the chain of corruption, switching off enzymes and
preserving the appearance of life in a Kellis mummy's hand.

COIFFED FOR DEATH, AN EGYPTIAN mummy meets eternity fashionably, above. Surprisingly, hair is one of the most durable parts of the body, often outlasting flesh, below. Researchers now use such locks to detect drug use in the ancient world. COURTESY PETER BENNETT.

YDE GIRL WINCES IN A Dutch museum, revealing a
single peglike tooth. Modern forensic examination shows
that the ancient teenager, one of Europe's famous bog
bodies, was probably stabbed, then asphixiated by an
unknown assailant. COURTESY DRENTS MUSEUM, ASSEN.

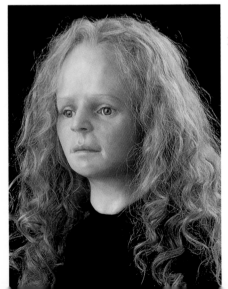

ALTERED BEYOND
RECOGNITION BY TIME
and the chemicals in a
bog's water, Yde Girl was
once a haunting beauty, as
British medical artist
Richard Neave discovered
after reconstructing
her face. COURTESY DRENTS
MUSEUM, ASSEN.

CAUGHT IN A TIME-LESS EMBRACE, the Weerdinge Men have been called the Netherland's oldest gay couple. Despite convincing evidence to the contrary, some experts still view bog bodies as social outcasts executed for transgressions—a theory picked up with tragic results by the Nazis. COURTESY DRENTS MUSEUM, ASSEN.

RED-HAIRED AND LONG-NOSED, CHERCHEN Man is one of several hundred Caucasian-looking mummies found in northwestern China. A resident of central Asia three thousand years ago, the lanky mummy contradicts theories about when China and the West first came into contact. COURTESY JEFFERY NEWBURY/DISCOVER MAGAZINE.

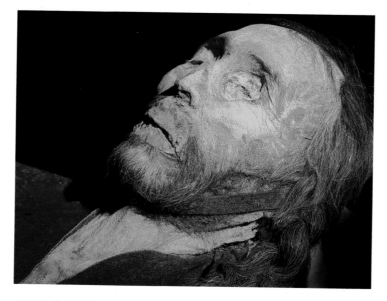

WHEN AMERICAN RESEARCHER VICTOR MAIR first laid eyes on Cherchen Man, he was greatly taken aback. The corpse closely resembled his own brother Dave. Mair became fascinated by the mummy's origins.

A THREE-MONTH-OLD CHERCHEN child lays swaddled in a shroud of red. Studies of DNA and textiles suggest that these Caucasian-looking mummies descended from European nomads who carried several key inventions—including writing—to China.

FOR CENTURIES, EUROPEAN ARTISTS DELIGHTED in using a transparent brown paint known as mummy, manufactured from the crushed bodies of Egyptian mummies. In 1903, the *Illustrated Mail* blithely showed its readers how a workman ground mummy bones for the pigment. COURTESY FITZWILLIAM MUSEUM, CAMBRIDGE.

FEW EARLY TRAVELLERS TO EGYPT could resist
packing home a mummy as a souvenir. During his famous
campaign on the Nile, Napoleon Bonaparte took a personal
interest in Egyptian antiquities. He eventually stowed two
mummy heads in his bags—one for his errant wife
Josephine. COURTESY CHESTER HIGGINS.

CAPITALIZING ON THE PUBLIC FASCINATION for
mummies, the press hounded Howard Carter after his
discovery of Tutankhamen's tomb in 1922. Carter refused to
compromise science for fame: modern mummy experts
sometimes find him a difficult act to follow. COURTESY MARY
EVANS PICTURE LIBRARY.

EXHUMED FROM AN ANDEAN PEAK in 1999 by archaeologist Johan Reinhard and his team, an Inca girl reclines in
frozen slumber. One of the most perfectly preserved mummies
ever found, the child was sacrificed to the gods more than five
hundred years ago. COURTESY *NATIONAL GEOGRAPHIC*.

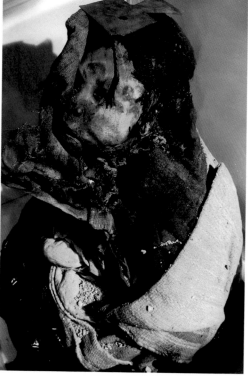

JOHAN REINHARD HAS EXHUMED EIGHTEEN Inca child mummies from the high Andes, including the famous Juanita, left, and a young girl from Mount Llullaillaco, below. The well-publicized finds beg a question: can science thrive in the media glare?

COURTESY *NATIONAL GEOGRAPHIC* AND REUTERS.

ST. ZITA AWAITS THE FAITHFUL in a basilica in Tuscany, an Incorruptible after more than seven hundred years. Recent studies suggest her preservation owes more to a quirk of early church architecture than to an act of God. COURTESY THE AUTHOR.

EAGER TO REPLACE THE CHURCH'S saintly Incorruptibles, Stalin and other Communist Party officials in Moscow created one of their own: Lenin. The work gave one of the embalmers a recurring nightmare. He dreamed he saw a fly buzzing inside Lenin's sarcophagus.

COURTESY REUTERS.

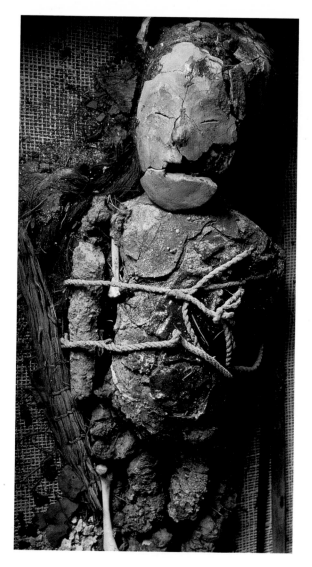

EARLY MUMMY EXPERTS WERE SUPREMELY confident they knew where mummification began: Egypt was the obvious birthplace. Current studies refute this. The earliest mummies, encased in claylike bodysuits, were made by the Chinchorro in Chile seven thousand years ago. COURTESY DAVID LIITTSCHWAGER AND SUSAN MIDDLETON/*DISCOVER* MAGAZINE.

LOOKING MORE ALIEN THAN HUMAN, a Chinchorro mummy gazes blankly at onlookers. The earliest Chinchorro mummies are those of young children. Mummification may have begun with a mother's unquenchable grief.

Gliddon was fascinated by America. He was thrilled by its immigrant energy, so different from the drowsy towns of the Nile he'd left behind, and he relished its freedom from convention. He was not at all perturbed by the inequality that wriggled like a giant worm through the American heartland. In his travels through the South, he didn't blink at the institution of slavery nor at the sight of gangs of black field hands picking cotton by hand. Nor was he put off by the attitudes of many white southerners who saw the black race as less than human. Gliddon, like many other European gentlemen of the age, happened to share these views.

So the young diplomat had been not at all averse to helping out a prominent Philadelphia scientist with his studies on the origins of race. Samuel Morton had published widely on subjects ranging from anatomy to geology, but he was best known for his work in physical anthropology. Like Blumenbach, said Lombardi, "Morton was an academic headhunter." He collected human skulls from correspondents in distant parts of the world, amassing what was later dubbed the American Golgotha. To conduct his studies, Morton measured various aspects of these skulls, including the cranial capacity. He believed this latter measurement was the most important of all, suggesting that it revealed not just brain size, but also intelligence. The larger the brain, the smarter the person. He filled each skull with either white mustard seed or lead shot, then measured the contents. From this he concluded that the largest brains were Caucasoid and the smallest were Negroid. That an elephant's brain was larger than that of a human being did not trouble him. Nor did scientific rigor. Studies by American paleontologist

Stephen Jay Gould have shown that Morton fudged his data—possibly unconsciously. He randomly pooled larger male skulls with smaller female skulls. He also seems to have packed Caucasoid crania tightly with seed and Negroid crania lightly.

Morton, as scholar William Stanton has pointed out in his book, *The Leopard's Spots*, privately believed that white people were destined to be masters and black people fated to be slaves. In Morton's view, God himself had created these differences, fashioning each of the races separately in the Garden of Eden. But the Philadelphia scientist lacked proof, so like Blumenbach he looked to Egypt for help. He had dashed off a letter to Gliddon, requesting assistance from the young vice-consul in obtaining a collection of ancient Egyptian skulls. Morton was keen to demonstrate that racial differences in intelligence dated back to the early days of Egyptian civilization, just short of the biblical date for creation.

Gliddon happily accommodated, corresponding at length with this new friend. He rounded up nearly one hundred ancient Egyptian skulls and twenty mummified heads and packed them off to America. The mummy heads proved particularly important to Morton. Some looked Caucasian to him, others like black Africans, and a few resembled mulattos. Morton was immensely pleased to see such racial diversity at so early a date. It lent further credence, he explained to Gliddon, to the theory of multiple creations. Morton then set about measuring cranial capacities. He was even more pleased. Ancient Caucasian-looking Egyptians had large brains; those who looked black possessed rather small ones. These disparities, concluded Morton, were "as old as the oldest records of our species." Both Morton and Gliddon were thrilled with the results, which seemed to bolster their theories of multiple creations. There had not been just one Adam and Eve, they concluded, but many—in fact, a pair for each of the races.

Inspired by Morton's work, Gliddon began scouring Egyptian ruins for other evidence that would support his mentor's theories. He took copious notes on tomb and temple walls that portrayed black slaves, ignoring the fact that these were war captives from powerful black kingdoms to the south. He paid close attention to the new dates emerging for the beginnings of Egyptian civilization. He also began planning his emigration to the United States. It occurred to him that he could earn a tidy living there by giving public lectures on Egyptology and promoting Morton's theories. Increasingly, Gliddon saw parallels between the Deep South and ancient Egypt. "Negroes were numerous in Egypt," he wrote, "but their social position in ancient times was the same as now, that of servants and slaves."

GLIDDON WAS A great hit in the United States in the 1840s. As a touring Egyptologist, he packed lecture halls from Philadelphia to Savannah, learning how to capture the public imagination. He always wore black, like a preacher, and spoke learnedly in language larded with scientific sounding words. He never saw a polysyllabic word he didn't like. But in spite of his bombast—or perhaps because of it— he became very famous. Leading scientists flocked to his lectures; prominent writers debated his ideas. Edgar Allan Poe made Gliddon a character in one of his lesser-known stories,

"Some Words with a Mummy." Poe seems to have thought Gliddon a bit of a fool. "It will be readily understood," observed Poe dryly, "that Mr. Gliddon's discourse turned chiefly upon the vast benefits accruing to science from the unrolling and disemboweling of mummies."

A shrewd showman, Gliddon went to great lengths to keep his lectures lively. He purchased an immense painted scroll by English panorama painter John Martin that depicted famous scenes along the Nile, from the Colossi of Memnon to the Pyramids of Giza and the harbor of Alexandria. As he lectured, stagehands busily rolled the scroll, giving the audience the illusion of riding a riverboat down the Nile. A pianist played what passed for Oriental music and Gliddon paced back and forth like a caged lion, picking up one, then another, of the more than six hundred props he liked to travel with, telling some fantastic tale about each. Reporters of the more discriminating sort were much amused. "Of Sampson's foxes he'd a tail," pilloried one critic, "Wrapped up in fair Delilah's veil / And in some antiquated pan / he'd had some toe-nails from Japan / And he declar'd he had a snail / Fresh from the back of Jonah's whale. . . ."

Even so, Gliddon was never quite satisfied. He dreamed of a bigger and better show. From his travels to England, he knew that nothing would pack the house like a mummy unrolling. He obtained a small shipment of mummies from a friend in Egypt who had visited a site known as Werda. Then Gliddon enthusiastically set about planning a grand affair for Boston in 1850. To prime his audience, he announced that he would unwrap the daughter of an Egyptian priest, information he claimed to have gleaned from deciphering hieroglyphs that covered one of the sarcophagi. The local press frothed at this news. In their excitement, however, reporters confused the daughter of a priest with a princess, transforming Gliddon's mummy into Egyptian royalty.

This only added to the enthusiasm of Bostonians. On the final evening of the lecture series, two thousand people— from poet Henry Longfellow and Harvard University president Jared Sparks to anatomist Oliver Wendell Holmes and famed Swiss naturalist Louis Agassiz—took their seats in the hall. "They were the crème de la crème of Boston's scientific community," noted Lombardi. "Everyone was there." In two earlier lectures, Gliddon had removed the princess's outer bandages in a kind of scientific striptease, tantalizing the audience while searching the linen for amulets and other treasures. That evening he planned on unveiling the princess in all her beauty. He sliced through the bandages and chipped loose the clots of resin. But as he tossed aside the last linen strip from her loins, a loud gasp arose in the front row. The princess had a generous penis. Gliddon was in a state of shock. "The mummy was clearly a man," said Lombardi, "and it was very embarrassing. Everyone in the audience began to laugh."

So stung was the Egyptologist by the ridicule that he quickly dashed off letters to Boston newspapers accounting for his error. The mistake, he claimed, arose from the poor handwriting of the coffin maker. But the damage had been done to his reputation as an Egyptologist—at least in the North. Humiliated, Gliddon retreated to the Deep South, where fewer hard questions would be asked about his credentials and his theories. He went to stay with Josiah Nott, a prominent New Orleans physician, a disciple of Morton, and a vocal supporter of polygenism. "Regarding Gliddon's slavery position," said Lombardi, "it was the perfect place to come."

Surrounded by congenial companions, Gliddon announced a new lecture series at New Orleans's Lyceum Hall and promised to unwrap yet another mummy. This would be a more intimate affair, as the Lyceum held only two hundred or so people. "The interesting thing," said Lombardi, "is that Gliddon announced this time that he didn't know a thing about the mummy. He said there was no evidence to point to the mummy's sex. I think he had learned to be quiet." This newfound discretion paid off. The New Orleans unrolling went off without a hitch. According to the *Daily Picayune*, Gliddon boasted to his audience that "if some of [Egypt's] savants could be resuscitated, they would conclude we had been apt pupils; and that we knew and did some things which they, in all the pride and perfection of their art and learning, were not quite up to." He then concluded the lecture by donating both of his unwrapped mummies to the city's medical school.

But Gliddon couldn't quite forget his public humiliation in Boston. He desperately wanted to salvage his scientific reputation. After Morton's death in 1851, he tried teaming up with Nott to write a definitive work on the origins of the races. Published in 1854, their collaboration bore the ponderous title *Types of Mankind: or Ethnological Researches, Based upon the Ancient Monuments, Paintings, Sculptures and Crania of Races and upon Their Natural, Geographical, Philological and Biblical History*. In it, Gliddon and

Nott outlined their theories in 738 pages of almost unreadable prose and mercilessly tiny type. But if they were expecting to win lasting scientific kudos and droves of new supporters, they were much mistaken. The book garnered poor reviews immediately and, within years, its central tenet, polygenism, was entirely discredited. Charles Darwin's new theory of natural selection and human evolution laid waste to all the old creationist ideas—including polygenism. And anthropologists ultimately abandoned simplistic attempts to define human races by such crude characteristics as skin color or cranial capacity.

Gliddon, however, didn't live long enough to witness this humiliation. Nor did he see the destruction during the Civil War of the Old South he cherished. Perhaps it was just as well. Struggling financially, the Egyptologist accepted work in 1857 with the fledgling British-Honduras Railway. He moved to Central America and never returned. He quarreled with his colleagues and was sacked from the railway within months of his arrival. In a Panama hotel, he committed suicide at age forty-eight, reportedly swallowing an overdose of opium.

ON MY FINAL afternoon in New Orleans, Lombardi took me to his small lab at Tulane. Little more than a back room in the university library, it was only a shade bigger than a closet, really, and yet it was the epicenter of Lombardi's world in New Orleans. Flipping on the lights, the young physician edged past a pair of ancient Egyptian coffins leaning against one wall and reached for a pair of latex gloves. Then he dramatically lifted the sheet from the table closest to the window. Lying on the table was the sadly crumbling body of the mummy that George Gliddon had unwrapped with such disastrous results in Boston.

Resting gently on a bed of soft white tissue paper, the man looked battered and worn, with a large, ugly, gaping hole where his nose had once stood. His face was as parched and cracked as dried mud, and his torso, or rather what remained of it, lay in tiny flakes and crumbs. It was impossible to say what had once been bits of pleura, heart, or kidneys. Not even his remaining bones lay in their correct position. It looked for all the world as if someone had put his body in a plastic bag and given it a cruel shake, and I pitied this man his miserable fate. He was destined for dust now, as sure as I was standing there. It was only a matter of time. He had been reborn at Gliddon's touch into a world of sorrow.

For months, Lombardi had been examining him delicately, trying to salvage something lasting from all this decrepitude. He had gently X-rayed what he could. He had measured and described and taken detailed notes. In doing so, he had discovered a final surprise. Easing his hand beneath the man's skull, he lifted it up into the air and cradled it in his hand. "The head was severed," he explained, "so they must have measured it and estimated the size, but they were very, very biased." Rotating his hand, he pointed with a latex finger to a small section at the back of the mummy's head. It took me a moment to catch his drift, but then I saw what he wanted me to see. A thick strip of linen bandage clung to the crania, cemented there by the embalmer's black resin. "They didn't remove all the bandages," said Lombardi, shaking his head, and I understood at once. The bits of linen would have made the head look larger, would have clinched Gliddon's case. Lombardi smiled as he watched my dawning understanding. "Perhaps Gliddon held it out in front of the people in the theater and maybe he said, 'Look at this big head. It's as large as the ones of modern people.' "

Gazing at this final duplicity, I understood at last how easy it was for the living to manipulate the dead, how simple it was to turn them to their own purposes, put words in their mouths, and fit a placard into their hands. The mummified dead are plastic to our touch and we the living can mold and arrange them however we choose. Scholars and scientists who fought for the dignity of humankind, who stood against bigotry and prejudice, whether they were aimed against the descendants of America's black slaves or the early inhabitants of China, had good reason to be suspicious of the everlasting dead. They looked harmless. But there were times when they carried a big club.

THE
MERCHANTS
OF MUMMY

⌐

A S DELICATE AS WE OFTEN are in our treatment of the newly dead, we are considerably less circumspect when it comes to human beings who perished hundreds or even thousands of years ago. Time, that great effacer of human memory, eventually turns us all into mere objects, simple arrangements of hard bone or heaps of fine dust that are valued—or not—according to the whims of the living. Death is a great leveler, it is certainly true, but the relative rarity of mummies sets them apart from all other kinds of human remains, endowing them with a special cachet. This mark of distinction has not always served the world's mummies well, however, for it has attracted the calculating eyes of the marketplace.

There have been many stories told over the years about the mummy trade. Some are undoubtedly true, but others are almost certainly apocryphal. The great American humorist Mark Twain seems responsible for one of the most tantalizing. While writing *Innocents Abroad* in the 1860s, Twain journeyed to Egypt, where he caught wind of a story that clearly captured his fancy. The trains that puffed across the Egyptian countryside, he wrote, were powered neither by cords of wood nor buckets of coal, as they were elsewhere at that time. The Egyptians had substituted something far more novel. "I shall only say that the fuel they use for the locomotive is composed of mummies three thousand years old, purchased by the ton or by the graveyard for that purpose, and that sometimes one hears the profane engineer call out pettishly, "D—m these plebians, they don't burn worth a cent—pass out a King!"

So striking was this brief sketch that Twain's tale has lodged itself firmly in mummy lore. No mummy expert has ever been able to authenticate the story, however, although several have tried and written about their frustration. Twain seems to be the only published source—and a rather suspect one at that, given his penchant for fiction and his own published disclaimer. "Stated to me for a fact," he observed of the train tale in a note to *Innocents Abroad*, "I only tell it as I got it. I am willing to believe it. I can believe anything."

Other accounts of mummy commerce are equally slippery, however, and deserve the same kind of caveat emptor. A particularly popular yarn relates to paper. During the mid-nineteenth century, American mills regularly recycled rags to make paper, since no one had yet discerned all the possibilities of wood pulp. As the demand for paper soared, so too did the need for old cloth, and during one shortage, several East Coast mills reputedly imported Egyptian mummies by the shipload and hired local women to strip them of their wrappings. The heaps of ancient linen were fed into mechanical beaters and rollers, which in turn churned out a brown wrapping paper that many grocers favored. According to paper historian Dard Hunter, the *Syracuse Standard* was so impressed that it published an entire issue on these sheets. But this mummy paper was not the saving grace that it seemed. Disease carried in the ancient linen wrappings is said to have spread through the mills: to prevent further outbreaks, the American government required the sterilization of all rags.

This story has all the classic elements of modern pulp fiction: greed, impiety, and stern retribution for the guilty parties. As such, it has aroused the suspicion of some mummy experts over the years. In the mid-1990s, Joseph Dane, an American English professor, went hunting for proof that mills had ever recycled mummy wrappings. He was unable to uncover a single shred. He came across no conclusive records of the trade nor even a single example of the paper—surprising given how novel these sheets would have seemed at the time. Moreover, if the mummy-linen edition of the *Syracuse Standard* had ever existed, it had vanished without a trace. "Nonetheless," concluded Dane rather cheerfully in a paper, "this appealing legend persists, and versions are found in standard paper histories both preceding and following Hunter."

Embellishing on the strange history of the mummy trade seemed rather like gilding the lily to me; it was quite fantastic enough on its own and needed no help from others. For hundreds of years, European grocers, apothecaries, paint makers, antiquities dealers, artists, diplomats, lords, dukes, and princes had snapped up Egyptian mummies whenever and wherever they could, buying them in bulk or purchasing them one by one. A great deal of money had changed hands. Reading brief accounts of this trade, I had grown increasingly curious about it. How, I wondered, had Europeans ever developed such an appetite for withered human flesh? And how far were buyers and sellers prepared to go to satisfy their hunger? The pursuit of answers led directly to the dust of mummies ground to pieces in the mortars of Europe's ancient apothecaries.

FEW SIGHTS INSTILLED such dread in the hearts of the sick and wounded in Renaissance Europe as the appearance of the local doctor. Carrying clinking bags of blood-stained knives and cradling murky jars of sinuous leeches, the physician was the sure harbinger of torments to come. European medicine had advanced little since the time of Hippocrates, and in the effort to improve upon classical remedies, European doctors had experimented blindly. Their treatments were little short of barbaric. They poured boiling oil on the bodies of gunshot victims. They seared the stumps of amputees with red-hot pokers. They slathered the skin of the syphilitic with toxic mercury and slit the veins of the anemic, bleeding them nearly two pints at a time until they were so feeble they could no longer rise from their sickbeds. Then physicians pulled out evil-looking devices resembling bicycle pumps for administering enemas to their patients. This they did as many as three or four times a day.

That so many perished in their physicians' arms is scarcely any wonder. Death must have seemed a welcome reprieve after days of medical torture. In such an age, Europeans were hungry for a miracle drug, any drug, that would free them from the most menacing ministrations of the medical profession. Mummy became that drug. Made from the pulverized flesh and bones of the preserved Egyptian dead, mummy was touted as a Renaissance panacea. Just a small dose, it was said, could cure any one of a host of ailments: poisoning, incontinence, migraines, abcesses, giddiness, paralysis, fractures, internal ulcers, contusions, concussions, scorpion stings, and vertigo. Mummy looked loathsome and it tasted vile. It brought on fierce heart pains and churned the stomach. It induced vomiting and invariably soured the mouth with a terrible taste. It was also very expensive. But all this seemed a small price to pay for freedom from the physician's torments.

Europe's wealthy intelligentsia swore by the drug. The French king Francis I, a patron of Leonardo da Vinci and the very soul of an enlightened Renaissance monarch, wore a small packet of mummy and powdered rhubarb around his neck to remedy any emergency. His daughter-in-law, Catherine de Medici, was equally enamored. As a young mother of thirty in 1549, she sent her own chaplain all the way to Egypt in pursuit of the ancient drug. Others were similarly besotted. The great English philosopher Francis Bacon praised the powder and attempted to analyze its powers. "Mummy," he pronounced, "hath great force in Staunching of Bloud; which, as it may be ascribed to the mixture of the Balmes, that are glutinous; so it may also partake of a secret Propriety; in that the Bloud draweth mans Flesh." Physicians across the continent agreed, prescribing it to anyone who could afford the price. Indeed, one eminent Genoese surgeon was so impressed that he listed it among the remedies that no village or ship should ever be without.

The great difficulty, however, was in finding an adequate supply. Real mummy was a rarity, for Egypt did not look kindly on people pillaging its ancient cemeteries. To stop the trade, authorities imposed stiff fines and dismal jail sentences, but this did not deter the adventurous. In 1586, Sir John Sanderson arrived in Egypt and set off promptly to see the pyramids and an ancient human burial ground, the Momia, that lay a few miles distant. Scrounging through dunes strewn with lengths of tangled linen and ragged bits of bone, Sanderson found a tomb lined with Egyptian mummies. He lowered himself into it by rope and rummaged about with great delight. "I broke off all parts of the bodies to see how the flesh was turned to drugge," he wrote later, "and brought home divers heads, hands, arms and feet for shewe." After slipping a bribe to local officials, he loaded six hundred pounds of mummified corpses on a ship bound for England and there sold them for a tidy profit.

Just how many other Egyptian mummies were shipped to Europe for this trade is unknown. But the traffic was immensely popular and surprisingly long lasting. For centuries, the English, the French, the Spanish, the Germans, and just about everyone else in Europe traded in mummies as curiosities and commodities. They bought them from antiquities dealers and exhibited them as souvenirs and treasures in glass boxes. Or they purchased them from tomb robbers and ground them up limb by limb to make medicine and manufacture artist's pigments. And this they did for many centuries. "People were still advertising in 1904 in London's *Daily Mail* for a mummy to make into pigment," marveled Sally Woodcock. "Mummy only died out because of the lack of availability of mummies."

Woodcock is a young English art conservator who works in London's Guildhall Art Gallery in the heart of Moorgate. She makes her living restoring old paintings, which is how she first got interested in the mummy trade. A cool and self-possessed woman in her mid-thirties, with chin-length straight black hair, a fringe of neat bangs, and a valentine-shaped face, she was dressed the day we met in casual clothes topped by a crisp navy and white striped apron. She looked scrubbed and immaculate, something of a feat under the circumstances. For weeks, Woodcock had been climbing up and down scaffolding to restore one of Guildhall's treasures, a sprawling eighteenth-century scene of a famous naval battle off the coast of Gibraltar. It was an immense piece of conservation work, but Woodcook was clearly enjoying herself. She described at some length both the history of the battle and the background of the painting, marshaling the minutiae of dates and personalities as effortlessly as a historian. For Woodcock, God was definitely in the details, and she mustered each fact as briskly as a general commands his troops.

She began delving into mummy commerce almost by chance. She was working at the time as a researcher at the Hamilton Kerr Institute in Cambridge, sorting through ledgers and papers that once belonged to Roberson and Co. A venerable old English firm dating back to the Victorian era, Roberson and Co. had been in the "colormen" business, assisting wealthy artists in their work. Roberson employees had ground pigments, stretched canvases, hiked finished paintings to exhibits, and generally helped out in whatever way their affluent clients desired. But some years back, the company fell on hard times, closing its doors and selling off its name. Its dusty records ended up under a sheet of polyethylene in a leaky attic. It was Woodcock's job "to make something of this stuff." While doing this, she came across something very odd. "What they had was a little jar, with bits of mummy—mummified human remains."

Woodcock had read at university about the predilection

of some European painters for mummy, or Egyptian brown as it was sometimes known. She had even seen it listed from time to time as a pigment in technical reports by fellow art conservators. But until she opened the small jar she hadn't given mummy much thought. Staring down at scraps of tarry human flesh, she was stunned and more than a little repulsed by the lengths some people had gone to for art. But as someone who loves rooting about in history and ferreting out the facts, she was also extremely curious. So she set about combing Cambridge's libraries for clues.

She learned, to her surprise, that the Egyptian mummy trade was born almost by accident, from a scholarly muddle over the translation of a few old Arabic medical books. The ill-fated texts concerned bitumen, an old catch-all term for asphalt and other similar natural hydrocarbons. Medieval Arab physicians, as it turned out, were very fond of bitumen. They employed it as a salve for cuts, bruises, and bone fractures. They also prescribed it as an internal medicine to treat everything from stomach ulcers to tuberculosis. But they achieved their best results from a specific type of bitumen, a black rock–asphalt that seeped from a mountain in the Darábjerd region of Persia. This substance was known locally as *mumiya*.

All this was clear enough; the trouble arose when European writers began translating these passages from Arabic. They were baffled by the word *mumiya* and some had ended up taking a stab in the dark at its meaning. Gerard of Cremona, a celebrated twelfth-century translator and a man of considerable erudition, had read classical accounts that described the use of bitumen in Egyptian embalming. So he assumed that *mumiya* referred to "the substance found in the land where bodies are buried with aloes by which the liquid of the dead, mixed with the aloes, is transformed and it is similar to marine pitch." Unfortunately, no one thought to question this definition, competent Arabic translators being rather few and far between at the time. So the idea that *mumiya* came from the embalmed Egyptian dead stuck in Western minds. Apothecaries in London, Paris, and Venice began clamoring for the new wonder drug, mumia or mummy, and people began referring to the ancient bodies themselves as mummies.

In some ways, this was very good timing. By the twelfth century, Europeans were traipsing back and forth to the Middle East in record numbers. It was the height of the Crusades. In Palestine, European knights learned firsthand of mummy as Jewish physicians daubed it on their injuries. The reputation of the drug for healing sword wounds and mending broken bones grew, and when the armies of Christendom finally limped home from the Middle East, they brought back not only an appetite for Eastern spices but a fancy for medicinal mummy. Thus the mummy trade was born, and by the early fourteenth century it was a flourishing business. According to the records of one Florentine merchant in the Bardi banking house, mummy was one of 288 spices and comestibles regularly imported into Europe.

Egyptian officials, however, were none too pleased by the bizarre new appetites of Christians. They cracked down as best they could on those smuggling mummy, making this a dangerous line of work. In 1424, for example, officials in Cairo rounded up a ring of grave robbers who had assembled a huge pile of mummies from local tombs. Under torture, the accused men confessed to their crimes, describing how they had stewed the mummies in vats, skimmed off the dark black oil in pots, and hawked the precious substance to European buyers, who paid as much as twenty-five pieces of gold per hundredweight. After recording these confessions, Egyptian authorities threw all the thieves in prison.

Fearful of arrest, some mummy merchants approached the trade from what they hoped would be a safer angle. They became mummy counterfeiters. In 1564, Guy de la Fontaine, a physician from the Spanish kingdom of Navarre, described some of their handiwork after paying a visit to a merchant in Alexandria. At de la Fontaine's request, the Alexandrian had displayed his inventory, a stack of thirty to forty mummified bodies. When the physician began to pepper him eagerly with questions about ancient Egyptian mummification practices, the merchant laughingly explained that he had embalmed the bodies himself. Some of the cadavers were recently deceased slaves; others were simply dead Alexandrians he had managed to acquire. The merchant had no idea what diseases they had perished from, nor did he particularly care. Mummy after all was just mummy.

De la Fontaine's story was not the worst to reach European ears, however. Other travelers of the age recounted even more troubling gossip about the counterfeiters' practices, accusing Ethiopian physicians of employing live victims to make mummy. "They take a captive Moor [sic], of the best complexion," noted one Friar Luys, "and after long dieting and medicining of him, cut off his head in his sleepe and gashing his body full of wounds, put therein all the best

Spices, and then wrap him up in Hay." After burying the cadaver in moist ground, added the friar, they dug their victim up and hung him to dry in the sun, "whereby the body resolveth and droppeth a substance like pure Balme, which liquor is of great price. . . ."

The gruesome tale was likely the product of an overactive imagination, but European intellectuals who heard such stories were much disturbed by them, and physicians who bothered to carefully test the drug grew leery of it. The brilliant sixteenth-century French surgeon Ambroise Paré, an early expert on the sterile treatment of war wounds, ranked mummy with such fictional panaceas as unicorn horns, noting that "this wicked kinde of drugge, doth nothing helpe the diseased. . . ." Other scholars, such as the seventeenth-century Dutch physician Petrus Baerdt, were shocked to think that what passed as some miraculous elixir from ancient Egypt was likely no more than the "arm or a leg of a decaying or hanged leper or of some whorehopper suffering from syphilis." And a few, like the Dutch writer J. van Beverwijck, took square aim at the trade on moral grounds, noting that it desecrated graves, rendered the dead into commodities, and turned "ourselves, like some fierce Indians, into cruel cannibals."

Still, many Europeans thought mummy preferable to the painful exertions of their doctors, and apothecaries kept dispensing the drug. When supplies of Egyptian mummy—counterfeit or real—ran low, shop owners freely substituted. In northern Europe, some pulverized the leathery bodies that turf cutters occasionally happened upon in the bogs. One enterprising merchant, Moses Isaak, let it be known that he would pay a good price for any such body recovered from the bogs of the northern Netherlands, and local villagers happily accommodated. Between 1784 and 1803, they sold twelve bog bodies to Isaak. Four were human. Two were dogs. Six were horses.

By the early twentieth century, even this bizarre supply seemed exhausted. Few apothecaries had any real mummy remaining in stock. According to the 1905 edition of *Hagers Handbuck der Pharmaceutisichen Praxis,* an important German pharmaceutical text, "The mumia which is met in trade is mostly only an imitation, consisting of resinous red-brown or brown-black pieces, mixed with some browned bone remnants and little pieces of linen. The mumia is stocked in pieces and powder. If one should obtain and give true mumia, don't forget to test for arsenic content, especially arsenic sulphide." Soon after, chemists began clearing their shelves of their mummy jars. No one wanted to be associated any longer with a trade in dead bodies.

ONE OF THE most astonishing things that Sally Woodcock turned up during her research was an article published in 1903 in London's *Illustrated Mail.* Entitled "Pictures Painted with Mummies," it contained several photographs. The afternoon I visited her, Woodcock showed me copies of them. The first depicted a middle-aged colorman from Roberson and Co. His sleeves were rolled neatly to his elbows and he stood in front of a bright window, resting his hands on a flat-faced grinding stone called a muller. Dark scraps of something that looked like licorice curled on a granite slab nearby. But it wasn't licorice. "See," said Woodcook, "he's grinding up a mummy. And those are the kinds of pallet knives you need because you scrape and grind, scrape and grind, and scrape the paint back into a pile. Then you grind it again."

Woodcock flipped to a second photo. It showed another Roberson employee. Elderly and hunched, with a full white beard and round face, he stood over a shiny cylindrical machine injecting mummy into a row of silvery paint tubes. Woodcock shook her head and then pointed to a third photo of a labeled tube. "There it is," she observed, looking up, a note of disbelief in her voice. "That's mummy."

No one knows just when artists first began daubing mummy onto their canvases. For centuries, apothecaries and colormen were closely linked—often they were one and the same person—so it is difficult to say whether they were dispensing mummy as a medicine to the sick or as a paint to the artists in their clientele. "You find colormen who sold pigments, canvases, and drugs," said Woodcock, "and in a lot of their recipe books, there's recipes for cures and there's even recipes for food. There's recipes for pickled onions next to arsenic green." But Woodcock thinks that Europe's artists picked up on mummy very early. She bases this belief on a text from 1598 she found at Cambridge. In it, the writer alluded to a still earlier treatise describing the use of mummy by Italian painters as early as the twelfth century.

That artists came to fancy a pigment made from mummified human flesh is not entirely surprising. European painters were continually experimenting with color, occasionally going to bizarre and lavish lengths to make a brilliant splash. To make a rich deep black, they packed scraps of elephant ivory tightly in clay pots and then heated them in kilns. To render the traditional blue robes of the Virgin Mary during the Renaissance, they bought an expensive gem, lapis lazuli, and ground it into powder. And in later times, they sought out ever more exotic sources. To obtain a beautiful golden yellow known today as Indian yellow, they purchased soil from India that was drenched in the urine of cows fed a special fodder—mango leaves.

So medieval European artists are unlikely to have blanched much at the thought of buying ground up human bodies. The bitumen-like powder made a lovely transparent brown color when added to oil or amber varnish, and it was almost impossible to duplicate without skillful blending of many other pigments. Mummified human muscles report-edly made the finest mummy, and artists loved the silky feel of it: it had a kind of sensual ease. "It flows from the brush with delightful freedom and evenness," wrote one nine-teenth-century English fan. "Thin films spread upon a white ground are extremely lovely and enjoyable by painters who understand and appreciate the refinements of their art." Mummy was also fairly versatile. Artists could apply it as a glaze or daub it lightly on a canvas to capture the buttery tones of shadows or the dark swaths on water in the middle distance. There was only one drawback from the aesthetic point of view. Mummy cracked terribly. Within a few years, a painting glazed with it looked much like a crocodile hand-bag. "It obviously was something that wasn't suitable," said Woodcock.

Some painters didn't care much about posterity, how-ever. Nor were they terribly concerned where the mummy on their palettes came from. During the French Revolution, artists obtained it wherever they could. Almost a year to the day after the overthrow of Louis XVI, France's new masters decided to commemorate the great revolutionary event. They dispatched a group of workmen equipped with hammers and crowbars to the royal abbey of Saint-Denis in Paris, the solemn burial place of most of France's kings and many of its queens. As a monk looked on in disbelief, the workmen began shattering the royal sepulchers, one by one, tossing the bodies into a mass grave north of the church. Then they pried open urns in the chapel and scooped out their contents, holding up the mummified hearts of the French kings. Some of the vandals toted these withered body parts off to a local apothecary, who paid them gladly and crushed them to make paint. According to one story, Alsatian artist Martin Drolling bought some of this sovereign paint and applied it to a portrait, which now hangs in the collection of the Louvre.

The vogue for mummy continued almost unabated in the art world throughout much of the nineteenth century. But by the late Victorian era, people were beginning to shrink from it. In 1881, the prominent London-based painter Lawrence Alma-Tadema was shocked to find his colorman at work one day casually grinding up bits of an Egyptian mummy. Alma-Tadema, who had made his reputation in part by painting Egyptian scenes of beautiful women in diaphanous linen gowns, had had no idea what mummy truly was. He hastened to relay the news to friend and fellow artist, Edward Burne-Jones. Burne-Jones, too, was stunned. After a moment's thought, he hurried off to his studio and returned with a tube of mummy in hand. He wanted to give it a decent burial. "So a hole was bored into the grass at our feet," noted Georgiana Burne-Jones later, "and we all watched it put safely in, and the spot was marked by one of the girls planting a daisy root above it."

BUT THE TRADE in mummies didn't die. Renouncing ancient cadavers as raw materials, many wealthy Europeans were decorating their drawing rooms with the actual dead, a fashion originally spawned by a young Corsican who dreamed of becoming another Alexander the Great. Born into a noble family and educated in a series of French military colleges, Napoleon Bonaparte was determined to leave his mark on the world. "I am destined to change the face of the world; at any rate, this is my belief," he once wrote his brother Joseph. In 1798, the young general believed his great chance had arrived: he had received orders from the French revolutionary government to conquer Egypt as a stepping stone to capturing India. Well aware that Alexander the Great had made his reputation in the East, Napoleon drew up ambitious plans: he decided to plant a French colony in Egypt. To lay a secure foundation, he recruited nearly 150 French scientists to accompany him and to furnish advice on all aspects of Egypt's natural history, ancient history, economy, and industry.

Napoleon found Egypt rather more than he had bargained for. No sooner had he taken Cairo than English warships slipped into the waters near Alexandria and sunk most of his fleet with its tons of scientific gear. But the French general and his scientists were not about to let a mere catastrophic defeat get in their way. While the young general tried tightening his hold on the country, his savants swept out into the countryside, observing, recording, and sketching. Some fell helplessly in love with Egypt's ruins. They measured the Sphinx, exhumed the Rosetta stone, mapped the Valley of the Kings, and marveled at the great temple of Amun at Karnak. They also vacuumed up antiquities, and even the young general himself was soon infected with the fever of collecting. When a combined English and Turkish force drove him finally from the Nile, Napoleon packed two mummy heads in his bags. One he kept for himself; the other he gave to his errant wife, Josephine.

Napoleon's army of scholars documented their travels up and down the Nile with exceptional thoroughness. Their final report, *Description de l'Égypt*, ran to twenty-four volumes; five were devoted to magnificent engravings of Egyptian antiquities and monuments. The French discoveries launched the discipline of scientific Egyptology and set Europe on fire with a seemingly unquenchable Egyptomania. "Everything now must be Egyptian," noted the English writer Robert Southey rather dryly in 1807, "the ladies wear crocodile ornaments and you sit on a sphinx in a room hung round with mummies and the long black lean-armed long-nosed hieroglyphical men. . . ."

With Europe aflame, the diplomatic corps in Egypt went on an unprecedented collecting spree. Sending their assistants into the field, they crated up antiquities for the new national museums that had opened their doors in Europe. Henry Salt, the British consul in Alexandria, acquired three huge collections of Egyptian antiquities, which included many splendid mummies. He sold one of his collections to the British Museum and a second to the Louvre in France. After his death, a third went up for auction in London. The most popular pieces were Salt's mummies. To keep the crowds rooted to their chairs until the end of the day, the auctioneers cleverly reserved the embalmed corpses for the last sales. One—"the mummy of a female of high quality, 5'4" high with its case highly painted and ornamented"—was a particular hit, commanding £105 before the hammer fell.

The new Egyptian exhibits further fueled the public fascination and crowds of wealthy young Europeans began converging on Alexandria and Cairo. Some stricken with tuberculosis thought of emigrating to Egypt, thereby taking advantage of the dry desert air. But most arrived on a grand tour of the Holy Land, wintering along the Nile before moving north in the spring to Syria, Lebanon, and Palestine. At the Great Pyramid of Giza, they hired local men—three per climber—to heave and pull them to the top. Along the banks of the Nile, they arranged for their transport south. A party of four could hire a private yacht known as a *dahabieh* and a captain known as *dragoman* for just £224, and sail the Nile for ten weeks attended by a cook, a manservant, and a cabin cleaner. "The traveler," noted one Lloyd's guidebook, "was a perfect king in his boat." In the afternoon sun, those aboard could laze under an awning on the deck, sipping tea from china cups, smoking a pipe, and gazing out at the crocodiles sunning along the banks. In the evening, they could dine on linen-covered tables set with crystal, silver candlesticks, and bottles of French champagne. And, of course, they could stop in whenever they chose at the towns and ruins and cemeteries that lined the Nile, picking up mementos of their voyage along the way.

Mummies were the most Egyptian—and hence the most desirable—of souvenirs and some travelers insisted on hunting for them on their own. At el-Cheguel Guil, the French novelist Gustave Flaubert and his companion Maxime Du Camp crawled wormlike through a black passage to an underground mummy grotto. "We have to drag ourselves along flat on the ground—exhausting," Flaubert noted later in his journal. "If one were alone, one wouldn't go very far; fear and discouragement would win out. We twist, descend, climb; sometimes to squeeze through I have to inch ahead on my side and several times go flat on my back, propelling myself by my vertebrae, like a snake." Flaubert hated it, but he found little relief in the grotto itself. Both he and Du Camp were terrified lest a stray spark from their candle set the entire chamber and its resinous mass of mummies ablaze. Just such a tragedy had claimed the lives of an American traveler and his party twenty years earlier. But the two French travelers weren't to be denied their trophies. Du Camp asked the guides to carry out a "supply of embalmed human limbs and crocodiles." Flaubert took only a mummified human foot. It sat upon his desk until he died.

More cautious travelers were content to buy mummies from dealers, but they had little guarantee that they could ever get the bodies home. In 1835, the Egyptian government tightened its grip on the antiquities trade, officially banning export of the country's ancient treasures. But even this did not stop determined collectors. In England, Rosalie David found the diary of a young woman who tried smuggling a withered cadaver aboard her boat with disastrous results. Removed from its dry tomb, the mummy began to decay alarmingly, and the cook, who had been in the service of Egypt's viceroy, soon sniffed out the secret. Terrified that he would report her to the authorities, the woman and her companion stole up to the deck one night and tossed the mummy overboard. Only the coffin made it back to England.

Some passengers relished the intrigue of smuggling, however, and in certain circles returning home with a mummy was regarded as an admirable sign of resourcefulness. "It would hardly be respectable," noted Father Geramb at one point to the Egyptian ruler Muhammad Ali, "to present oneself in Europe without a mummy in one hand and a crocodile in the other." Such respectability called for new levels of deviousness. It was simply impossible to cram a whole mummy into most steamer trunks, and larger shipping containers attracted too much official attention. So European tourists began demanding smaller mummies, specifically sawn-off heads, hands, and feet. Sellers suddenly found themselves in the grotesque business of dismembering bodies, and all their hewing and chopping resulted in the strange wealth of ancient body parts that floats around Europe and North America today. Nearly every major museum owns a collection of such mummified hands and feet. Some possess heads mounted in Victorian glass cases, suitable for the mantel. They were, after all, perfect Victorian keepsakes—exotic relics from someone's great Egyptian adventure, wizened badges of courage, bittersweet reminders of the death that awaits all, and clear tokens of life everlasting—in one form or another.

Even so, it wasn't easy to keep a mummy intact in the cold damp of an English country home, and many were lost entirely over the years. At the Manchester Museum, David has been trying to track down dozens of Egyptian mummies mentioned in Victorian journals and diaries in hopes of gathering samples from them for her mummy tissue bank. Occasionally she finds them in odd places, stuffed in the attics of private homes or crammed into a corner of a backroom in a public school. "We went to see one in North Wales a few months ago," she said, "and that was a stately home. The current owner's great-great-grandparents brought it over from Egypt as a souvenir."

Occasionally, however, some of these imported mummies make it onto the open market. In the mid-1990s, an antique dealer in Wiscasset, Maine, put an ancient Egyptian mummy up for public sale in his shop. Reputedly brought to the United States in the 1920s by a wealthy shoe manufacturer, the mummy had been exhibited for years in a small family-owned museum. When the museum closed its doors, the mummy was sold to an antique dealer in Wiscasset. The dealer believed his new purchase to be the rarest and grandest kind of mummy, an ancient Egyptian princess. For such a rare treasure, he asked a handsome price: $20,000. When a reporter from Boston dropped by his shop, she was appalled to see a human being offered for sale. She began making phone calls. By the time she was done with the matter, the United States customs service had launched an investigation of the mummy and placed a seizure notice on it.

But the mummy was not quite as advertised, noted writer David Hewett in the *Maine Antique Digest* in 1997.

When Egyptologists from the Boston Museum of Fine Arts arrived in Wiscasset, they noticed—with a surprise rather similar to that of unroller George Gliddon earlier—something unexpected curled along the princess's groin. It was a shriveled penis. No one else had ever spied it there. In all likelihood, guessed the Egyptologists, the mummy was an ordinary temple priest. Hearing this, officials at the Egyptian embassy in Washington waived their right to recover the body. In Egyptian terms, the mummy was simply too commonplace to bother with. But outside the land of the Nile, Egyptian mummies had become rarities. The temple priest's mummy remains on sale. According to one Internet report, the shop owner declined a swap of four rebuilt Harley-Davidson motorcycles: it wasn't enough. "I heard of a guy who sold a mummy hand," the dealer allegedly told reporters. "The guy got $40,000 for just a hand. Come on, I'm willing to sell a head, a chest, hands, arms, and legs—an entire mummy—for $40,000."

Crass as these remarks sound, it bears remembering that few of us are entirely innocent of trade in the mummified dead. As much as we deplore trafficking in the ancient dead, most of us have taken part at one time or another in this commerce. The days of pulverizing mummies to fill paint tubes, as Sally Woodcock discovered, or grinding them in mortars for medicine have mercifully vanished, but a new kind of mummy economy has emerged to take its place, a kind of mummy.com. Capitalizing not on real flesh, but on the steady delivery of sensational new mummy stories and images, it seeks to satisfy our seemingly insatiable appetite for the everlasting dead. Today mummies are big business, and the modern media does its best to serve up a steady diet of mummy movies, mummy documentaries, mummy television specials, mummy advertisements, mummy Web sites, mummy posters—and, of course, mummy books.

And in this, I am no better than any of my colleagues. In choosing to write about the preserved dead for magazines and books, I, too, have begun trading in their withered flesh.

CELEBRITIES

⌒

T HE MERE MENTION OF A new mummy discovery has a tendency to set editors' pulses racing. And the more extraordinary a mummy is, the more concerted the barrage of reporters becomes. In the late fall of 1922, for example, an obscure English Egyptologist pulled off one of the most glorious mummy discoveries of modern times: the finding of the boy king Tutankhamen. Howard Carter had roamed desert ruins along the Nile for thirty-one years, working side by side with some of the greatest excavators of his day. He knew, as one writer put it, "almost every yard of sand in the Valley of the Kings." But Carter was little pre-

pared for the press storm that overtook him when he
announced that he had found the tomb of the boy king
Tutankhamen. Almost overnight, Carter found himself in
the kind of limelight generally reserved for heads of state
and Hollywood leading ladies; he and his colleagues were
almost blinded by the glare. "No power on earth could shelter us from the light of publicity that beat down upon us,"
he lamented shortly after. "We were helpless and had to
make the best of it."

This was no easy matter, for a mob of reporters and
photographers laid seige to the excavations. Dressed in
straw boaters, Harris tweeds, rumpled white shirts, and
loosened ties, they hovered each day like crows on the high
exterior wall above the tomb, waiting for the slightest
glimpse of the newly famous Egyptologist and the tomb he
worked upon. They were hungry for news that would satisfy
their readers back home and they tried their best to charm
Carter, an abrupt, irascible man who proved little suscepti-
ble to their wiles. When all their blandishments failed, they
resorted to pure hounding. Finally, an exasperated Lord
Carnarvon, the patron whose deep pockets funded the dig,
attempted to chase them all off by signing away exclusive
rights to the story to the London *Times*.

That did not put an end to the media bombardment,
however. Letters flowed in from film companies offering
huge sums of money. And determined reporters continued

hunting down any shadow of a rumor about the excavation and Tutankhamen. One of the most creative journalistic minds belonged to Arthur Wiegall, a former inspector of antiquities at Thebes. Wiegall had inveigled his way into a job as a correspondent for London's *Daily Mail* on the strength of his Egyptological connections. He naively expected preferential treatment, but Carter was not one to play favorites. The gruff Egyptologist scorned all members of the press pretty much equally. So Weigall was forced to improvise. Denied access to real news from the dig, he fed his editors a torrent of wild tales that considerably embellished the myth of the mummy's curse.

It was Wiegall, for example, who broke the story of Carter's ill-fated golden canary. Carter had brought the bird as a pet to Egypt and his Egyptian crew, who had never seen such a bird before, quickly adopted it as a mascot and a token of good luck. But luck, as it turned out, really wasn't on the canary's side. After Carter opened Tutankhamen's tomb, a wandering cobra insinuated its way through the bars of the bird's cage and devoured the unfortunate creature. In Weigall's dispatch, this bit of reptilian stealth was drenched in mystical significance. Weigall couldn't resist pointing out to his readers that the cobra was the same species as the golden snake that writhed across Tutanhkamen's mummy mask.

Carter made a point of ignoring such lurid tales. The

mummy's curse, after all, was a media invention, fabricated from a series of coincidences. Carter himself lived on for sixteen years after he opened the boy king's tomb, scornful of such fictions to the end. "All sane people should dismiss such inventions with contempt," he once snapped. Instead, he dedicated himself to the preservation of Tutankhamen's tomb and all its contents. With a handful of researchers—chemists, anatomists, and others—he recorded its treasures and slowly unwrapped the mummy of the boy king. Carter was desperately curious about the cause of the young man's death, but despite a careful examination, the team was unable to hazard a guess. So Carter respectfully returned the young pharoah to his coffin and laid him to rest once again in the Valley of the Kings.

Carter refused to compromise science. He brilliantly preserved Tutankhamen's many treasures, and for this Egyptologists are exceedingly grateful. But Carter stuck to a difficult path in his work. Few modern mummy discoverers are able to remain so magisterially aloof from the press, perhaps because there are so few archaeological patrons like Lord Carnarvon around today to fund their work. Indeed a kind of strange symbiosis has arisen in recent years between the modern media and some mummy experts, and this has raised difficult questions about the role of the media in modern mummy science and the trans-formation of the preserved dead into public figures.

AT 22,110 FEET, Mount Llullaillaco is one of South America's highest mountains. It stands just 721 feet lower than Mount Aconcagua, the highest peak on the continent, and its summit is subject to wild buffeting winds and sudden blinding snowstorms. Rising straight out of the pebbled plains of the Atacama Desert in northern Argentina, Llullaillaco is not a place for casual travelers. Indeed, it is not always a place for seasoned climbers. In the spring of 1995, an American mountaineer vanished while attempting a solo ascent. When climbers from the Chilean military and local search and rescue teams set out to hunt for him, they had to abandon the pursuit before reaching the summit: the weather had closed in dangerously. Yet for all its perils, Llullaillaco holds a strange distinction. Atop its summit, four miles above sea level, lies a major Inca ruin, complete with stone walls. It is the world's highest archaeological site, and in the spring of 1999, Johan Reinhard, a prominent American explorer, mounted an expedition to excavate it.

Among many other things, Reinhard is an Andean archaeologist and a highly respected one at that. He has won his greatest fame as the discoverer of the young Inca girl popularly known as Juanita, or the Ice Maiden, but he has exhumed many other such bodies from Andean mountains. In 1999, after nearly two decades of exploring South American slopes and three previous expeditions to Llullaillaco, Reinhard believed that at least one and possibly more Inca children lay buried on the peak of the towering mountain. He believed they would be dressed, as Juanita had been, in fine robes and entombed with all their perfectly preserved grave goods: exquisite Inca bowls; shawl pins; and tiny gold, silver, and shell figurines. He also suspected that these children would be unlike any other mummy he had ever found. Buried at 22,100 feet, they would be frozen, in all probability, never once having thawed from the moment of death. If that were the case, they would be the best preserved and most photogenic mummies ever recovered from the ancient world. Determined to find them, Reinhard teamed up with a young Argentinian archaeologist and called on his veteran team of Peruvian climbers and students. Then Reinhard raised enough money from the National Geographic Society to mount a major expedition to Llullaillaco in the spring of 1999.

He planned the ascent for March, hoping that the heavy snowstorms that generally shroud Llullaillaco earlier in the season would have vanished by then. In this, however, he was disappointed. Battered by bad weather, he spent the first four days of the expedition cocooned in his tent just two hundred feet beneath the summit, worrying that all his considerable efforts and planning were about to come to naught. But on day five, the morning clouds dissolved into a faded blue sky; to the east, white-dusted peaks could be seen stretching to the horizon. Reinhard and his team set out for the summit, trudging single file up the steep slope with ice axes in hand. At the top, Reinhard found an encouraging sign. The ruins of Llullaillaco had escaped the hard icy crust that forms on other peaks with repeated freezing and thawing. Llullaillaco wouldn't require the kind of bone-wearying excavation that Reinhard had become accustommed to over the years. But that was not to say that the dig would be easy. Temperatures at the summit regularly plunged to 35 degrees Fahrenheit and the thin air contained just 40 percent of the oxygen it did at sea level. Such a threadbare supply of oxygen starved both the body and the brain. It produced nausea, brutal, skull-splitting headaches; quick fatigue, and poor judgment. It could also bring on potentially fatal pulmonary and cerebral edema. Llullaillaco's peak was not a place for amateurs.

Reinhard and his team, however, were very experienced. After just a day and a half of digging, one of the Peruvians, Arcadio Mamani, turned up a frozen body. It was a boy of about eight sitting with his knees drawn to his chest. His face was buried in the folds of a frozen carmine-red tunic. Reinhard urged his team to press on. A second mummy, swaddled in cloth and entombed with a spectacular white-feather headdress, emerged just as he and a colleague were lifting the boy from his tomb. A few days later, the team encountered a third body, a young girl. Reinhard eased back the fabric from her face and shoulders. Lightning had singed her chest and charred her nose and mouth. Still, her face was exquisitely beautiful. Her cheeks were plump and full with baby fat, her lips soft and round. She looked, to Reinhard's amazement, as if her eyes would flutter open at any moment.

Reinhard and his team carried all three bodies back to the Argentine city of Salta. There conservators went to work. They unwrapped the cloth draped about the head of the second body, gently pulling back the textile. Their patient work revealed a young teenaged girl, whose delicate oval face was still eerily lit by a golden, lifelike glow. Bits of green coca leaves clung to her upper lip. Her hair, plaited by someone's loving hands five hundred years ago, glistened in the light. Reinhard was very pleased. The girl seemed immaculately well preserved, even down to her internal organs. According to the images from the CT scans, blood still welled in her heart, as well as in that of the other two children—something never seen before in the Inca mummies. "I doubt that more perfectly preserved mummies will ever be found," Reinhard marveled in his subsequent *National Geographic* article.

Both the public and the press were thrilled by these discoveries. So, too, were many Andean archaeologists. Passages from the Spanish chronicles suggest that the children of Llullaillaco were sacrifices made by the Inca to their gods, but these texts include few details of the dramatic rites. Archaeologists were keen to find out who these children were and what had happened atop the mountain peaks. The children from Llullaillaco had much to tell them. "Johan's been able to do something that no other archaeologist could have done," praised Daniel Sandweiss, an Andean archaeologist at the University of Maine. "He's accessed a set of data that the rest of us would never see, and it's important data. It talks about important events in the Inca world."

But not everyone was so impressed by Reinhard's finds; indeed, some seasoned researchers shook their heads in puzzlement. Since 1995, they said, Reinhard had conducted an unprecedented mummy hunt in the high Andes. Financed in part by the National Geographic Society in Washington, he had hired local climbers and enlisted South American archaeologists to locate the once-sacred tombs of similar Inca children. In just four years, he had mounted nearly half a dozen expeditions, exhuming eighteen of these rare child mummies. But Reinhard's record as a researcher and advocate of the preserved dead, said critics, left something to be desired. His first major discovery—dubbed Juanita in honor of Reinhard, whose first name is often translated in Spanish as Juan—is one of the most important mummy finds of the twentieth century. Yet scientific research on it had stumbled badly. Hastily given over to public display just eight months after her discovery, Juanita had produced relatively few published scientific studies. "Juanita," said Sonia Guillén, a former member of Reinhard's research team, "was a big fiasco in my opinion."

Just what had gone wrong wasn't immediately apparent, but some experts believed that Reinhard had inadvertently opened a Pandora's box when he stumbled upon Juanita. The spectacular nature of this mummy find, they contended, fueled public fascination around the world, creating a vast hungry public market for news and photographs of the frozen Inca girl. The resulting media barrage turned Juanita into a public figure and triggered a bitter battle in Reinhard's research team, as various interests competed for control of the find. In the end, said some critics, it was not the scientific team but *National Geographic* that made certain key decisions in the project and sparked an unprecedented mummy rush in the Andes.

After a career filled with accolades, Reinhard was stung by such criticism. In his home near Franklin, West Virginia, the anthropologist clearly felt maligned by all the mudslinging. A sturdy, big-boned man in his mid-fifties possessed of cool blue eyes, thinning silver hair, and a jutting lantern jaw that hinted—accurately, as it turned out—at a testy, combative nature, he was determined to set the record straight. The National Geographic Society, he explained, had never meddled in the project's key decisions. Instead, the American media giant had supplied several critical things that the impoverished Peruvian government could not, including much-needed funds for mummy conservation in Peru. As for his own motives in mounting expeditions in search of other frozen Inca children, Reinhard maintained that they were simple and straightforward. Far from engaging in photo and film opportunities or a mummy rush, he had undertaken the climbs as rescue missions to scientifically excavate and preserve the mummies from grave robbers, who were eager to plunder silver and gold and who were willing to use dynamite to blast away the enveloping ice to get at it. "To me, you don't show respect for these sites by leaving them for the looters," he observed.

Reinhard, one of South America's most experienced mountaineers, had seen ample evidence of such blasting and looting himself. For more than twenty years, he had been combing the slopes of the high Andes for traces of the Inca, ever since fellow climbers had invited him on their expeditions to South America in 1980. Reinhard was thirty-seven at the time. Possessed of a Ph.D. in cultural anthropology from the University of Vienna, he had been living in Nepal, studying the remote forest tribes and pursuing his deep love of climbing. To pay the bills, he had conducted freelance anthropological research, made a few ethnographic films, and worked as a camp manager for the 1976 American expedition to Everest. But he was restless and very footloose. He had never married nor had he any children, so he happily signed on for the trip to South America.

In Santiago, he came across a booklet on several mysterious Inca structures that perched on lofty peaks throughout the Andes. As a climber and anthropologist, Reinhard was immediately intrigued. Andean archaeologists believed that these strange ruins were places where the Inca had worshipped the sun or sent signals to those in distant villages. Reinhard wasn't so sure. "Not having gone through academic training in Andean archaeology or cultural anthropology, I just let my mind roam." In the Himalayas, early tribes had worshipped mountains as protectors and it occurred to Reinhard that something similar could have taken place in the Andes. "But I never thought I'd be able to figure out why the Inca had been going up on those peaks."

He is intrinsically drawn to mysteries, a trait that he inherited from his father, a postal department detective, and he loved the idea of investigating these enigmatic places on his own. As a high school student in New Lenox, Illinois, he had once saved up enough money from his summer jobs to head off to Brazil alone for a solitary adventure. There he had acquired a fascination for foreign cultures, a taste for scuba diving and other extreme sports, and a penchant for solitude, all of which became his trademarks in his later years. "From the age of sixteen, none of my friends could understand my way of thinking or my way of seeing things," he said.

So, after reading the pamphlet on the mountaintop

Inca ruins in Chile, he started to investigate. One afternoon, while returning from one of these forays, he encountered an old man with a string of donkeys. Reinhard struck up a conversation, describing the stone-walled ruins he had just visited. The old Chilean had never seen them himself: he and other local people avoided the mountaintops, for they were dangerous places. Still, he told Reinhard that in two weeks' time people would be gathering for a ceremony to worship the peak the ruins were on. In the Andes, he explained, people believed that the mountains were gods who controlled the rains, the fertility of the fields, and the health of the llama and the alpaca herds. This belief was fundamental to Andean life. Reflecting later on what the old man had told him, Reinhard realized that South American archaeologists had overlooked this practice of mountain worship when they interpreted ancient sites in the Andes.

Reinhard set up a new base of operations in Peru and Bolivia. "I liked the idea that there was a lot to see and do and explore that didn't seem well known." For the next fifteen years, he doggedly scaled one Andean peak after another, often by himself, searching for Inca base camps and summit sites. In the process, according to one prominent alpine historian, he bagged more high altitude peaks in South America than any other known climber. Reinhard was in his glory. "What I wanted to kill was the attitude that archaeologists couldn't do archaeology at altitude, because when I started in 1980 that was the prevailing attitude."

He loved the freedom of the work, but it was also a dangerous time. For much of it, Peru was locked in a deadly civil war, with Maoist guerillas known as the Sendero Luminoso on one side, and the Peruvian army on the other. Between 1980 and 1990 alone, the combatants killed 17,000 people, Peruvians and foreigners alike. In the face of such hostilities, most North American and European archaeologists left for Chile and other safer countries, fearful for their own lives and those of their students. Reinhard, however, stayed. Traveling and working alone, he became adept at slipping in and out of Sendero regions quickly and quietly, without attracting attention. One friend from that era, American cultural anthropologist Gary Urton, recalled how Reinhard took a similar tact in his personal life. In Cuzco, "Johan would just appear and then he'd be there and then he was gone. And then you'd see him two years later."

By all accounts, he lived a meager existence. He depended on odd jobs and others to help him get through the year financially. "I had a girlfriend," he told me, "who had a free house, so I didn't have to pay for housing—most of the year anyway." On one occasion, the National Geographic Society kicked in with some grant money, as did a few other funding agencies. In 1987, Reinhard won a Rolex Award for his studies: it paid for three years of research. By such threadbare means, he found and mapped more than forty mountaintop ritual sites and published widely on this work, winning generous praise from several prominent Andean archaeologists. Helaine Silverman, a leading authority on the prehistoric Nazca people of South America, called his book on the Nazca lines "the most satisfying and simplest explanation" she had seen. Others were equally impressed. In 1992, Bolivia awarded Reinhard the Puma de Oro, its highest honor in the field of archaeology.

By his late forties, Reinhard had reached the top of his game. He had not only been accepted, but lauded by prominent Andean anthropologists and archaeologists. "He was interested in what the Inca were doing at high altitude, and nobody else worked on that," said Gary Urton, "so for many years, he really made significant contributions." Then, in 1995, this quiet existence came to an end with his discovery of a frozen Inca mummy on the slopes of Mount Ampato in Peru.

REINHARD HADN'T SET out to find mummies. He had seen two Inca children recovered by other climbers during his early visits to South American museums, but neither of these preserved bodies had made much of an impression. "I had no fascination with the mummies originally," he recalled. In September 1995, however, he decided to climb Mount Ampato in Peru with a friend in order to photograph a neighboring volcano lofting an ashy plume hundreds of feet into the air. He wanted the images for his slide collection. On the day of the discovery, his climbing partner, Miguel Zarate, was temporarily walking ahead while Reinhard made some notes. Zarate spied a tuft of brilliant red against the ashy ice. It was a miniature feather headdress on a carved shell figurine from the Inca period. A few minutes' search turned up two similar statuettes. Greatly excited by this, Reinhard and Zarate spread out to comb the region.

In a crater below, Zarate noticed a rough cloth sack. It occurred to both climbers that it could be a mummy bundle, but they immediately dismissed the notion: it seemed so improbable. When Zarate tried to lift it, they got an eerie surprise. The leathery face of an Inca girl gazed at them blankly. Reinhard decided then and there to carry her and the figurines down the mountain: it was, he knew, an extremely important find. The mummy weighed almost as much as a slender living girl, and this meant that she had frozen, like the famous Iceman of Europe, and not freeze-dried the way most of the other known Inca children had. After her tumble down the slope, her head had dried in the air, but her torso and limbs were still wrapped in protective layers of cloth, exquisitely preserved. This increased her scientific value enormously.

Traveling almost nonstop by foot, donkey, and bus, Reinhard and Zarate managed to tuck her into a freezer at the Catholic University in Arequipa two and a half days later. To their immense relief, ice still clung to her outer tunic. Word of the find spread quickly around the university. It seemed obvious to local archaeologists that the girl was one of the *capacocha* children. The *capacocha* was among the most sacred of all Inca rituals. According to the early Spanish writers, the Inca hoped that by giving up something as precious as human life, the gods would look more favorably on their prayers, letting loose the rains needed to water the valleys and green the fields, water being a scarce commodity in the Andes. The Inca also believed that a *capacocha* sacrifice could ward off pestilence or other natural calamity or bestow wisdom and good health on a new emperor, thereby bringing prosperity to the entire Inca empire.

By tradition, the Inca consigned only their finest possessions to their gods. For the *capacocha*, they chose their children. The victims, according to historical records, had to be healthy and perfectly formed, without a flaw to be seen anywhere on their bodies. In one account written in the 1570s, an Inca woman told the Spanish that she had been selected for sacrifice until somebody discovered a little blemish on her skin and set her aside. Often the child stood just at the threshold of adulthood, a bit younger than marriageable age. Reinhard believed that this was to ensure the purity and virginity of the human offering. But some other Andeanists questioned this, pointing out that the concept of virginity was not terribly important in traditional Andean culture. Instead, these anthropologists theorized that the Inca probably picked human beings who were at the height of their vital powers, possessed of all the joy and animal spirits of a young teenager.

Andean scholars agreed, however, that the ritual was one of immense importance to the Inca. In the fifteenth century, for example, a prominent lord from Cajatambo agreed to give his daughter, a girl "beautiful beyond exaggeration," for the *capacocha*. He accompanied her first to the Inca capital of Cuzco in a procession so holy that local villagers hid away as it passed by their doors: anyone trying to stop it or hinder its progress was immediately put to death. In Cuzco, the Inca emperor awaited the arrival of the lord and his daughter and other similarly chosen children from elsewhere in the empire. Seated upon a golden throne in the city's central square, the emperor greeted them solemnly and prayed to the sun, while priests distributed small cakes to the children. Long days of celebration and ceremony followed. When they finally ended, the lord brought his daughter home. By the time she stepped foot in her village, the girl was reconciled to her fate and gave a little speech. "Finish with me now," she reportedly told her kin, "because the celebrations which they did for me in Cuzco are quite sufficient." So the child was taken to a mountaintop visible for miles around. Someone dug a deep shaft there, lining it with ceramic pitchers and silver bowls. Then they lowered her into the grave and covered it over with stones. That was the last that the Inca saw of her.

Entombed in the mountain, the girl became a guardian spirit to her community. People trekked to her grave to ask her advice on important matters, and it was said that she spoke to them in the voices of the priests who attended her. Reinhard had little doubt that the slender Inca girl from Ampato had met a similar fate.

AFTER ASSURING HIMSELF that Juanita was safe and sound at the Catholic University, Reinhard began making urgent plans. He fully expected there were more frozen children and more Inca grave goods on Ampato and he was keen to rescue them: he worried that looters would destroy them once the story had broken. A major expedition to Ampato would require money, however, far more than Reinhard had at his disposal. So he called George Stuart at *National Geographic*. Stuart, the magazine's staff archaeologist, had just become acting chair of the society's powerful research and exploration committee. A rumpled, genteel southerner, Stuart has a passionate interest in the prehistory of Latin America. Indeed, his own son David is one of the world's leading authorities on Mayan hieroglyphical writing. Listening to news from Arequipa, Stuart was captivated.

Reinhard also wanted to find experts to help preserve the body from deterioration. He asked Catholic University colleague Jose Antonio Chavez to contact Sonia Guillén, a prominent Peruvian physical anthropologist whom Reinhard had met over cocktails a few years earlier in Cuzco. Guillén was an expert on the mummies of Peru's coastal desert. She was also the director of a major new mummy research facility, Centro Mallqui, near the Peruvian city of Ilo, and she had taken a strong interest in Reinhard's research. Indeed, she had asked him to call her if he ever came across a *capacocha* child. Hearing of the new find, she readily agreed to help out. In Austria, studies of the famous Iceman were reaping a scientific windfall—new data on ancient European clothing, medicine, infectious diseases, diet, agriculture, and environments, thanks to the efforts of nearly 150 scientific consultants. Guillén hoped to do something similar. "The dream," she recalls, "was that this would be possible with Juanita."

From Washington, Stuart swiftly wired funds for the return expedition to Ampato. Stuart's colleagues at the National Geographic Society began making arrangements for a photographer and film crew to cover the expedition. The timing of the discovery seemed particularly fortuitous, for the society was going through a rocky time. Competing for readers with the new Internet media and a host of specialist magazines, the society's flagship magazine, *National Geographic*, had taken a severe beating in circulation. In just six years from 1989, it had lost nearly two million readers. To bolster the $463-million-a-year enterprise, society executives had recently created a for-profit arm that included its television operation. Intense coverage of a major new mummy discovery—a perennial favorite of readers and television viewers—could help boost the society's fortunes.

With funding from Washington, Reinhard teamed up with Chavez and recruited sixteen climbers and archaeologists to assist in the excavations. Together, the expedition members headed off to Ampato, where they camped for three long weeks. At 19,200 feet, they found the tombs of two more Inca children, complete with a host of Inca artifacts— a scattering of figurines and finely painted plates and pots and an assortment of more mundane items, such as spoons, drinking vessels, and sandals. But to the disappointment of all, neither of the new bodies was as finely preserved as Juanita.

Back in Arequipa, Reinhard turned to the pressing problem of preserving Juanita. Already Guillén had called several prominent mummy experts for advice, including Art Aufderheide and two Austrian anthropologists, Konrad Spindler and Horst Seidler, who were leading the research on the Iceman. The consensus was that Juanita's dried head had to be kept at a lower humidity than the rest of her body and her clothes. This would be a difficult feat, however, and Guillén could see no way of pulling it off in the simple facilities available at the Catholic University in Arequipa. "There was no infrastructure [there]," she recalled, "not even the idea of how to do research with any type of body."

So the discussions dragged on, as the team wrestled with the problem. Reinhard found these meetings difficult to sit through. His colleague and close friend, Jose Chavez, the dean of archaeology at Catholic University, was growing increasingly irritated with Guillén. Chavez suspected that Guillén was quietly pursuing her own agenda, for she maintained that the best place to keep and study Juanita was in her own mummy research facility in Ilo. But these assertions grated at Chavez. He hoped that Juanita would bring funding for a new conservation lab in Arequipa, creating another mummy-research center. Reinhard was uncomfortable with the increasingly heated bickering. A solitary man, he had great difficulty in keeping the team running smoothly.

Further adding to tension was the mounting media frenzy. The Austrians arrived in Peru with a German television crew from Spiegel-TV; they wanted to film their own documentary on Juanita. Meanwhile, the Peruvian press had begun clamoring for news on the find, and Peruvian documentary makers had embarked on a bidding war for rights to Juanita. Others were also beseiging the team. One firm approached Reinhard with a bizarre proposal: it wanted to extract eggs from Juanita's ovaries. These, it suggested, could be used for a daring experiment. By fertilizing the ova with modern sperm, the team hoped to create an Inca baby.

Reinhard dismissed the Inca in vitro proposal out of hand. He also arranged for a postponement of the German documentary and tried to hold the Peruvian press at arm's length. *National Geographic* had obtained first publication rights to the story in exchange for funding for the return expedition to Ampato and for conservation work on Juanita. "This was, and still is, a standard clause for all grants given out by the National Geographic Society," Reinhard explained. Indeed, the American archaeologist was writing the article himself in hopes that the ensuing publicity would bring in scarce research funds for Juanita. But dodging the local press proved extremely difficult: Peruvian reporters had begun besieging Guillén and her colleagues for tidbits of news.

In Lima, government officials began mulling over plans for a major museum exhibition of Juanita. This touched off another heated battle among the mummy experts. The Austrians were deadset against any public display of mummies. Spindler and Seidler had done much soul-searching about the ethics of exhibition during their own studies of the Iceman. They saw nothing wrong in examining the dead for the benefit of science and the knowledge of humankind, but they considered all public display of ancient bodies a callous act of disrespect. A well-preserved mummy, they argued, was as recognizable as a modern corpse. As such, it demanded a similar degree of protection and privacy from prying eyes. Even the best-intentioned museum exhibit attracted thrill seekers: galleries filled with mummies were little better than carnival sideshows and chambers of horror.

Quite apart from these ethical considerations, the Austrians also believed it impossible to both preserve and display a frozen body. No one had yet designed an exhibition case capable of regulating temperature and humidity sufficiently to ward off condensation and bacterial growth on human flesh. After discussing the matter at length, Spindler, Seidler, and Guillén agreed that the wisest approach was to stabilize Juanita and get on with serious scientific studies. Guillén and the Austrians particularly wanted to examine the young Inca girl by three-dimensional CT scanning, for they regarded this as the next best thing to an autopsy. In Austria, Spindler and his team had gleaned much valuable data from such CT scans of the Iceman, and they offered Reinhard the use of their facilities and their experienced staff.

Reinhard listened to these discussions with mounting irritation. He was beginning to feel extremely pressured. High-ranking Peruvian government officials, including President Alberto Fujimori, were all in favor of exhibiting Juanita: such a show could spark new interest in the country's rich Andean past and the resulting press coverage could attract droves of tourists, who had steered clear of the Andes since the civil war. Reinhard was privately opposed to the idea of placing Juanita on exhibit, but he felt he had little choice in the matter. "We had to show Juanita," he told me. "Government officials were coming and demanding to see her."

Privately, he confided his predicament to staff at the National Geographic Society, who agreed to help him find a suitable case for conserving Juanita. "It needed to be done," recalled Stuart. "I think, too, they realized that it had great potential as public relations, either positive or negative, but both to the extreme." Quietly, society staff began making phone calls. The Carrier Corporation, an American refrigeration company also known for its climate-control system for the Sistine Chapel, offered to build two $250,000 customized display cases for Juanita free of charge, certain that the ensuing hoopla would more than compensate for the costs. At Johns Hopkins Hospital in Baltimore, radiologists agreed to conduct expensive stereolithic CT scans *pro bono*.

When the National Geographic Society presented these offers to Reinhard, it added a proposal of its own. If Juanita was to journey to the States for the scans and the customized case anyway, it would be a prime opportunity for an American exhibit. Where better than in the National Geographic Society headquarters in Washington, which was close to Johns Hopkins Hospital? The society often mounted exhibits on its research projects there. Moreover, such a show would attract intense press coverage for Peru and publicize the plight of the mummies. Reinhard was pleased, but the final decision wasn't his. The Peruvian government owned the mummy. Before reaching a decision, Peruvian officials sought advice from advisory committees of lawyers, archaeologists, conservators, and physical anthropologists. All four committees approved the mummy's export.

In Lima, Guillén was stunned by the news that Juanita would be traveling to the United States and the National Geographic Society headquarters. With its immense influence, the society had gone far beyond funding research and reporting the news. This was disturbing enough to Guillén and to the Austrians, who felt increasingly left out of the major decisions over the mummy. But there were also other key issues. Guillén could scarcely believe that the society had succeeded in cornering an exhibit of one of the most important Peruvian archaeological finds of the past century, displaying it to Americans before a public exhibition could be arranged in Peru and before scientists had had an opportunity to study the body thoroughly. She worried that such an exhibition would offend the sensibilities of Native Americans, who opposed the display of aboriginal remains. Furious at the prospect, she mounted a spirited public protest in Lima's most important newspaper, *El Commercio*, enlisting the support of prominent Peruvian anthropologists.

The Austrians were equally incensed. To argue their case, Spindler and Seidler arranged to meet officials from Catholic University and Peru's National Institute of Culture at a lunch at the Austrian embassy. By the time dessert was served, Seidler and the Austrian ambassador were fuming: their luncheon companions refused to back down from the plans. Outraged, the Austrians, too, went public with their criticism. Spindler accused *National Geographic* point blank of cultural imperialism. "What is being done there," he observed to a *New York Times* contributor, "is, from my point of view, a mixture of Hollywood and Disneyland against a background of trying to achieve successful sales, while science makes a crash landing."

In Peru, Reinhard was stung by the reaction. "He was really under pressure as the tall gringo on the make," recalled Stuart sympathetically. "It is always a position of extreme vulnerability in public relations." Nevertheless, Juanita was shipped to Johns Hopkins Hospital in Baltimore in May 1995, just eight months after her discovery. There she underwent CT scanning and biopsies and was sent on to Washington, where she was installed in the National Geographic Society headquarters for a monthlong exhibition.

The display proved immensely popular: more than 100,000 people squeezed through the doors. "They physically couldn't get any more people through," recalled Reinhard. "There were times when there were lines going around the block and people waited three hours. And you only had four minutes inside." Hillary Clinton stopped by to see her. So did Alberto Fujimori. And soon everyone was talking about her. Even Bill Clinton cracked a famous joke about her at a political dinner. A fellow Democrat had earlier quipped that Republican presidential candidate Bob Dole was so old that he had dated the Inca mummy in high school. Clinton picked up the theme. "I don't know if you've seen that mummy," remarked the president during a speech to the audience, "but you know, if I were a single man, I might ask that mummy out. That's a good-looking mummy."

AFTER HER STINT in Washington, Juanita was flown back to Arequipa, where she was placed on display. Curious visitors gazed in awed silence at her icy body, but as they came and went, prominent Andeanists in North America were beginning to ask questions. They were hungry to learn more about Juanita and her two frozen Ampato companions. Spanish colonial records had etched a rough sketch of the *capacocha* ceremonies, but the descriptions lacked many vital details that would shed critical light on the workings of Inca society. In particular, Andean archaeologists and anthropologists wanted to know exactly what had taken place on the remote peak and how the children had been chosen for this fate and how they had died.

Aware that his colleagues were waiting, Reinhard wrote a brief article for *National Geographic* describing some of the key findings from the CT scans. While examining the images, Johns Hopkins radiologist Elliot Fishman had noticed a dark two-inch-long fracture curling along the right side of the girl's skull. More ominously still, her brain seemed to have been pressed to one side of her cranium. To Fishman, it looked as if a hemorrhage from one of the major arteries in the brain had pushed the tissue to one side before death. He had seen similar injuries many times before in emergency room cases when assailants beat their victims with baseball bats. From this, Fishman concluded that Juanita had been clubbed to death on the remote Andean mountaintop.

But this confident diagnosis and reconstruction of Juanita's death puzzled some leading Andean researchers. Indeed, they found the scenario rather hard to believe. The whole point of the *capacocha* rite, observed Sabine MacCormack, an American expert on Inca religion, was to offer the gods a perfect human being. Inca authorities had deliberately sought out flawless children, discarding those with even a slight skin blemish. Why then bludgeon one of these nearly perfect victims, violating the child's body with a blow? It was not as if the Inca didn't have other, gentler methods at their disposal. On the Chilean mountain El Plomo, priests had likely given a *capacocha* boy an intoxicating corn beer before lowering him into a mountaintop tomb. Inside the tomb, the boy had drifted off to sleep, gradually freezing to death. MacCormack strongly suspected that Juanita met a similar fate: "I think [her] death was by exposure and intoxication."

Other researchers were similarly skeptical. In his extensive studies on human sacrifice in the more ancient Moche culture in Peru, physical anthropologist John Verano had noticed a striking sexual pattern to ritual executions. Adult males were generally the ones who suffered brutal, violent deaths. Executioners severed their heads or sliced open their throats and drank their blood, or sometimes they ripped their hearts out while they were still beating. Verano believed that these males were likely captives taken during warfare. Women and children, he observed, received very different treatment. They died more gently. Quite often, executioners strangled them with a special knot that helped extinguish consciousness quickly.

Verano found it hard to believe that an Inca priest would have clubbed a beautiful young child in the head. Moreover, he had doubts about Fishman's diagnosis. If an assailant had battered Juanita to death, he explained, she would have bled profusely. But textile experts had detected no bloodstains on her clothing. It was quite possible that the skull fracture had happened after death, not before. "You know this mummy fell one hundred feet or more down the side of a mountain," observed Verano in his New Orleans home, "and it may have landed on its head. So if it had a fracture, that would not be a surprise at all. This is a five-hundred-year-old body that has been through all kinds of changes—burial, defrosting, falling down a mountain, being carried on a bus, and all these other kinds of things."

Fishman and his colleagues had arrived at the conclusions they did, suggested Verano, because of their experience with living or recently dead patients. They are not experts in the varied changes that ancient bodies go through over hundreds or thousands of years. That is the specialty of physical anthropologists and mummy experts such as Verano, Guillén, and Seidler. Fishman and his colleagues, said Verano, had "never worked with mummies before."

In his West Virginia home, Reinhard vigorously defended

the head-injury theory. During his own research, he had come across accounts from three Spanish chroniclers describing the sacrifice of *capacocha* children by a blow to the head. This form of execution, he maintained, was a far kinder and swifter death than that of burying someone alive or of strangling him. "I know this," he explained, "as I've been knocked out cold six times in my life and I never knew I was hit until I woke up." As for the ability of Fishman and his team to make the diagnosis, they were eminently qualified. One of the Johns Hopkins team members, he noted, had seen over one hundred deaths caused by blows to the head, far more than Verano ever had, and the fractures exactly resembled Juanita's.

To resolve the matter, Verano hoped that Reinhard or his colleagues would publish all the available CT data so that others could evaluate it. But that, it seems to me, is one of the sad disappointments of the Juanita project. For all Guillén's early hopes that the young Inca teenager would one day tell researchers as much about ancient Andeans as the Iceman had to say about ancient Europeans, Juanita was still something of a cipher to the scientific world, even five years after her discovery. Relatively little has made its way into the scientific press.

Reinhard maintained that there were good reasons for this. His co-director on the project, Chavez, had been absorbed in establishing a mummy-conservation laboratory and a mummy museum in Arequipa and in traveling to Japan for the yearlong exhibition of Juanita there. Reinhard, who had recently been appointed an Explorer in Residence at *National Geographic*, had been equally preoccupied. In addition to raising funds and mounting more than half a dozen major expeditions to the Andes in search of yet more Inca shrines and their mummies, he had been lecturing on his finds, serving as a consultant on television documentaries, penning articles and field reports on his later mummy discoveries, and co-authoring a major scientific book on his Llullaillaco finds.

The work that still lay ahead of him on all his mummy finds, however, seemed enough for several careers. Still Reinhard appeared reluctant to wrap up his fieldwork in the high Andes. He hoped to rescue yet more mummies from the avarice that had turned ancient cemeteries elsewhere in Peru into pitted moonscapes and had robbed so much of South America of its ancient birthright. In our conversations, he repeatedly stressed the importance of retrieving the Andes' rich treasures and priceless scientific information before looters reached them with their sticks of dynamite. The pace of looting, he explained, had greatly accelerated in recent years. Better mountaineering gear had enabled more climbers to ascend to high elevations. Greater poverty in South America had driven local villagers to greater lengths of desperation. Higher prices commanded by artifacts had made plundering all the more lucrative.

I didn't doubt any of this. But I wondered how many looters would have thought to risk their lives climbing South America's highest mountains, were it not for what they had seen in the press of Juanita and of Reinhard's other finds. "It's a double-edged sword, these discoveries," conceded Stuart sadly. "If you find a spectacular site and publicize it, people go in there and tear it apart." And this struck me as terribly sad and tragic. It was Reinhard who had carried science to the highest peaks in South America, exhuming and retrieving the ancient dead in conditions so bitter and brutal that they pushed the human body and mind to the extremes of endurance. He had gone where few archaeologists could hope to follow, and he had succeeded admirably, thanks to his immense physical strength and stamina and mountaineering experience, in retrieving fragments of the past for science. For this, he has rightly received great acclaim and respect. But in doing so, Reinhard may have sadly hastened the destruction of some of the very mummies he hoped to save.

THE

INCORRUPTIBLES

~

T HE BITTER, UNREMITTING COLD OF the
high Andes had worked a kind of miracle on some of
those frozen in their snowy tombs. It had gone far beyond
the crude mechanics of preservation and the mere attenua-
tion of a physical existence, salvaging something rarer
still—the semblance of life. It had kept flesh golden, lips
carmine, skin supple, eyes moist. Indeed, all that seemed
lacking was the flush of warmth, the moist exhalation of
breath, and the flutter of motion. In preserving those frozen
children, nature had demonstrated its mastery over time,
performing feats of eternity that made human morticians

look feeble and sick. I was amazed by those lost Andean children and I was very moved. But I can't say I was terribly surprised. Nature, I had come to realize, is highly inventive when it comes to staving off corruption. She does not always need the remote Andean cold to preserve the eerie appearance of vitality.

I first began to appreciate this during a visit I paid one sunny spring morning to the Necropolis Company in England. Hidden away discreetly behind a concealed door and up a narrow winding staircase in an old funeral parlor in the London suburb of Kingston upon Thames, the Necropolis Company did little to advertise its peculiar trade. Founded in 1852, the same year that Charles Dickens began writing *Bleak House*, the Victorian firm was in the business of exhumation, namely digging up the dead and moving them someplace more convenient. It was, according to its staff, an important trade in Great Britain: there were simply too many old cemeteries lurking in too many high-priced neighborhoods, especially in London where virtually every block seemed to harbor some ancient burial ground or another. The Necropolis Company specialized in trundling off the ancient dead with dignity and, in the last two decades alone, had carried them away from more than 125 old churchyards, hospital grounds, cemeteries, and prison yards. During one removal alone, in Islington, they had exhumed 15,000 people.

Over the years, the firm's operations manager, Roger Webber, had seen virtually everything in the moldering bodies and skeletons line. A somber, melancholy fellow in late middle age, he had gazed on the bodies of young women reduced to mounds of grayish-white grave wax, the soaplike substance that formed as fat decomposed in water. He had seen caskets slopping with coffin liquor, the dark liquid that pools from rotting flesh. He had smelled the reek of putrefaction and seen skeletons grinning shamelessly as they trailed tatters of clothes and rags of human flesh. He had witnessed a lot of things he didn't want to talk about. But the thing that had really impressed him was not the festering dead, but the centuries-old preserved bodies that he and his crews sometimes stumbled upon in rain-soaked English burial grounds.

So taken was Webber with these ancient cadavers that he offered to show me pictures of them. The Necropolis Company, as I learned, made a practice of photographing each of its projects, carefully documenting its grim work. Webber had some of these photos at hand in his dark, wood-paneled office. He didn't know if I wanted to see them, but of course I did, so I moved my chair around the big mahogany table and edged closer to him to see the photos.

He had not been exaggerating. The album he produced contained several haunting photos. The most amazing was of a middle-aged Victorian matron who had perished in 1839. Dressed for the tomb in a white cotton bonnet, white winding sheet, and shroud, she gazed out at the world with weary eyes, a look of pinched annoyance on her face.

Death, it seemed, had not been a welcome visitor. But it had treated her kindly nonetheless, preserving her almost intact. Webber and I studied her face, and a note of awe crept into his voice as he recalled finding similar bodies. "Sometimes you see coffins that have been buried for two hundred and fifty years," he told me. "You look into the viewing plate and the body's been perfectly preserved—no deterioration at all, still color to the eyes and the skin a sort of pinkish color."

Such mummies, he conceded, were rather rare in England. When he and his colleagues exhumed the Islington cemetery with its fifteen thousand bodies, they found only two such mummies. I asked Webber why he thought this pair had been spared the fate of everyone else in that damp cemetery, and he mulled it over before replying. During Victorian times, he explained, wealthy families had often splurged on heavy oak or elm caskets caulked with Swedish pitch and sheathed on the outside and lined on the inside with heavy lead. Such coffins were intended to be indestructible, but in most cases, the lead linings had merely oxidized and corroded, exposing their contents to all the usual agents of corruption. But if one of these caskets happened to be interred in heavy clay soil, a vacuum sometimes formed about it, sealing off the corpse from water, bacteria, and insects, everything that customarily nibbles away at a cadaver.

It was a good, sound scientific explanation, but I sensed that try as Webber did to rationalize such finds, he found them at heart mysterious and rather wonderful. These bodies were just so unlike the general rule of thumb in exhumation, with all its grave wax and coffin liquor and terrible putrefaction: they seemed to be ruled by some other dispensation. A practical, down-to-earth man, Webber carefully avoided using words like miracle, but he couldn't help but feel astonished in the company of such cadavers. And as I sat beside him, gazing at the photos, I felt a shiver of awe. I wondered who these people were and what kinds of lives they had lived and why they had been singled out for this strange form of immortality when so many others of their age had rotted into the ground.

It struck me later that this sense of awe was similar to that of the medieval European villagers who had exhumed the preserved bodies of famous martyrs or devout nuns centuries after their deaths. The medieval Catholic Church had regarded their preservation as miraculous and it had given these bodies a special name—the Incorruptibles. The Church had often beatified or canonized them and great cults of the faithful had grown up around them. After seeing Webber's photo album, my curiosity was aroused. I wanted to know how much of the saintly incorruptibility in medieval Europe was due to conditions readily explained and scientifically understood, and how much fell into the realm of something far less explicable—the world of miracles and divine grace.

〜

SELDOM IN HUMANITY'S long history has the body been held in such pitifully low esteem as it was in medieval Europe. It was the body, after all, that deceived and betrayed the soul, that tempted and sinned and craved and desired, that lusted after the soft breasts of the neighbor's wife or ached for the sweet beauty of the gardener's boy, that struck an innocent child in anger or beat a importunate beggar in wrath, that hungered greedily for rich pastries and stealthily hoarded sacks of gold, that coveted rich jewels and schemed for another's land, that puffed up with pride in public and slept all day long while others toiled. It was the body that led the way to the fires of damnation and suffered the eternal torments of hell. For all these reasons and many more, pious Catholics heartily despised the body and treated it accordingly. They fasted. They self-flagellated. They wore hair shirts. They mortified the flesh. The body was, after all, the root of all evil.

But amid all this abnegation, there was one striking exception. Not all bodies were reviled by the medieval clergy in Europe. Among dutiful Catholics, hundreds of cults sprang up around the corporeal remains of saints. Such bodies—or rather, what remained of them—were deemed sanctified, for the Holy Ghost, it was said, once lived within them, healing the sick, dispensing words of wisdom, and embracing the humble and poor. This had forever left its mark on frail human flesh and bone. These had been transmuted by the alchemy of faith into something holy and, as such, the remains of saints possessed great powers for the good. "God Himself fittingly honors such relics by working miracles in their presence," observed the great thirteenth-century Italian philosopher and theologian St. Thomas Aquinas. The bodies of saints, in other words, were divine lightning rods, capable of attracting miracles.

Over the years, hagiographers recorded many tales of such miracles. Those performed by St. Zita, a humble Tuscan servant and a contemporary of Aquinas, were a case in point. When church officials exhumed her body years after her death, sight reputedly returned to the blind, movement to the paralyzed, health to the fevered, life to the withered, fertility to the sterile, and speech to the mute. Moreover, the miracles did not end there. St. Zita's body revealed no trace of decay: she had been preserved whole and intact, an Incorruptible, and so she remains today, as I discovered while paying my respects to the wizened saint in a medieval church in the small Tuscan city of Lucca. In the glass-sided reliquary, her gaunt face was smooth and her hands soft and supple-looking. Her lustrous nails gleamed. But for the dark color of her skin and the antique style of her dress, she looked as if she could easily have risen from her brocade bed and strolled the streets of fashionable Lucca, attracting hardly a second glance from passersby.

The Roman Catholic Church has unearthed many such Incorruptibles in its long history. During the 1970s, American writer Joan Carroll Cruz set about trying to count them, combing the hagiographies of hundreds of Catholic saints for any mention of physical preservation. When she found one, she wrote to the saint's shrine for confirmation. By such means, she tallied 102 Incorruptibles, from Saint Cecilia, the second-century Roman martyr, to Saint Charbel Makhlouf, the nineteenth-century Lebanese monk whose body continued to exude blood and perspiration more than sixty years after his death. Almost certainly other Incorruptibles exist, their bodies encased in dusty reliquaries in forgotten country churches. But they have been sadly forsaken over the years, even by the faithful. "I don't think that any count is possible," explained Ezio Fulcheri in his office at the University of Genoa. "Not even the bishops know how many there are. You see, there are so many churches that have been closed and are neglected now."

Fulcheri is an authority on the Incorruptibles, or, as he prefers to put it, the mummies of saints. A pathologist by profession, he runs a rooftop lab at one of Europe's largest and busiest hospitals, San Martin, where he teaches a score of young residents in blue jeans and trendy miniskirts how to detect cancer cells in surgical biopsies and how to diagnose birth defects in the cells of fetal tissue. For most people, this would be a depressing line of work. But Fulcheri, as I discovered during my stay in Genoa, is a jolly, happy man beneath all his responsibilities. Brisk and energetic in the lab, with a tendency to talk in succinct point form, he is an expansive bon vivant in the after hours. More Teutonic than Italian-looking, with short, neatly combed blond hair and austere steel-rimmed glasses, he loves amusing gossip, five-course meals, and an abundance of Liguria's finest wine, preferably all together.

The son of a country doctor from the neighboring Piedmont region, Fulcheri takes his work seriously, but not himself. In his aging lab with its spectacular view of all Genoa spread below, he has chosen to dispense with much of the customary medical hierarchy, creating the warm, cheery atmosphere of a treetop nest. Fulcheri likes to put people at their ease, and just a half hour after we met, he had casually introduced me to most of his staff and students, made me an espresso himself in the lab's cluttered closet-sized kitchen, and generally helped me feel right at home. He had also, unknown to me at that moment, sent a welcoming bouquet of flowers to my hotel room.

Married to a fellow pathologist and the father of two-year-old twins, the forty-seven-year-old physician was in constant motion. He seldom sat long and drove far too fast, narrowly missing a pedestrian the day he took me out on a tour of local saints. But despite the chaotic whirlwind he lives in, Fulcheri manages to radiate a sunny energy that knits together his staff, students, and even strangers into a moveable extended family. At a lunch bar one day, I watched in amazement as he instinctively went to the rescue of a young stranger with a furiously wailing baby. The other patrons had studiously ignored the ear-splitting din. Not Fulcheri. He walked over and began playing unself-consciously with the shrieking infant. He made silly faces. He cooed and gurgled. He lifted the baby out of its mother's remarkably yielding arms and rocked it gently. Before long just about everyone in the cafe was smiling—even the baby.

Somehow, Fulcheri had done it: he had tuned in to the baby's wavelength. When mother and child finally left, he saw them to the door, waving after them like a proud grandfather.

With his zest for life and his delight in all its trimmings, Fulcheri seems very much a man of the here and now. But as a young high school student, he had been fascinated by classical history and literature, and when he finally finished his medical training, he began dabbling in research on the splendid collection of Egyptian mummies at the Egyptian Museum in Turin. He loved studying their ancient diseases, for this combined two of his great loves—medicine and history. It was while moving in the circles of Italian Egyptologists that he received a peculiar, irresistible phone call in 1986 from Monsignor Gianfranco Nolli.

A prominent Egyptologist, Nolli was the inspector emeritus of the Vatican's Egyptian Museum, which houses many of the antiquities that ancient Roman travelers had plundered from Egypt. But Nolli also served the Vatican in a lesser-known capacity—as a consultant to the Congregation for the Causes of Saints. This august body, composed of nearly two dozen cardinals, archbishops, and bishops and assisted by a small core of ecclesiastical investigators and scientific consultants, works out of a brick and stone building near St. Peter's Square. Its chief duty is to examine the lives, writings, and purported miracles of people of extraordinary holiness, referring those it deemed most worthy of recognition as saints, blesseds, and martyrs to the pope for his final decision.

Nolli had been given an unusual project by the Congregation. He was looking for a pathologist to assist him in some of its more difficult aspects. Fulcheri, a devout Catholic, agreed to meet him in Rome. Nolli lived in a three-story house whose aging rooms were filled to the ceilings with books. With alert, darting eyes that seemed to take in everything, the elderly priest explained to Fulcheri that he had long made a study of the ancient connections between the Holy Land and Egypt and Egyptian mummies, and it was on account of this latter speciality that the Congregation had approached him with an unusual request. They wanted him to preserve the body of the dissident Ukrainian cardinal Josef Slipyj, who had recently died. And they wanted him to do so with an Egyptian-style embalming.

Slipyj, it transpired, was a strong candidate for canonization. A vocal opponent to Communism in Ukraine, the cardinal had been arrested and sentenced to hard labor in the Siberian Gulag at the end of the Second World War. After eighteen years of privation, Slipyj had been exiled to Rome, where he died in 1984. Fulcheri had never heard this story before, but he understood at once why the Vatican wanted the prelate preserved. "Sometimes there is a man or woman that the people love, and for this reason they want to preserve the body for a cult and in many cases for political reasons," he explained to me. "Some people spend a lot of time in church and there was an idea to have the body there to remind them." The Vatican worried that as Communism faded in Ukraine and a new era of religious tolerance dawned, other religions might gain a strong new foothold in the country. The Roman Catholic Church did not want Ukrainians to forget its long history in Eastern Europe, nor its bitter opposition to the old Communist regimes. If Slipyj were canonized, his splendidly preserved body could help jog Ukrainian memories.

Already Nolli had recruited several other prominent Italian scientists for the project, including Nazzareno Gabrielli, the director of scientific research at the Vatican Museum. A chemist by training, Gabrielli had devised a variety of solutions to replace the traditional resins and oils favored by Egyptian embalmers. But Nolli still needed a pathologist skilled in histology, the science of cellular composition and structure. Fulcheri offered his services. So, a few weeks later, the Genoese pathologist joined Nolli and the others in the underground crypt of St. Sophia in Rome, where Slipyj's body had been buried.

Turning the crypt into a makeshift lab, Fulcheri and his colleagues lifted the prelate's body from its coffin and laid it out on a rough table. The cadaver was still intact, but the flesh had begun to darken appreciably with decay. Following the methods of the ancient Egyptians, the team removed the brain and viscera and cleansed the cardinal's internal cavities. Then they immersed the body in a chemical bath designed to switch off enzymatic decay. All the while the team took detailed photos of the body and scribbled copious notes. "We recorded how we began to work, what we did, what substance we employed, what the concentration was and why," recalled Fulcheri, "because it's mandatory to preserve the body for the future."

Over the next four months, the team immersed the cardinal in a series of chemical solutions, each slightly different from the other and each designed to advance the process of mummification. At the end of a year, Fulcheri collected tissue samples, embedding them in protective paraffin wax and slicing them thinly to make slides. Slipping these under the microscope, he compared them to those he had prepared before the mummification began. He was terribly pleased: the processes of cellular decay had slowed almost to a standstill. Nolli and Fulcheri declared the mummification a success, and they immediately informed the Congregation of their results. Shortly after, the Vatican flew Slipyj's mummified corpse to the capital of western Ukraine, Lviv, where it was buried in the crypt of a cathedral, pending canonization.

Fulcheri was fascinated by the work. It was the start of a strange new career for him as an expert on the mummies of saints.

THE TWENTIETH-CENTURY CATHOLIC Church had not hesitated in calling on science for help in preserving a future saint. But Fulcheri had little idea whether it had done so in earlier times. There had been many times in its history when the Church had regarded science suspiciously as a rival orthodoxy. Moreover, it was unclear how much the Church could have benefited from science in an earlier age. The popular European and North American tradition of embalming, with its chemicals and cosmetics and short-term preservation, developed quite late. Indeed, it was not until the seventeenth century that European anatomists and chemists began experimentally injecting substances as diverse as wine, turpentine, alcohol, vermilion, lavender, and rosemary into the arteries of animal and human cadavers. And such short-term forms of preservation did not become widely available to the public until the late nineteenth century, when American enterpreneurs began embalming thousands of Confederate and Union soldiers slaughtered on the battlefields of the Civil War.

Still, Fulcheri was intensely curious about the Incorruptibles. Soon after finishing the work with Slipyj, he received another call from Nolli. After exchanging pleasantries, the priest asked Fulcheri for his help once again, this time with an official examination of an important medieval Tuscan saint, Saint Margaret of Cortona. Such an examination, known in church circles as a canonic recognition, was intended to root out fake relics—which had once abounded and which medieval poet Geoffrey Chaucer had once satirized—and to help conserve real remains. It was also conceived as a miniature fact-finding mission to learn more about the life of a saint. Hagiographies were notoriously unreliable, for they were often penned by uncritical admirers and laced with legends and literary conventions.

The saint in question was a thirteenth-century Italian mystic, St. Margaret of Cortona. According to the history, St. Margaret had been the daughter of a simple Tuscan farmer. As a farm girl, she had attracted the eye of a wealthy young man. Living openly as his mistress, she flaunted his finery and bore him a son, scandalizing the countryside. After nine years of this affair, her lover suddenly went missing, and she discovered his body in a shallow grave. Regarding this as a sign of God, she asked public pardon, then devoted her life to good works. In 1279, when the army of Charles of Anjou threatened to lay waste to Cortona, the citizens appealed to her to pray for their deliverance. St. Margaret reassured them—correctly as it turned out—that their city was in no danger. Charles signed an armistice soon after.

After death, the body of St. Margaret resisted decay. As

one of the Incorruptibles, she attracted thousands of devout Catholics every year to her magnificent Gothic tomb in the cathedral in Cortona. She was the source of much wonder. Her body, noted Joan Carroll Cruz in *The Incorruptibles*, "is light in color and dry, but completely whole. Even the eyes are full and all the nails of the feet and hands are still in place—truly a miraculous preservation which has existed for almost seven hundred years."

To examine such a body, the Congregation for the Causes of Saints needed a medical specialist: Fulcheri readily volunteered. In Cortona, he joined the other examiners, taking the oath required of all participating at such proceedings: he vowed to respect the saint's remains, to take nothing from them, and to tell the truth about his findings. Only then were he and his colleagues permitted to break the reliquary seals and carry the saint's body to a private area in the cathedral. As a representative of the bishop looked on, Fulcheri gently removed the saint's clothing. As he lifted the hem of her dress up over her legs, all those assembled began to murmur. Several long incisions streaked along her thighs; other, deeper cuts ran along her abdomen and chest. Clearly made after death, they had been sewn shut with a whipstitch in coarse black thread. St. Margaret, it seemed, had been artificially mummified.

Fulcheri pored over the historical and ecclesiastical records. At the time of her death in 1297, Margaret was a beloved figure in Cortona, the founder of an important hospital and the worker of many miracles of healing. Cortona's citizens were sure that she was a saint and they were determined to see her body preserved so that their city might benefit from the miracles that God might choose to perform in its presence. "So at the time of her death, the people asked the Church to embalm her," observed Fulcheri. According to the records, they made this request publicly, yet over the centuries knowledge of it had been lost. People assumed, given the state of her body, that she had been preserved by an act of God. Earlier canonical recognitions performed on her body had done little to set the record straight. The examiners had detected the fragrance of unguents and spices about her, but they had been too embarrassed to give her a full physical examination. "They had drawn back her vest, but just a little to be modest," said Fulcheri.

Those who preserved St. Margaret had done so remarkably thoroughly, excising her internal organs and drenching her skin in fragrant lotions. Their handiwork reminded Fulcheri of ʹthe techniques employed by the ancient embalmers of Egypt. Mulling this over, the pathologist wondered whether the resemblances were merely coincidental—the results of independent invention by two different cultures at two different moments in time—or whether at some point in the distant past, the Catholic Church had borrowed something from the great Egyptian tradition of mummification, adapting it to its own purposes.

The Bible, after all, had established an important precedent. In the Old Testament, Joseph, the church patriarch who was sold into slavery in Egypt as a youth and rose to become the governor of Egypt, had commanded his servants to embalm the body of his father. Elements of this practice had likely lingered in Palestine for more than a millennium. The New Testament relates how mourners at the holy sepulchre anointed the body of Christ with natural preservatives made of plants. Indeed, Nicodemus arrived at the tomb carrying a hundred-pound weight of myrrh, the resin of choice for Egyptian embalmers, and aloes, an antibacterial residue from the various species of *Aloe* that flourish in southern and eastern Africa. "Then took they the body of Jesus, and wound it in linen clothes with the spices, as the manner of the Jews is to bury," notes the Gospel of St. John. According to tradition, the stone used for this anointing still stands in the Church of the Holy Sepulchre in Jerusalem.

Imbued by faith, the early Christian fathers were determined to follow the example of Christ in every possible way. "If Christ, as the head of the Church, was oiled and embalmed," said Fulcheri, "they thought that important people and holy people should be oiled and embalmed, too." So early Christians began anointing the bodies of the holy with natural preservatives and wrapping them in linen, simple acts that greatly aided the mummification of many saints. When the first Christian missionaries journeyed to Rome, they brought these customs with them, and the use of such preservatives soon became well established in Europe. According to early historical records, fourth-century Christians in Umbria lovingly entombed the body of Saint Emiliano with "aromatic resins and precious perfumes and white linens" and Christians continued anointing their saints and martyrs with such substances for more than a millennia after this. In 1697, for example, an Italian surgeon left a list of twenty-seven powered herbs and drugs that he had employed to preserve the body of St. Gregorio Barbarigo.

Myrrh, aloes, and frankincense, another favored Egyptian resin, headed the list. "So the ideas from Egypt were transferred to Palestine," observed Fulcheri, "and then they came to Europe."

But while some Europeans were saturating the bodies of saints and martyrs with preservatives, others, as Fulcheri discovered, were taking more extreme steps to preserve human bodies. This they did in the name of the state. Across Europe, the death of a monarch created considerable political turmoil and anxiety. To soothe doubts, royal families were forced to show their courts and foreign dignitaries that a king or queen had truly departed and that someone new could rightfully assume the vacant title. In practice, this meant placing a regal cadaver on display until it could finally be buried. But the custom posed a serious problem. It could take weeks for important foreign dignitaries to arrive for a state funeral and by that time the cadaver would be a festering mess. So in royal courts from London to Vienna, physicians were called upon to fend off rot from their sovereigns until the cadavers could be tucked safely in the tomb.

Historians are unsure just when European doctors got into this morbid business: records are scarce, and Europe's royal families have never been terribly keen on permitting researchers to prod and poke the remains of their ancestors. But records suggest that one of the earliest cases took place in the late summer of 1087, when physicians were called in to preserve the body of one of England's most famous kings, William the Conqueror. William had died rather unexpectedly after a riding accident while surveying the burned ruins of Mantes, the French city he had just razed. His steed had stepped on a burning ember and, as it reared up sharply, threw the obese monarch hard against the pommel of his saddle. The resulting injury did what all William's enemies at the Battle of Hastings could not: it killed him. Shocked by this, his family and courtiers began hastily arranging a funeral. To preserve the dead king's body, they called in physicians to cleanse it and to remove the internal organs. But even these measures proved inadequate. By the beginning of the funeral, William's immense body was bursting at the seams with fetid gases and, to the horror of all, suddenly exploded inside the church, sending the nobles fleeing from their seats.

Fortunately, not all court physicians in Europe were such bunglers. Indeed some became so skillful at human preservation that they succeeded in keeping the bodies of their sovereigns from harm's way for centuries. During the 1980s, Italian pathologist Gino Fornaciari had the rare opportunity of examining some of their best handiwork. An expert on mummification, Fornaciari was given permission to examine dozens of ancient bodies interred in wooden coffins in the Basilica of San Domenico Maggiore in Naples, the final resting place of the royal family of Naples during the Renaissance. In all, Fornaciari and his team studied the remains of three kings and one queen, as well as the bodies of various other prominent Neapolitan princes and nobles of the fifteenth and sixteenth centuries. The pathologist was much impressed. Half of the bodies had been expertly mummified by contemporary physicians. Evisceration incisions ran down their abdomens. Holes pierced their crania for brain removal. Bits of herbs such as rosemary, laurel, wormwood, and myrtle still clung to the insides of their abdomens. Pine resins saturated their skin. "Even in the case of the coffins," noted Fornaciari later in a paper, "preference was shown for resinous substances which were thought to favor the preservation of the body."

The complex methods employed by the court physicians were very similar to those applied to St. Margaret. But Fulcheri could not make out the reasons for taking such drastic measures with a saint. The embalmers of Cortona had gone far beyond the traditional anointing of the holy, carving into her sacred flesh and excising and removing most of her internal organs. The church records offered no explanation, so Fulcheri began hunting elsewhere for clues, searching to see if he could find other similarly mummified saints in Italy. Perhaps, he reasoned, their histories would shed light on motives.

His research turned up only five similar cases—St. Clare of Montefalco, Blessed Margaret of Metola, St. Catherine of Siena, St. Bernadine of Siena, and St. Rita of Cascia. All had resided in the Italian provinces of Umbria and Tuscany. All had lived within a relatively short period of time, from 1297 to 1447. And all were mystics of a type fashionable in northern Italy during the fourteenth and early fifteenth centuries. Their followers were determined to preserve their bodies, but as Fulcheri could see from the records, a simple anointing had not served their purposes. Some mourners were eager to remove the internal organs for saintly relics to be sent to churches elsewhere. Others wanted to search the organs themselves for certain distinguishing marks. St. Clare of Montefalco, for example, had once told her followers, "If you seek the cross of Christ, take my heart; there you will find the suffering Lord." The nuns who had known her so well during life took this remark literally. After she died, they cut out her viscera and began poring over it for signs of divine grace. They extricated three gallstones, which they regarded as symbols of the Holy Trinity. Inside her heart they discerned signs of cardiac disease affecting the saint's papillary muscles and nearby valves and tendons. This abnormality, they concluded, resembled the outstretched body of Christ on the cross.

NOT ALL THE Incorruptibles, however, could be chalked up so neatly to the work of ecclesiastical surgeons. Some, such as St. Zita, the wizened saint I had admired in Lucca, revealed not a trace of human intervention. When pathologist Gino Fornaciari examined her body during the 1980s, he detected no sign of preservative unguents or resins on her skin. Nor did he find any incisions on her seven-hundred-year-old cadaver. St. Zita was whole and complete, possessed of all her internal organs. She and others like her—St. Ubald of Gubbio, Blessed Margaret of Savoy, and St. Savina Petrilli, to name only a few—had escaped decay by means of some other agency. As a scientist, Fulcheri suspected the hand of nature. He wondered whether certain environmental conditions had brought about the saints' preservation, for many had been interred before canonization in distinctive burial vaults beneath church floors.

The peculiar design and location of these vaults had been determined early in Church history. During the first century A.D., the Roman emperor Nero had found it politic to persecute Christians. An extravagant and unpopular ruler, he had been accused of setting a great fire in Rome to clear ground for a new palace. To deflect these rumors, Nero pinned the blame on Christians. He ordered the arrest of a great multitude of them and had them dragged to the Circo Vaticano. There, in front of all Rome, he had them set ablaze, torn apart by dogs, and hung from crucifixes. As his victims cried out in agony, Nero himself mingled among the audience dressed as a charioteer. When he finally had his fill of this cruel sport, the victims' families claimed the bodies, interring them near the circus or in the undergound tunnels of Rome's catacombs.

Such persecutions continued sporadically at the hands of other emperors. So when the Christian convert Constantine finally assumed power in Rome in the early fourth century and gave Christians freedom of worship, they breathed an immense sigh of relief. They retrieved their martyrs from catacombs and makeshift graves and began reburying them in safer, more glorious tombs under the altars of their new churches. In Rome, Constantine himself ordered the construction of a magnificent new cathedral, the Basilica of St. Peter, whose altar capped the original tomb of the disciple, one of Nero's victims. From that time on, the relics of a martyr or saint were tucked beneath the altar of every new Roman Catholic church that rose in Europe. Indeed, an early word for these churches was *martyrium*.

The new church architecture ushered in a new funerary fashion. Pious Christians were no longer content to bury their dead in ancient cemeteries and catacombs: they wanted them to lie inside the church, as close to the altar as possible. So Italian church builders came up with a simple plan. To accommodate the dead, they constructed burial vaults beneath the church floors, creating places of worship that effectively doubled as mausoleums. In these vaults, bishops were buried closest to the altar; priests and monks were entombed a short distance away from it. Kings, who ruled by divine right, were interred next to them and the nobility were inhumed a little farther off. By the medieval era, even a few wealthy merchants and their families had managed to buy their way into these vaults. Only the great unwashed were laid to rest in cemeteries outside the eaves. Christian churches had become houses of the dead, and rather exclusive ones at that.

Lying within church walls, the vaults were holy places, but some also offered another major advantage. Carved out of the cool ground or lined with alkaline stone, they had both chemical and climatic environments conducive to mummification. "They had all the right technical conditions for the preservation of mummies," observed Fulcheri. "The temperature in these crypts is quite low, and there is little temperature difference between summer and winter, so it is very easy to keep the human body there. So for this reason, a lot of the people who are exhumed from there are well preserved." In effect, some of the vaults served as superb natural mummifiers, preserving their trove of dessicated flesh for centuries.

Future saints were often laid to rest in these vaults until they were exhumed during beatification or canonization trials. By then, the tombs' microclimate had dessicated their flesh, turning it to the texture of old leather. If there was any confusion among officials about which body belonged to the saint, they sometimes picked the best preserved one, for incorruptibility was taken as a sign of holiness. Ordinary Europeans had no idea that nature had such preservative power and at a time when nearly every villager or city dweller had seen rancid corpses strewn along the streets during plague years or smelled festering cadavers piled high on a battlefield after a disastrous defeat, an ancient cadaver seemed a miracle.

By the Enlightenment, however, churchmen were beginning to ask questions about incorruptibility. The most observant had noticed that some saints began decaying almost as soon as they were removed from the burial vaults. This raised uncomfortable doubts about the saints them-selves, so in 1734 a particularly scholarly pope, Benedict XIV, published the first of four volumes on saints, raising the standard for incorruptibility. Only those bodies that remained soft, supple, lifelike in color, and fresh-looking for many years, ruled Benedict, without any subsequent disinte-gation and without any meddling by morticians, would be deemed miracles. But this didn't solve the problem. There was still room for interpretation about who was or wasn't incorruptible, and the devout frequently gave a favorite can-didate considerable latititude. To demonstate that a saint's arm was still supple enough to bend, some examiners frac-tured the limb, allowing the forearm to flop loosely. "It's not a great sight today," conceded Fulcheri.

On occasion, bound by love, some went further still to preserve the incorruptibility of a saint. Several years ago, explained Fulcheri, Monsignor Nolli, who is now dead, visited the convent of the Poor Clares in the Italian town of Assisi. There the priest paid his respects to St. Clare, the thirteenth-century founder of the order. As a young teenager, St. Clare had fallen under the influence of St. Francis of Assisi. Running away from home in 1212, she had taken her vows and become famous for her many miracles. Twice she saved Assisi from the swords of its enemies and it was said by the townspeople that she could see things that others couldn't. During her final illness, an image of the Mass conducted in the Basilica of St. Francis, on the far side of town, appeared on her wall. St. Clare watched it with pleasure. In recent decades, the thirteenth-century saint became the patron saint of television.

Unknown to many, there was an irony in this. St Clare was not all that she seemed. The day that Monsignor Nolli went to visit the saint, who rested in a glass case behind a heavy ironwork grate in an Assisi church, he saw that her skin was unnaturally brown and opaque. He also noticed a sprinkling of dust gathering beneath her hands and alongside her face. She did not look at all like a seven-hundred-year-old person should. Nolli asked for permission to examine St. Clare with Fulcheri, Gabrielli, and two of their colleagues. When they opened the grate and the reliquary, they saw that St. Clare was not a mummy at all. Instead of soft supple flesh, Fulcheri and his colleagues found a silver mask and a silver mannequin of the saint. Inside it were the saint's bones all tied together with silver wire, cloth, and pitch.

The Poor Clares intended no ruse. At some point in the distant past, St. Clare had simply gone the way of all flesh.

"So considering that the saint was very much adored," observed Fulcheri, "they took whatever bones there were and created a body around them. Instead of having an urn or reliquary made up, they made a *corpus sanctos*—a holy body." Such a complete body was a much more inviting object of contemplation and love than a mere collection of bones. In this, the Poor Clares were merely following a little-known church tradition. Elsewhere in Europe, the pious fashioned similar holy bodies. Recent studies by researchers at the University of Padua suggest that as many as seventy now grace European churches.

Over the centuries, some of the devout came to believe that the silvery St. Clare was flesh and blood. But the nuns' efforts to dress up St. Clare's remains had been sadly misguided. Rather than protecting her bones, they had attracted hungry insects. Fulcheri and his colleagues feared that the creatures would soon devour all that was left of the saint, so they requested and received permission to conserve what remained of her in a human-shaped reliquary with a porcelain mask. It was the first time in a century that any man had stayed in the convent. The nuns, rather than objecting to such an invasion, treated Fulcheri and his colleagues with great affection. As the scientists worked, they sang the same Gregorian chants that the Poor Clares had sung seven hundred years ago when St. Clare died and her soul ascended to heaven. "It was," said Fulcheri, "a poetic moment."

Influenced perhaps by such discoveries, the Roman Catholic Church has now virtually abandoned the old notion of incorruptibility. It no longer accepts physical preservation as one of the two miracles required before a saint can be recognized by the pope, and in recent years incorruptibility has gone much the same way as the old Latin Mass and the medieval vision of hell as a place of brimstone, fire, and eternal physical torment. But this did not bother Fulcheri, nor diminish or alter his own personal faith a whit. "Why should I change my ideas?" he asked, a bit testy that I had even presumed to ask in the first place. "The saints are a natural phenomena. Okay. St. Clare is not a mummy, only bones. But my devotion to St. Clare is exactly the same. It hasn't changed."

But try as it will, the Vatican will never be able to completely quell the sense of astonishment, the strange moment of recognition we often feel in the company of one of these bodies. Blended equally of awe and desire, it is too much a part of who we are and too much a reflection of our deepest desires to relinquish easily. Such ancient flesh holds out proof of a power—whether divine or natural—so prodigious and loving that it chooses to keep our fellow humans just as they are through eternity. It is an amazing affirmation, a testimony to our significance in a universe so often stony with indifference. It holds out hope that death will not be the end of us, that there is some salvation from the final annihilation that we fear awaits us all.

DESPOTS

B ACK IN VANCOUVER, I THOUGHT about the
stories that Fulcheri told of his experiences as a mum-
mifier and examiner of the holy dead. I understood his fascination, and in part I shared it, but I couldn't help but
notice the eerie disconnect between the humble faith of the
devout and the chill logic of the Vatican, which had not hesitated to call in the whole bristling arsenal of science to preserve a dissident Ukrainian cardinal. I wondered—although
I felt rather guilty for harboring such thoughts—whether
the Vatican intended on disclosing to the people of Lviv
what it had done to Cardinal Slipyj, explaining how it had

surgically altered and chemically enhanced his body for eternity. Or would Rome choose another course of action? Would it remain silent, allowing Ukrainians to draw their own conclusions about the cardinal's preservation at some distant time in the future?

What struck me most in Italy, however, was just how deep the reverence for preserved bodies runs in the Catholic world, and how easily those in positions of power can turn this to their advantage. The prelates of Rome had capitalized upon this ancient veneration to inspire the faithful and to advance the Church's own political agenda, but they were not the only ones to profit from it. Others in Europe, far more ruthless, had also sought to exploit it, and they had done so on occasion with particularly disastrous consequences. Indeed, during the 1980s, radical nationalists in Serbia had used veneration for the ancient preserved dead to prepare the way for ethnic cleansing.

The Serbs are a people with very long memories. As Orthodox Catholics, they live along the edges of the ancient cultural faultline that divided Christian Europe from Moslem Asia. Conquered by the Ottoman Turks in the fourteenth century, they fomented rebellion after rebellion for nearly five hundred years, until at last they won their freedom in the nineteenth century and later united with other Slavs to found Yugoslavia. It was a fragile union. Serb nationalists hated sharing the reins of power, particularly with Yugoslavia's sizable Moslem population. By the late 1980s they had begun scheming to seize control of the entire country. As an intregal part of their plan, they promoted a dramatic public tour of a fourteenth-century Serb prince, Lazar.

It was Lazar, a popular local hero, who had led the ill-fated defense of Serbia from the Turkish invaders. Enjoining his fellow Serbs to leave work on their farms to follow him in June of 1389, the prince and his forces met the invaders on Kosovo Polji, "the field of blackbirds." In the heat of the clash, Serb knights managed to slay the Turkish leader, Sultan Murad I. But the death of the sultan did little to curb the ferocity of his forces. The Turkish army slaughtered the Serb knights in their heavy chain-mail armor, leaving the battlefield littered with glinting corpses. They also captured the kingpin of the Serb defense—Lazar himself, who was beheaded a month later.

The Orthodox Church canonized Lazar as a martyr. His followers carried his body to a monastary at Ravanica, where he was revered for centuries as an Incorruptible. Few things, reasoned extreme Serb nationalists in the late 1980s, were likely to inflame Serbs as much as a glimpse of the murdered prince, whose mummified remains had by then become little more than bones. That he had so deteriorated did not matter to Serbs: the devout offered their prayers as a procession carried Lazar from Bosnia and Croatia to

Kosovo. Two years later, the new Serb leader, Slobodan Milosevic, spoke to more than one million people on the ancient Kosovo battlefield, stirring nationalism to fever pitch. Portraying himself as the reincarnated Lazar, Milosevic rode to power, unleashing war and the atrocities of ethnic cleansing and forcing tens of thousands of Moslems to leave their homes in Kosovo.

Milosevic understood exactly what he was doing, but he was not the first politician to see the glimmer of gain in the relics of the ancient dead. From the Russian Revolution to the darkest days of the Cold War, Eastern European Communists had capitalized on ancient Christian beliefs surrounding the preserved dead. While suppressing the Catholic Church in Eastern Europe, dispatching priests to the firing squads and archbishops to the frozen camps of the Gulag, they had cynically borrowed pages from Rome, creating their own brand of Incorruptibles.

⌒

NUMBER 2 KRASIN Street looks much like any other modernist Soviet-era office building in Moscow. Situated just a brisk ten-minute walk from the walls of the Kremlin, it blends into its drab surroundings with a kind of artless camouflage. On a recent March morning, the bland gray facade was the same color as the muddy slush in the street. The blackened skeletal trees out front looked exhausted and defeated, as trees do throughout Moscow at that time of year. The sign over its doorway drew scarcely a blink from a passerby. It read, in Russian, THE SCIENTIFIC RESEARCH AND METHODOLOGICAL CENTER OF BIOMEDICAL TECHNOLOGIES. As with so many other things in the former Soviet Union, however, the placard out front did little to convey the eerie reality within. At 2 Krasin, some of Russia's finest medical minds toiled, as they had for decades, on a bizarre quest: to transform dead dictators into the most perfect mummies the world has ever seen.

In this, the staff at 2 Krasin had been singularly successful. Thanks to its ministrations, Vladimir Ilyich Ulyanov, better known as Lenin, lies seemingly untouched by time in his austere Red Square mausoleum. Dead for nearly three-quarters of a century, Lenin remains a major public figure in Russia, as much a part of popular culture and political discourse in Moscow as many living politicians. And Lenin is just one of the triumphs of the Mausoleumists, as the secretive aging morticians at 2 Krasin Street are privately known. Their client list reads like a Who's Who of the Cold War— Joseph Stalin, Ho Chi Minh, and Kim Il Sung.

I had arrived in Moscow by appointment to meet and talk with the Mausoleumists, but I had unwittingly picked a bad time. The United States, Canada, and other NATO members had just begun bombing Belgrade after Slobodan Milosevic's assault on Kosovo. Young Russians were up in arms about the devastation being wreaked on their old Serb allies, demonstrating angrily in front of the American embassy. To prevent things from getting out of hand, the Kremlin had sent out the army to guard the embassy from the sea of sullen faces on the street. My interpreter, Natalia, an

English-language professor from St. Petersburg, was worried sick. Her students were desperate to run off to Yugoslavia to volunteer for the army. But I found it hard to gauge the depth of Russian rage. A click of the remote in my hotel room produced a popular Moscow television program: the American cartoon *Beavis and Butthead*, dubbed into Russian.

Nonetheless I felt very nervous heading off to my first meeting at 2 Krasin Street, and my sense of anxiety was not exactly allayed inside the door. Against the far wall, a receptionist sat behind a lone desk, looking very small in a very large and empty-looking foyer. She stared at Natalia and me, took our names and made a discreet call on a rotary phone, whispering something into the receiver. I glanced around the foyer, searching for some other sign of life. There wasn't any, only a door standing ajar in an empty corner room. At one time, 2 Krasin Street had boasted its own KGB monitoring, but circumstances were clearly not what they had been. To help pay the bills, the Mausoleumists and their associates had been reduced to leasing out space to two businesses virtually unheard of in the old Soviet era: a travel agency and a bank.

A secretary finally appeared and led the way up the stairs past a dusty-looking bust of Lenin the revolutionary and into a small elevator. A formaldehyde odor wafted in the air as staff in white lab jackets squeezed in beside us. On the third floor, the door parted on a large carved wooden panel showing Lenin beaming down benevolently. The secretary led the way down a narrow corridor and ushered us into an immense echoing office stripped bare of any personal photos or effects. At the far end behind a desk sat a dapper-looking man in his early sixties. It was Juri Denisov-Nikolsky, the senior Russian researcher responsible for Lenin's body. Short and rotund, with graying hair swept back neatly from his face, he spoke an eloquent, old-fashioned kind of Russian and wore a look of frank curiosity on his face. As we talked, I began to see that he had been looking forward to this meeting. He loves to spar.

Denisov-Nikolsky wasn't at all what I had expected. I had imagined someone dry, humorless, difficult, and rather self-important, which was how he had come across on the phone to Natalia. He isn't. He is a stickler for detail, yes, but he is fond of a laugh, particularly when it can be had at others' expense. His thick unruly black eyebrows hop and dance frenetically above his eyes when he is amused, which seemed to be much of the time in my presence. First of all, however, he had to take Natalia and me up to the office of the director of the institute for an official grilling that would decide whether he could talk to me at all. This, it soon became obvious, was going to be an ordeal. But after Natalia and I had somehow scraped through, we all headed back downstairs to schedule a meeting. Denisov-Nikolsky loosened his necktie like a man about to have a good time.

The next morning when we arrived, he was in a jovial mood. He greeted us amiably and made fun of me when I alluded to what I had read about the secrecy of the Mausoleumists' methods. "So I guess I just made a great mistake in coming into contact with a person like you," he said, with a broad conspiratorial grin. "I should live isolated and away from the outside world." Seeing him so relaxed and amused,

I began to feel ridiculous. It occurred to me that perhaps I had read too many John Le Carré novels. So I began to ask him detailed questions about the methods that he and his colleagues used to preserve Lenin. He declined to answer. I asked how many people the Mausoleumists had embalmed. He refused to give out the information. I requested permission to see the Mausoleumists' labs. I had heard, although I didn't mention this, that they featured large liquid tanks containing human cadavers that dated back to 1949. I wanted to see them. Denisov-Nikolsky changed the subject.

He was, however, slightly more willing to talk about other things—including his own background. Like his fellow Mausoleumists, he is a member of Russia's old medical elite. He was born in Azerbaijan, the son of an engineer, and he graduated from one of the best medical schools in the then Soviet Union, St. Petersburg's Military Medical Academy. He has a Ph.D. in anatomy, with a speciality in the morphology or structure of human bone. Among other things, he is an expert on osteoporosis, the abnormal loss of bone tissue that plagues many postmenstrual women, and he has lectured widely on the subject in Russia. He lives comfortably in Moscow, though not as comfortably as he did before the drastic devaluation of the ruble in the late 1990s, and has traveled broadly. He is married to a fellow doctor and medical researcher. His daughter is a doctor and his grandson is about to enter medical school. He is a member of the prestigious Academy of Medical Sciences.

Much of his spectacular climb up the ladder in the Russian medical establishment was due to his labors as a Mausoleumist. In 1970, Denisov-Nikolsky had just finished a stint as a young medical expert for the Russian army and as a researcher for a Moscow medical institute and was at loose ends when he received an important referral to Sergei Debov. Debov was the biochemist who headed the laboratory belonging to Lenin's Mausoleum, as the research facility was then known. A pioneer of Russian work on DNA and a vice president of the Russian Academy of Sciences, Debov was an erudite and charming man who was on the lookout for a first-rate medical researcher. He and his fellow Mausoleumists had a good thing going. In return for their silence and their research on new and better ways to preserve the dead, they each were given their own laboratories. These were relatively well stocked and equipped with up-to-date scientific gear—a novelty in much of Soviet science. Debov and his colleagues also had the freedom to pursue their own research interests. This, too, was a novelty. A post at 2 Krasin Street ensured a spacious, comfortable apartment in Moscow, a good deal of foreign travel, the best schools for one's children, and all the medals and honors that a grateful government could bestow. Denisov-Nikolsky signed on.

After nearly thirty years of such work, he became the guardian of the lab's secret formulas for Lenin's care. Some Russian reporters, impressed by the body's lifelike color and look, had accused him of secretly substituting a wax model. When I asked him if it were true, Denisov-Nikolsky laughed. Twice a week, one or another of the Mausoleumists inspected the body for signs of deterioration. Every eighteen months or so, Denisov-Nikolsky arranges for Lenin to be lowered by elevator into a subterranean laboratory beneath the Mausoleum. This lab is kept at a constant temperature of 60 degrees Fahrenheit—a beautiful spring day in the parlance of the Mausoleumists. There it is stripped of its clothes, checked for signs of decay, and immersed in a vat of chemicals. Then it is raised again several weeks later into the world of the living.

BY SUCH ELABORATE means, Lenin, the driving force behind the Russian Revolution, the founder of Europe's earliest concentration camps, and the architect of Soviet-style terror, has eerily outlasted all his comrades and contemporaries. The last time Lenin's wife, Nadezhda Krupskaya, saw him in 1938, she is said to have shaken her head sadly. While she had aged, she muttered to a guard, her husband looked exactly the same as he did the day he died. It was a fate that neither she nor Lenin had ever wished for. Lenin himself was frankly contemptuous of those who made dead revolutionaries their idols. His wife shared these views. Shortly after her husband died from a stroke in January 1924, she wrote a letter to the Soviet newspaper *Pravda*. She demanded that her husband be given a plain burial in a simple grave. "Do not let your sorrow for Ilyich find expression in outward veneration of his person," she warned. "Do not build memorials to his name."

Lenin's would-be successors ignored her. Even before Lenin was dead, Joseph Stalin had proposed embalming the revolutionary so that Russians could get used to his death gradually. At the time, neither Stalin nor his ideas were taken particularly seriously. When Lenin died, observed Denisov-Nikolsky, "plans were made to bury Lenin and the grave was even dug and the day of the funeral was named."

Delegations from across Russia struggled to make the funeral on time, but in the dead of winter, many were held up on the roads. The Kremlin ordered that Lenin be temporarily embalmed according to funeral practices popular in the West. This would allow delayed delegations to pay their respects to Lenin. But five weeks later, the crowds of mourners had not thinned and brown patches had appeared on the skin on Lenin's head. These were worrying signs of decay.

Stalin, who was beginning to gather up the reins of power, insisted that Lenin be permanently installed in Red Square. The bodies of Russian Orthodox saints were preserved under glass in cathedrals across the country. Why not inter Lenin in a shrine where pilgrims from the grieving nation could pay homage? It was an incredibly cynical idea. Lenin, after all, had launched a vicious campaign against the Russian Orthodox Church. Indeed, he took such a personal interest in the Church's destruction that he had asked to see daily lists of the priests to be put to death. But Stalin astutely observed that Lenin's campaign had left a huge void in Russian society. Stalin had been raised in a deeply religious household and had even attended a theological seminary. He knew that a successful Communist government would have to supply something to replace the Orthodox saints. Stalin offered up Lenin.

No one had ever tried to preserve a human body exactly as it had been at the height of life, not even the ancient Egyptians. "People in Egypt mummified their great leaders so the souls could live together with the bodies," noted Denisov-Nikolsky. "They didn't aim to keep the exact appearance of the mummies and that's why we'll never know what Ramses V looked like." But Stalin envisioned perfection. He wanted a body that the Russian public could immediately identify and worship, a body that was even more lifelike—and hence more holy—than those of the saints. A Committee for the Immortalization of Lenin's Memory was hastily convened. One of its members, Leonid Krasin, a close working associate of Lenin, advocated freezing his old friend like a side of beef. But after conducting a few experiments with other corpses, Krasin gave up. He realized it would be extremely difficult to maintain the body at the exact temperature required. Moreover, moisture was bound to collect on the inner surface of the sarcophagus, accelerating putrefaction.

With no one else to turn to, the committee reluctantly handed Lenin's body over to a pair of untried morticians, biochemist Boris Zbarsky and anatomist Vladimir Vorobiov. Vorobiov had a local reputation in the city of Kharkov as a preparer of anatomical specimens for medical classes. He flayed, incised, and chemically treated human corpses to reveal the minutiae of their anatomy. His cadavers were instructive for medical students, but never very pretty. Zbarsky, on the other hand, was a cocky young Jewish biochemist eager to make his way in the new Soviet system. He had never worked with the dead before, but he had persuaded himself that with his knowledge of chemistry and Vorobiov's grasp of anatomy, they could preserve Lenin for decades just as the Kremlin wanted. Zbarsky was willing to risk everything on this belief. He knew that failure would lead directly to the firing squad.

In March of 1924, he and Vorobiov moved into a cellar below Lenin's temporary wooden crypt in Red Square. Initially, the young biochemist refused to touch the famous cadaver: he couldn't bear to handle a dead man. He expected Vorobiov to carry out all the procedures, but the astonished anatomist refused. According to one story, Vorobiov threw a medical gown over to his young associate one day, suggesting that henceforth they do everything together. Zbarsky reluctantly agreed and they got down to work. They ordered vats of chemicals—formalin, glycerin, alcohol, ethanol, potassium acetate, quinine chloride, gutta-percha, and honey. They also contacted Alexander Pasternak, the brother of the famous Russian writer Boris Pasternak, the author of *Dr. Zhivago*. Vorobiov wanted Pasternak, an accomplished artist, to do a detailed watercolor of Lenin's body. This could then serve as a permanent record of Lenin's skin color, his liver spots, and warts. This rendering, which sprawled over nine sheets of paper, would become the standard against which their work could later be judged. There was no time to spare. The water in Lenin's eyes was evaporating: his closed eyelids were shrinking ghoulishly into their sockets. Also, the muscles of his lower lip were retracting, creating the beginnings of a grimace. Worse still, Lenin smelled.

Zbarsky and Vorobiov worked around the clock with their assistants. They ate and slept in the crypt. They never publicly divulged exactly what they did to Lenin. But according to Zbarsky's son Ilya, who followed in his father's footsteps as a Mausoleumist and later wrote a fascinating book about his experiences, the team first eviscerated Lenin, then flushed out his body cavity with distilled water and acetic acid. They injected him with formalin and lowered him gently into a formalin bath. He looked like an exotic fish in an aquarium. Eventually the two morticians hauled him out and dried him off. Then they dunked him repeatedly in a bath filled with glycerine, potassium acetate, water, and quinine chloride—the same solution, claimed Ilya Zbarsky, that was used for maintenance treatments on Lenin.

Four months after they began, the work was done. The Kremlin invited Lenin's family to come take a look. Dimitri Ulyanov, Lenin's brother, was stunned. He said Lenin looked even better than he did when the family last viewed him a few hours after death. Relieved to hear this, the Kremlin installed the body in an elegant, pyramid-shaped mausoleum in Red Square. For his efforts, Zbarsky received a huge sum of money for the time, twenty-five thousand rubles, which he spent on clothes and lavish dinner parties for his friends and party contacts over the next three years. The nervous strain of the previous months had imprinted itself painfully on his imagination, however. He had a recurring nightmare: in his dreams, he told one reporter, he saw a fly buzzing inside Lenin's sarcophagus.

Zbarsky and Vorobiov continued to minister to Lenin, visiting the Mausoleum twice a week. But despite their great triumph, they never managed to ingratiate themselves with Russia's new master, Stalin. Vorobiov disliked the small Georgian intensely and, on occasions when he had drunk too much, didn't mind saying so in the company of others. This was very unwise: Vorobiov died under mysterious circumstances in 1937. Zbarsky hung on longer at the Mausoleum, but in 1952 he was purged and imprisoned in one of Stalin's anti-Semitic campaigns. He died soon after. One of his students, Sergei Debov, began tending to Lenin's needs, and before long Debov and the Cold War carried the Soviet brand of immortality to new heights.

IN AN ELEGANT sunlit apartment on Begovaya Street, Lyudmilla Debova dabbed a tear from her eye as she watched her husband, Sergei Debov, on videotape. Debov, who took part in the mummification of Stalin, Ho Chi Minh, and many others, had died of skin cancer in 1995. But Debova kept his study just as it was when he was alive, a shrine to her husband's memory. After spending an afternoon with her and her vivacious sister, Valentina Victorovna, I felt as if I knew him, too. Debov's well-thumbed books—the collected plays of Shakespeare, coffee-table books on Monet and Degas, field guides to shells and fossils, biographies of Martin Luther King Jr., and other twentieth-century luminaries—still lined the shelves of his study. The tangerine plant Debov had carried back from Hanoi still flowered in a corner window. The dried crocodile he had collected in Angola still sat on a ledge. And the little lacquered liquor cabinet he had been given in North Korea, that was there, too. Debov, it transpired, had always brought back mementos when he traveled abroad. "The whole world is represented here," said Victorovna proudly.

The videotape showed a tall, distinguished-looking man in his early seventies with thick black-framed glasses. He looked relaxed and slightly bemused as he answered questions from a Russian television journalist. The sudden death of Stalin in March of 1953, he explained, took the Mausoleumists by surprise. For nearly a quarter of a century, Stalin had ruled the Soviet Union with a terrible cunning, eliminating all opponents and spreading terror from the frozen reaches of Siberia to the prosperous countryside dachas outside Moscow. Stalin had seemed both immortal and invincible. Signing daily death-sentence lists of five thousand people at the height of the great purges of the late 1930s, he spent his evenings sipping Georgian wine and reveling in American westerns and comedies screened in his private theater.

Stalin's would-be successors immediately bestowed their country's greatest honor upon him. They ordered the Mausoleumists to prepare their chemicals. For Debov and his colleagues, this was a frightening prospect, for Stalin had died under suspicious circumstances. In the Kremlin, rumors of poison were flying, for it was said that Stalin's face had turned black just before his death and that he had hurled curses at all those who huddled around him. Debov and his colleagues feared that if they turned up evidence of poison, there would be a bloodbath in the Kremlin, where Stalin's successors eyed each other hungrily like circling hammerhead sharks. If there was any hint that the Mausoleumists had concealed such evidence, it would be the Gulag or worse for them all. On the videotape, a Russian television reporter asked him if he was afraid. Debov smiled a little, hesitating. "Nobody wished to do the postmortem examination," he conceded finally, "so a college student was found to do it."

Fortunately, the student discerned no hint of foul play. Stalin had died of a stroke. But the team did not have an easy time preserving his body. Stalin's face was pocked and pitted, something tactfully omitted from official portraits of the Soviet leader. This meant that the Mausoleumists had to find a way to make the scars disappear. Eventually they called in lighting specialists who devised a system of twinkling lights that softened Stalin's pockmarks and hid his wrinkles, making him look years younger and far more pleasant than he ever had in life. When the body was at last ready for viewing, Debov called the Kremlin and asked for a set of clothing to dress him in. "An aide brought a shabby worn-out uniform and an old pair of boots," recalled Debova. "Sergei was very surprised, but it turned out that's all that Stalin had. He just slept on an army bed and led a spartan life."

When the Mauoleumists were done, Stalin's body was exhibited in a glass-topped sarcophagus next to Lenin in Red Square. For a while, lines of the curious extended far down the pavement, but they quickly tapered off. Later, a young woman stood up at a Communist Party congress to describe a dream she had. In it, Lenin had spoken to her, saying, "It is unpleasant for me to be beside Stalin who brought such misfortune to the Party." After that, a group of men from the Kremlin appeared late one night in 1961 at the Mausoleum. They brought papers and an ordinary wooden coffin. Debov and his colleagues helped them lift Stalin from his glass sarcophagus and lay him in the coffin. Then they watched as soldiers nailed the lid shut and carried it out to a freshly dug grave behind the mausoleum. Debov never saw Stalin's body again.

BUT THE MAUSOLEUMISTS were not terribly concerned by Stalin's sudden fall from grace: by that time, they had their hands full of work. Other Communist states were lining up to have their own version of Lenin, so whenever somebody prominent died—from Mongolian strongman Horloogiyn Choybalsan to Angolan revolutionary Agostinho Neto, and from Bulgarian party boss Georgi Dimitrov to Czech Communist leader Klement Gottwald—the Mausoleumists got a call from the Kremlin. The instructions varied shrewdly from case to case. The rulers and despots of minor client states, such as Mongolia, received the cheapest, most ephemeral form of Soviet mummification, while those who presided over nations critical to Russian foreign policy benefited from the most lavish attentions that Debov and his team could manage.

Ho Chi Minh, the North Vietnamese leader who had delivered such a stunning blow to the confidence of the American military, warranted red-carpet service. He died of a heart attack in 1969, at the height of the Vietnam War. With instructions from the Kremlin, Debov and his colleagues packed a plane full of chemicals and equipment and flew to Hanoi. The North Vietnamese seemed very anxious about the embalming. The American army had begun searching for Ho Chi Minh's body, after hearing rumors that the North Vietnamese would trade all their prisoners of war to get it back. So Hanoi had been forced to go to elaborate lengths to protect the corpse, moving it from cave to cave. One morning, Debov and his colleagues woke up to see an American tank churn past their camouflaged shelter. "The team was guarded," said Debova, "but still they saw the cannon of the tank pointed at them."

Further adding to the tension were technical problems.

It was the first time the Mausoleumists had worked with a body whose skin was not pink-white. They weren't exactly sure how to preserve the correct pigmentation. They tested various solutions on human cadavers of similar color in Hanoi until at last they found something that worked. They were immensely proud of the finished product. Debov later told his wife that Ho Chi Minh was better preserved than Lenin himself. The North Vietnamese leadership were very grateful. They awarded Debov their highest medal, the Hero of Labor, and presented the departing scientist with a precious keepsake: a pair of vases made from an American warplane they had shot down.

Indeed, wherever Debov traveled as a Mausoleumist, his hosts showered him with honors and gifts. They threw elaborate banquets and pandered to the team members' private hobbies. "Debov loved to fish," says Debova, "so wherever he went, they organized fishing trips for him." When North Korean president Kim Il Sung died in 1994, Debov and his team flew to the capital Pyongyang, where they were put up in the dead leader's palace. In a country of famines, "they were treated like czars," said Victorovna. Kim Il Sung's reclusive successor and son, Kim Jong-il, happily posed for photos with them, and when Debov returned to Moscow, his suitcases bulged with presents, including a bottle of gold-flecked liquor. Debova still had it. She brought it out and kindly offered me a drink. When I declined, a look of relief crossed her face. "It's Korean," she said, wrinkling her nose, "so it's not very good."

The reputation of the Mausoleumists seemed unassailable, but even so, a few famous names from the Cold War slipped through their hands. The phones at 2 Krasin Street were maddeningly silent in the late summer of 1976, for example, when Mao Tse-tung died in China. Sino-Soviet relations were horribly strained at the time. The Chinese didn't dare ask for help. Instead they sent a small delegation to Hanoi, hoping to weasel the Russians' secrets out of those who tended to Ho Chi Minh. The Vietnamese refused to divulge a thing. In Beijing, the new leadership realized it would have to go its own way in preserving the Great Helmsman. The Chinese, however, were greenhorns at this work. In their nervous attempt at perfection, the appointed embalmers injected Mao with liters more formaldehyde than standard medical texts prescribed. "The results were shocking," observed Mao's personal physician, Li Zhisui, in his published memoirs. Mao's face became as swollen and distended as a soccer ball. Formaldehyde seeped from his sodden skin. His bloated ears stood out like inflated flippers along the sides of his head. Only hours of frantic salvage work by Li and his associates returned Mao to some semblance of himself.

THE MAUSOLEUMISTS TOOK a secret glee in these stories. They weren't at all sorry to hear of their Chinese comrades' troubles. But by then, unknown to Debov and his colleagues, the glory days of 2 Krasin Street were almost over. The old Soviet Union had begun staggering like a drunk under the weight of economic stagnation, and Eastern Europe couldn't wait to dispose of its puppet governments. In 1989, Berliners finally tore down the concrete slabs of the hated Berlin Wall and then reunited, while Romanians arrested Communist leader Nicolae Ceausescu and his wife, videotaping their executions for public television. A year later, Bulgarians deposed their own Communist leaders, then angrily desecrated the Stalinist mausoleum of Georgi Dimitrov, who had been mummified by the Mausoleumists. Dimitrov's family hastened to fetch the corpse, which they quickly cremated in order to avoid further indignity.

In Moscow, people seemed equally keen to rid themselves of the past. At the instigation of Boris Yeltsin, a fierce critic of the old Soviet regime, the Russian republic declared its sovereignty, effectively dismantling the Soviet Union. The old Soviet flag with its hammer and sickle disappeared from the Kremlin walls, and statues of Lenin came clattering down onto the cobblestones. Russians talked longingly of burying Lenin's body, claiming that peace would never come to the land until the architect of the Russian Revolution had been evicted from his grand tomb in Red Square and buried in the cold ground where he belonged. But the Kremlin hesitated: if Lenin were buried, who could guarantee he would rest in peace? Dead as he was, Lenin had many, many enemies. Kremlin officials cast about for a tidy solution. One rumor had it that they considered auctioning off the body to a foreign buyer, thereby removing the troublesome corpse from harm's way while earning a tidy sum for the government.

The auction, of course, never took place. Yeltsin failed miserably in his attempt to jump-start the Russian economy, the old Communist guard flexed its muscles once again, and the optimism that had swept through the streets of Moscow vanished. Lenin's body still remained safely ensconced in

Red Square. But at 2 Krasin Street, his minders were bitter men. In his echoing office, Denisov-Nikolsky rapped the table hard in frustration. Since 1991, he explained, the Russian government had virtually ignored him and his colleagues, embarrassed, it seemed, by their mere existence. Indeed, the government had paid not one ruble toward the upkeep of Lenin. "Nothing!" said Denisov-Nikolsky, almost roaring, his face a livid red.

The financial starvation had led to desperate measures. To pay their bills, the guardians of Lenin had entered into a business relationship with a Russian funeral company, Ritual Services. The firm catered to Moscow's nouveaux riches, which in practice often meant catering to the Russian mafia. Initially, the Mausoleumists served as consultants, helping to pretty up and preserve cadavers for families who could afford such luxuries, but relations with the company had quickly soured. Denisov-Nikolsky and his colleagues had severed all connections. The anatomist refused to discuss the details, but it was clear that the falling out hadn't been on ideological grounds. Indeed, the Mausoleumists welcomed any wealthy customers, even Americans. "If a rich Texan wished to preserve himself, his wife, or his mistress, then why not?" observed Denisov-Nikolsky. "If someone suddenly gets the wish to be embalmed, we're open. We're willing to do it."

Clients weren't exactly pounding down the doors, however. To help stay afloat, the Mausoleumists were reduced to accepting handouts from a public trust fund established by a prominent Russian journalist. It was a humiliating state of affairs for a group of scientists who once stood at the pinnacle of official Soviet science. It was also a very worrying one.

Lacking financial support, the Mausoleumists had no incentives to attract a new generation of medical researchers to their ranks. Young Russians wanted to go where the money was, explained Denisov-Nikolsky, derisively rubbing his thumb and forefinger. Moreover, Russia's finest medical talent wanted to do something more satisfying than work on dead bodies, especially when there were few perks to compensate for this sacrifice. Without new blood, the aging Mausoleumists were in danger of becoming extinct. And signs of the end were everywhere. The Mausoleumists had nearly exhausted the supplies of embalming chemicals they had stockpiled in better times, said Denisov-Nikolsky. They were unable to afford to buy new stores. Outside, as if to underline these contentions, a secretary clattered away on a manual typewriter.

Like most of his colleagues, Denisov-Nikolsky hated the thought that Lenin's body might one day end up as worm food. He had sunk the best and most productive years of his medical career into the work at the Mausoleum and he was not about to see his pet project fall to wrack and ruin. He was proud of what he and his colleagues had achieved. Over the past thirty years, he said, he had detected no trace of decomposition or putrefaction in the cadaver. Lenin, the revolutionary, seemed to be in a perfect state of limbo—a feat never before accomplished by human morticians—and he desperately wanted to see how long it would stay that way. "This has been a very great achievement by Soviet science," he insisted. "It doesn't have any analog anywhere in the world. So to stop, to cease this work would greatly affect the achievements and developments of Russian science."

For more than half a century, the Soviet government

had gone to immense lengths to keep its revolutionary saint whole and intact. It had siphoned off the best minds of its medical schools, students whose brilliance could have been put to work healing the living, and sent them instead to toil upon the bodies of dead men. It had paid lavishly for the preservation of Lenin in his granite tomb, while millions of Russian peasants had perished from starvation during the great famines of the thirties. It had elevated the craft of the mortician into a science and lavished every honor conceivable on a group of men whose main contribution to society was to tend cadavers. All this it had done to preserve the dead.

Denisov-Nikolsky knew all this, but the scientist in him regretted nothing. Lenin, he maintained, was now a great scientific experiment and, as ironic as it sounded, he was loath to let something as ephemeral as politics get in the way.

CHILDREN

⌒

THE MAUSOLEUMISTS HAD GLADLY SATIS-
FIED their curiosity, peeking into a rarefied world of
privilege denied to most, but they had never lost sight of
who they were and what they were doing. They had as fine
a sense of social distinctions as any equerry at Bucking-
ham Palace or any chargé d'affaires at the White House,
something I had discovered quite by chance one afternoon
at 2 Krasin Street. I had been chatting with one of the oldest
Mausoleumists, seventy-nine-year-old Yuri Romakov, and I
had asked him whether he himself would like one day to be
preserved with all the skill his colleagues could muster.

Romakov stared at me through rheumy eyes and tried stifling his disbelief, but he was clearly shocked. Such mummification, he informed me coldly, was only suitable for truly exceptional people. Ordinary folk, he implied, were scarcely worthy of such attention. Indeed, they should be content with whatever nature chose to unleash upon them—fungus, mold, rot, maggots, and beetles.

Romakov, good Communist as he once was, saw little irony in this. Nor was he alone in such sentiments. For hundreds of years in Europe and Asia, morticians skilled in the science of mummification had gone about their work selectively, reserving physical immortality for a privileged few—the rich, the powerful, the holy, the high, and the mighty. Through their adroitness, the celebrated had managed to escape the worst excesses of death, remaining whole, intact, and still eminently presentable to adoring crowds. As a result mummification had become a sort of status symbol in some circles—a visible sign that someone had not only arrived but left in considerable style, and that in between he had been widely loved, revered, worshipped, and blindly followed.

When the famous Italian opera star Enrico Caruso died in Naples in the summer of 1921, for example, his fans were beside themselves with grief. Caruso, they believed, was the greatest tenor who had ever lived, a man whose voice possessed such supple warmth and richness that they could scarcely imagine setting foot again in an opera hall without him. Caruso had understood his fans' ardor. As souvenirs, he left them more than 240 recordings of his favorite arias and popular songs, but even these were not enough to satisfy his many admirers. They wanted to gaze again on his sturdy, good-natured face, with its deep cleft chin, and his thatch of dark curls. Taking pity on their grief, Caruso's widow permitted the morticians of Naples, who were renowned for their skills as mummifiers, to preserve her husband and lay him out in state at the Hotel Vesuvio in Naples.

On the day of the funeral, a crowd of 100,000 admirers jammed the streets of Naples to watch Caruso pass by in a wreath-adorned hearse. But this did not put an end to public mourning for the man with the haunting tessitura. Fans continued to clamor to pay their respects, so the Caruso family arranged to display his mummified body in a glass casket in a cemetery above Naples. For seven or eight years, opera lovers made their pilgrimages to the tomb, weeping at the sight of Caruso and leaving bouquets of flowers as tokens of their love; Caruso's friends regularly gave him fresh changes of clothes. But the tenor's widow hated the public spectacle her husband had become. It seemed to her an indecency. At last she convinced Italian authorities to help her remove his cadaver to a marble sarcophagus in a private mausoleum.

Caruso's fans had been loath to part with the great tenor: he had seemed more like a god on the stage than any mere mortal and they had expected him to live forever. Now that he was dead, they craved a glimpse of his face to remind themselves of the joy he had once brought them. Italy's superb morticians had kindly granted them this wish.

I confess that I like to imagine Caruso surrounded even in death by friends and admirers. A man of enormous physical vitality, the great tenor had once taken immense delight in sketching sly caricatures of his associates. I suspect he would not like to be alone in death. The story of his preservation gave me pause for thought about the original human impulse that lay behind mummification. I wondered if human societies had always been so attached to the great among them, and whether this reverence for remarkable people had given rise to the idea of mummification. Had the first morticians gone to work on someone as rare and extraordinary as Caruso? Or had they devised this form of immortality for another, less transparent purpose, one now forgotten by the living?

EARLY MUMMY EXPERTS were supremely confident that they knew where the mysterious and rather arcane art of preserving the dead began: the answer seemed obvious to all. Egypt was the land of the mummies, the place where desert sands rippled with tattered strips of yellowed linen and bits of withered flesh. Classical writers left little doubt that it had long been so. Even before Alexander the Great had led his armies from his home in Macedonia and Julius Caesar had staggered into the arms of his betrayers on the Ides of March, travelers had penned descriptions of the curious trade of the embalmers along the Nile. Impressed by such lines of evidence, nineteenth-century mummy experts saw little need to look any further for clues: no other early civilization in the ancient world, it seemed, was so brilliant, so mystical, and so apt to have discovered the intricate secrets of preserving the dead.

This blind faith colored much later scientific thinking and led inevitably to some rather grand theories. In the years leading up to the First World War, for example, a prominent Australian anatomist, Grafton Elliott Smith, set aside his autopsies of Egyptian mummies and began scrutinizing mummification methods around the world. He plowed through obscure anthropological texts on the embalming practices of Madagascar tribes and peered at photos of child mummies unearthed in the American Southwest. He combed histories of the Spanish conquest and examined the peculiar pattern of incisions on mummies from the Torres Strait. When he was done, he arrived at what might be called a grand unified theory of mummification, which he published in a book entitled *The Migrations of Early Culture*. In it, Smith, the man who had amassed the collection of mummified penises that so disturbed his family, concluded that the ancient Egyptians were much more than the inventors of the art of embalming. They were also its chief evangelists, carrying their distinctive culture and the secrets of Egyptian mummification around the ancient world, even to the far shores of South America.

Many of Smith's colleagues shook their heads at this theory, with its quirky assumptions and sweeping generalizations, but some did not. Novelist H. G. Wells was sufficiently intrigued to popularize it in his own book, *The Outline of History*, and at University College London, archaeologists began busily exploring the idea of an ancient Egyptian diaspora. But as fascinated as some British intellectuals were by Smith and his splendid ideas, the Australian mummy expert proved no visionary. His grand unified theory was little more than a house of cards. No evidence ever surfaced of ancient Egyptian morticians in such faraway places as Indonesia and Mexico, as Smith had suggested. And in the 1980s, a series of stunning archaeological discoveries in Chile revealed that another society had stumbled upon the secrets of mummification long before the Egyptians. More than two and a half millennia before morticians along the Nile began waving flies away from cadavers, coastal dwellers in Chile had begun skillfully preserving their dead along the parched edges of the Atacama Desert, fabricating mummies of such singular beauty that they continue to haunt South Americans today.

The Chinchorro mummies, as they are now known, are the world's oldest mummies. Concealed within iridescent black and red masks and bodysuits, they personify, quite literally, the human desire to transcend the frailties of the body and the distintegration of self. Elevating death into something reassuringly, hauntingly beautiful, they are among the most complex mummies ever made in the ancient world. "I'm still mesmerized by the care the Chinchorro put into reconstructing these bodies," said anthropologist Bernardo

Arriaza, "because very often we tend to be shocked by the dead. We don't want to be around them. But it's hard to distance yourself from these mummies. They are not just archaeological artifacts, they're human beings who were trying to be preserved."

Arriaza is a leading authority on the Chinchorro mummies and his devotion to these ancient bodies is legendary. I first met him at the Mummy Congress, after he had given a paper on his latest research, and I was immediately struck by the fervor in his voice whenever the talk turned to the Chinchorro. A Chilean from the vineyard country south of Santiago, Arriaza teaches physical anthropology at the University of Nevada in Las Vegas, a strange place for a man of his interests to end up. But Arriaza, as it turned out, has never given up Chile. He dreams of returning, taking his American wife and young American son with him. But until then, he remains staunchly Chilean at heart. A Chilean flag drapes one of the walls of his office in Las Vegas and on the monitor of his computer flashes his own personal screen-saver: a superb photo of one of the Chinchorro mummies.

As a kind of restorative, Arriaza returns each summer to Chile, working long hours on the collection of ancient bodies at the University of Tarapacá. In between these journeys, he analyzes, lectures, and dreams about Chinchorro mummies. At any one time, he had half a dozen different schemes on the go to help preserve and protect them. He is working with local artists to create a portfolio of painted portraits of the Chinchorro mummies. He is writing popular articles and directing amateur videos. He is even mulling over a plan for mummy performance art at the

Burning Man Festival held each year in Nevada—anything to get these ancient mummies better known.

In short, Arriaza is something of a dreamer when it comes to the Chinchorro. But to look at him, there is little hint of a man whose waking thoughts constantly circle around something so old and so cold in the ground. In his early forties, Arriaza is olive-skinned and disconcertingly handsome, with hazel-green eyes, angular chin, chiseled features, and a heavy five-o'clock shadow. He wears a goatee, smiles infrequently, and dresses for comfort, not style, in rumpled polo shirts and khaki pants. He looks more like an artist than a scientist—a painter, perhaps—and this and his air of careless self-absorption seem to have a magnetic effect on many women, even those who have never laid eyes on him. On one occasion, after I had finished writing a magazine article about his work, a young fact-checker called breathlessly out of the blue from New York with a pressing question. "Is he really as good-looking as he is in his photos?" she asked, sighing audibly.

I am never entirely certain whether Arriaza realizes the effect he has on women. But there is a legendary quality to it. His wife, Vicki Cassman, told me that she had gotten to know him while he was conducting autopsies on mummies at the museum at the University of Tarapacá, an atmosphere about as seductive as a funeral parlor. To make matters worse, Cassman was a young conservator at the time. She was ethically, morally, and emotionally opposed to anyone destroying fragile mummies and hated the thought of someone cutting into their brittle flesh. Logic suggested that she should have detested Arriaza. But after just a few days of watching the young anthropologist, she fell head over heels in love.

Arriaza had begun working on mummies in Arica by a lucky chance. His father was a former miner and had relatives in Arica, so Arriaza had enrolled at university there. When he graduated, he'd gotten a job at the local museum. In his second year, the museum had received a call from someone at the local water company. A crew had been out bulldozing a channel for a new waterline along the sandy lower slopes of a local promontory, El Morro. The bulldozer blade had suddenly bitten into some sort of cemetery, but not anything recent. The ground was littered with a handful of strange-looking bodies. Arriaza and some of his colleagues hustled out to take a look. By the time they arrived, a big crowd had begun to gather. The officials from the water company were trying to keep them back. In the sand were pieces of five masked mummies.

Arriaza and his colleagues knew at once what they were. In 1917, the famous German archaeologist Max Uhle had accidentally exhumed a few similar mummies while digging in Arica. After that, researchers had turned up the odd masked mummy here and there along the north coast of Chile. They were exceedingly rare, but everyone agreed that they belonged to an early Andean people whom Chilean archaeologists had dubbed the Chinchorro, after a beach where one of their villages first came to light. The Chinchorro had lived and died by the whims of the sea. They had fished with intricate knotted nets, harpooned sea lions, consumed hallucinogenic plants from the Amazon, adorned themselves with necklaces of lapis lazuli and exotic bird feathers, wrapped cotton turbans around their heads, and lived in villages of reed or skin-covered huts whose floors were plastered with clay and seaweed.

But no one knew very much about their mummies, for there had never been a discovery to match the one at El Morro. Over the next few months, Arriaza's colleagues recovered ninety-six Chinchorro bodies scattered helter-skelter over seventy-five square feet of sand. Many were artificially mummified and of these each had a molded paste mask bearing a slightly different expression. It almost seemed as if the Chinchorro morticians had tried to capture an abstract likeness of the person within. A few of the mummies were clumped together—a woman with pendulous paste breasts, a man with a paste penis, and several children—as if they had belonged together as a family. But other than that and the fact that most faced out to sea, there were no orderly graves and very few grave goods. It almost looked as if the mummies had never really been intentionally buried at all.

This seemed odd to Arriaza, but he didn't have much time to mull over its meaning. He had begun working for Marvin Allison, a well-known mummy expert and pathologist from the University of Virginia who had taken on the analysis of the mummies. Allison wanted to age and sex each of the Chinchorro bodies and look for signs of disease. An autocratic, difficult man, he was a great believer in autopsy, but between the newfound Chinchorro mummies and the natural mummies he was already studying, there were simply too many bodies and too little time for thorough analysis. He needed an assistant, someone he could train to gather the necessary data and perform mummy autopsies. So he chose Arriaza, giving the young Chilean an intensive crash course in pathology and anatomy.

Arriaza was in awe of Allison and his immense knowledge of anatomy, anthropology, pathology, and South American prehistory. He was also fascinated by the thought of working on the rare mummies that Uhle had first described sixty-four years earlier. So he began soaking up all the lessons that Allison generously imparted. But as he began dissecting a few of the most fragmented Chinchorro mummies himself, Arriaza felt a deep, unexpected sorrow. He hated adding to the indignities these bodies had already suffered. Moreover, he found it almost impossible to ignore their humanity and artistry. With the help of colleague Vivien Standen, he began recording every step he took and every layer he cut through, hoping to reconstruct on paper exactly how each mummy had been made.

Soon, however, even these elaborate efforts seemed woefully inadequate. After thinking things over, he informed Allison that he wouldn't be doing any more mummy autopsies. The pathologist was infuriated about having to take over the remaining dissections. By this point, however, Arriaza couldn't bear to see any more destruction. He began a kind of covert operation, hiding away mummies to keep them from Allison's hands.

THE CHINCHORRO BODIES that Arriaza had managed to save are housed at the University of Tarapacá in Arica, just down the street from the fabled Restaurant of the Dead. I badly wanted to see them. I suspected that no photos could ever do them justice, and I wanted to learn, if I could, what had prompted the Chinchorro to begin making such elaborate mummies so very long ago. Arriaza seemed pleased to arrange a visit. So, on a Friday afternoon in May, I scrambled out of a cab to meet him on the dusty University of Tarapacá campus. A short walk brought us to a small garagelike building set in a field of olive trees. A faded sign on the door read LABORATORIO ARQUEOLOGIA TIERRAS ALTAS, a legacy I guessed from some previous occupant.

Inside, Arriaza brushed absently past a broad sunlit counter where someone had laid out dozens of old human bones in neat rows. Scattered between were patches of crinkled tinfoil, each cradling a blackened mummified human foot or a hand. A strong mucilaginous smell wafted up from the table: it was the scent of ancient human bone warmed by sunlight. Arriaza, however, took no notice. Trading a joke with Vivien Standen, he reached for a set of keys and unlocked the door to the back room. Flicking on the light, he stepped to one side. Along the far wall were rows of shelving units that stood almost to the ceiling. Each was lined with heavy gray boxes. It was a good deal less than state-of-the-art storage for such important mummies, but it was all that the university could afford.

Arriaza walked over to one of the shelves. With immense care, he eased off the lid from one of the boxes, revealing a tiny outstretched body on a bed of sand. In the soft light, I bent over to take a closer look. It was a child, no more than a toddler, covered in a crumbling, flaking layer of blue-black clay. The tiny eyes of its mask were closed and its mouth drawn shut as if sleeping, like some primitive African idol or a modern Henry Moore sculpture. The effect was very beautiful. But its small body was slowly falling to pieces. A network of deep cracks and fissures zigzagged like ugly open wounds across the paste upon its torso. Sticks and human bones poked out from a sleeve of human skin, where the protective clay had dissipated into powdery dust. It looked as if one more shaking, perhaps even one more nudge, would be the end of the child: the body had the sad look of a badly used doll or a battered child. I wanted very much to protect it.

Arriaza slipped the lid back on gently. Then he showed me another Chinchorro mummy, and another, until at last we had looked at seven or eight. Almost all were children. As I straightened and looked around at all the small boxes, I realized that I was standing in a morgue of the very young. That they had died thousands of years ago took away none of the chill of that silent place and its boxes. Some of the children had been only old enough to take their first swaggering baby steps; others had been unable even to crawl. And a few, the most touching of all, had perished in their mothers' wombs. But each child, no matter how small or how young, had been exquisitely prepared for eternity with tiny paste masks and bodysuits. "It's the emotion of love that's represented here," said Arriaza gently, "taking all that care to mummify a little fetus. That is very, very touching."

Such tender concern is a rarity in human societies, explained Arriaza. Among most modern societies, stillborn babies and young infants seldom receive much in the way of funerals or send-offs, for they have yet to become full members of society. "In some parts of the world, if you are not baptized, you are not even considered to be a person," Arriaza noted. But the ancient Chinchorro had clearly seen things in a different light. They had known and under-stood—as grief counselors do today—that the pain parents feel after the death of a child is not commensurate with age: the loss of a day-old infant can be just as devastating as that of a two-year-old. "The Chinchorro seemed to honor all human beings whether they contributed to society or not," observed Arriaza in one recent paper, "paying particular attention to those who never reached their potential."

That the Chinchorro should have understood the psy-chology of grief so well is understandable: they had a good deal of experience with it. In an age before modern medicine, Chinchorro infants had regularly fallen victim to a host of bacterial, parasitic, and viral infections. Indeed, one in every four Chinchorro children perished before reaching the age of one. This meant that nearly every Chinchorro mother had suffered the agonizing loss of at least one of her children: undoubtedly, some mourned many more. Arriaza, good sci-entist that he is, could not say for certain what effect this had had on them, but he believes that it was considerable. Indeed, he suspects that such grief had driven Chinchorro parents to invent mummification in the first place, for only children were intentionally and elaborately preserved in the earliest Chinchorro cemeteries.

This made a touching kind of sense, since modern psy-chiatric studies have revealed just how traumatizing the death of a child is for most parents. Never expecting that their child—the object of their deepest affections—would die before them, grief-stricken mothers often enter into an altered state of consciousness that they describe as some-where between life and death. In such a state of mind, wrote

Finnish therapist Leena Väisänen, they frequently experience eerie dreams and abnormal psychic and physical phenomena. They long for the babies they have lost and feel an unbearable sense of emptiness and yearning that resembles physical pain. Indeed, most of these women are unable to stop acting as mothers, even though their children are gone. Biologically and hormonally driven to keep their infants alive, they yearn to continue caring for them. In these circumstances, wrote Väisänen, a mother "is constantly preoccupied with the baby, the grave, and death." They want to stay as close as possible to their infants. Often this need is so overpowering that they create phantom babies in their minds to replace the children who were lost.

Under the sway of such grief, a Chinchorro mother could easily have conceived of the idea of preserving and beautifying the body of her infant. Such a notion may well have become the heart of a soothing ritual handed down for generations among the Chinchorro. Similar ceremonies, after all, are held in other cultures. In Japan, for example, grieving parents take part in a ceremony to call upon a Buddhist god known as Jizo, the custodian of crossroads, to guide the soul of their stillborn children to safety. In honor of this event, they buy or make babylike statues, dress them in baby clothing, then place them along country roads or in the halls of temples. Chinchorro parents may have done something similar, with a mummified child as the focus instead of a mere statue.

Certainly some of the elaborate ministrations involved in making a mummy would have filled the need of mourning mothers to continue caring and tending for their lost children. The earliest mummies, noted Arriaza, had taken weeks of finicky work. The Chinchorro had delicately removed the child's skin, rolling it off delicately like pantyhose, then stripped the body to bare bone. After reinforcing the skeleton with sticks, they tied the skeleton back together again, plumping it out with bunches of reeds. Then came the artistry. Daubing on a thick ashy paste that dried like clay, they molded facial features and bodily contours, then slipped the skin back over the body and crowned the head with a wig. This left only a final coat of shimmering blue-black paint. This they made from tiny particles of manganese that peppered the sand of a local Arica beach. To obtain enough of this metal pigment to paint a child, someone had to sift through handfuls of sand for many hours— busywork that might have appealed to a heartbroken mother. Then they had to mix the manganese with water and apply it to the mummy with a fine grass brush, polishing it to a smooth iridescent gleam.

Seeing a lost child reborn as a beautiful new being may have eased the heavy hearts of mourners, noted Arriaza. "When a person dies, he gets separated from society and that's going to be a shock for the living. The dead person is in a kind of limbo. But when the Chinchorro had finished preparing the body, the person could be brought back into society again and this would have been a celebration of the dead." With their children restored to the world of the living, Chinchorro parents wanted to keep them close. Rather than burying the gleaming bodies deep in the ground, they seem to have lain them gently, like living people, on the sand. For years afterward, families tended them faithfully, gently painting and repainting all their tiny nicks and dents.

Such a ritual must have helped ease the sorrow of loss, for Chinchorro families continued to perform it for more than three thousand years. But as the centuries passed, the ceremony evolved and changed. Instead of reserving mummification only for the very young, families preserved all their kith and kin tenderly. Everyone was treated the same. "Whereas the Egyptians considered only kings and other exalted citizens worthy of mummification," noted Arriaza, "the Chinchorro accorded everyone in the community, regardless of age and status, this sacred rite." The Chinchorro also began to envision the dead in a subtly different way, creating mummy masks to reflect this. Instead of scratching two lines for eyes and another for a closed mouth, they punched two tiny holes for eyes and drilled another, larger one for a mouth. By these simple acts, the Chinchorro mummies suddenly gazed out intently at the world, awake, alert, ready to listen to the living. "The Chinchorro did not separate death from life," said Arriaza. "The eyes of the mummies were open, their mouths were open. So for the Chinchorro, the dead were not dead. They had just gone through a change of state."

Capable of communicating through the voice of a priest or shaman, such transcendant beings made superb go-betweens with the spirit world. They could advise, counsel, intercede, and wield their considerable influence on behalf of their kin. The Chinchorro must have happily poured out their troubles to them, for it was natural for families to speak to their ancestors. In time, the dead became almost as essential to life as the living, and so intimately linked were the two that this bond lasted almost as long as the Chinchorro themselves. When the mummy makers finally vanished under mysterious circumstances from northern Chile around 1100 B.C., they left behind their greatest treasures— sandy slopes adorned with painted mummies, which the desert and the wind slowly enshrouded in sand.

THE IMMENSE REVERENCE and love that the Chinchorro felt for their mummies did not die with them, however. It became deeply embedded in the lives of Andean people along the coast and nearby mountains, although later societies took a simpler approach to preserving the dead, well aware that dry desert air would do much of the work for them. Many chose to bundle up cadavers in immense absorbent cotton shrouds that soaked up the body's moisture, speeding the drying needed for mummification. It is possible that some went further still. On Peru's southern coast, archaeologist Julio Tello found evidence that the Paracas people removed the internal organs from their illustrious dead and dried their remains by fires before wrapping them in some of the finest woven cloth ever produced in South America. Other researchers have disputed these finds, however.

Be that as it may, no Andean society kept the faith in mummies burning as fiercely as the Inca. The Inca believed that the preserved dead were still alive. They also believed that these withered bodies were willing to offer their wisdom and lend their life force to that of nature to ensure bountiful harvests. In return for all this, the living had to treat them with respect and tend to their physical needs. They had to give them coca leaves to chew and beer to quench their thirst. They had to help them urinate by lifting the hems of their tunics at appropriate moments. They also had to ensure that they were properly dressed and sheltered, and, in the view of some scholars, this explains why each new Inca king built his own palace and acquired his own servants and estates through taxation. The splendid house and property of his predecessor would be needed for his predecessor's mummy and commemorative cult. "Some people have argued that that's the reason the Inca kept expanding their territory until the Spanish arrived," said Arriaza. "They had to look for new places to conquer. Their previous lands belonged to the dead."

Indeed, it could be said that the might of the great Inca empire, which stretched from the rain forests of Colombia to the deserts of northern Chile, rested on mummies, for seldom did Inca emperors make a major decision without first consulting the preserved bodies of their ancestors. Deeply grateful for their advice, Inca sovereigns paid them every possible respect. When Atahualpa fell captive to the Spanish during a treacherous ambush at Cajamarca, he sent one of his own lords with a small party of Spanish officers to Cuzco to gather up the ransom. In the Inca capital, the officers set to work immediately on the temple of the sun, prying off its outer golden plaques with copper crowbars. Then they entered a large house nearby. There the plunderers found a woman in a golden mask fanning two royal mummies. The bodies were dressed lavishly in rich ornaments and held beautiful gold staves in their arms. Pizarro's men immediately set about stripping them of their finery. But avaricious as they were, they stopped short. Atahualpa, a proud man, had begged them not to take everything: one of the mummies was his own father.

With this rich ransom in hand, the Spanish leader Francisco Pizarro had little further need of his royal captive.

He tried and convicted the Inca emperor on trumped-up charges, then sentenced Atahualpa to death by fire, the Spanish punishment for idolators. For Atahualpa, this was an unbearable thought. Being reduced to ashes meant that he could never become a mummy or enjoy eternity as an honored ancestor among his descendants. To escape this miserable fate—one that the Inca had reserved only for their most detested enemies—the emperor converted to Christianity just shortly before his execution, taking the baptismal name of Juan de Atahualpa. This entitled him to death by strangulation and a Christian burial in the ground, where his body might naturally mummify.

In the months that followed, Pizarro tightened his hold over the Inca, until at last he secured the city of Cuzco. His army looted the temple of the sun, and Pizarro himself moved into the largest of the Inca palaces, which had housed the mummy of Atahualpa's father. But the stories of the mummified sovereigns disquieted many of Pizarro's men: they reminded them uncomfortably of the saintly Incorruptibles they had left behind in Europe. How, they wondered, could such miraculous preservation have taken place among such blatant heathens? The Spanish priests hastened to set their minds at rest. Trained during the Spanish Inquisition, the priests had learned to detect any whiff of the devil's work. Demons, they explained, were masters of deception. They were capable of assuming many forms to hoodwink the naive—even that of an Incorruptible. As such, the mummies had to be stamped out. And this had to be done with all the efficiency the new Spanish colonial authorities could muster, which was considerable.

Alarmed, the Inca quietly spirited away as many of the royal mummies as they could into the countryside. The word for these bodies in Quechua, after all, means "something precious and carefully kept." And for nearly two decades, they concealed the mummies of their imperial family in small villages outside Cuzco. But in 1559, a clever Spanish official in Cuzco, Juan Polo de Ondegardo, began a concerted search for them. He managed to ferret out the hiding places of several, retrieving the bodies of at least three Inca emperors and two of their consorts. The Spanish were astonished by their appearance. "The bodies were so intact," wrote the chronicler Garcilaso de la Vega later, "that they lacked neither hair, eyebrows, nor eyelashes. They were in clothes just as they had worn while alive, with llautas [bands] wrapping their heads, but no other sign of royalty."

Polo and his associates made little secret of their discoveries, creating quite a stir. According to de la Vega, "They carried them in white shrouds through the streets and plazas, the Indians dropping to their knees, making reverences with groans and tears, and many Spaniards removing their caps." Still Polo couldn't quite bring himself to destroy the Inca sovereigns, even though he knew they were a potent political force. Under orders from the Spanish viceroy, the Marquis de Canete, he dispatched the bodies to Lima, where they were put on public display in 1560, forming a kind of early mummy museum. Finally in 1580, the Spanish authorities decided to dispose of the withered cadavers. They gathered up five of them and buried them beneath the courtyard of one of Lima's earliest hospitals.

But that was not the end of the Inca mummies. Unknown to the Spanish, the love of the preserved dead permeated the length and breadth of the Inca empire. Far beyond Cuzco, there were thousands of humbler mummies, each as intertwined and enmeshed in the lives of ordinary people as veins and arteries are in human flesh. The mummies were just as essential. In the Andes and the Atacama Desert, people did not see death as the end of life. Instead they believed it was just the beginning of a new and more influential phase as a revered ancestor who could lend assistance to the living. In mountain caves and burial houses across the Andes, humble farmers visited mummies of their local leaders by moonlight, bringing corn beer and coca leaves for their comfort. They mended the mummies' clothes and spilled out the sorrows of their time. They sought advice from them on all important matters, even soliciting their opinions on marriage partners for their children.

When the Spanish authorities finally understood the extent of this mummy religion in the Andes, they were horrified. They believed—rightly—that Christianity could never take root in a land possessed of such powerful beliefs. So the Spanish clergy embarked on a campaign modeled upon the Inquisition. They decided to extinguish the ancient worship of mummies and other idolatries in the region. They rode out into the countryside and began searching for mummies hidden in caves and remote mountain shrines. Slowly, one by one, they confiscated the ancient bodies and arrested their tenders. Their successes gave them confidence. They wrote detailed how-to guides for finding mummies, complete with a list of ready-made interrogation questions for their protectors.

. These guides greatly honed their skills as mummy hunters. In 1607, for example, one well-trained Spanish clergyman went to work in the small Peruvian town of Huarochiri. Francisco de Avila sought out and arrested native priests, seized a large pile of mummies, and carted the whole lot off to Lima for an auto-da-fé in the city's largest square. At Avila's beckoning, soldiers tied one of the unrepentant native priests to a stake at one end of the plaza and stacked mummies and other sacred objects in a bonfire pile at the other. As Peru's viceroy looked on, Avila preached to the people of Lima in Quechua, exhorting them to give up their mummies and other idols. Then he theatrically lit the bonfire. As the dead bodies crackled in the flames, he ordered the recalcitrant native priest brought forward for a public flogging. This done, he exiled the unfortunate man to a Catholic house hundreds of kilometers away in Chile. Then Avila dismissed the somber crowd.

In the decades that followed, there were many other similar spectacles, and these, even more than the conquest itself, took the heart from the Andean people. They couldn't bear to see their beloved mummies so brutally treated. "See, these people did not fear death," said Arriaza. "What they really feared was death without the possibility of coming back. So when the Spanish burned and buried the Inca mummies and other mummies, the Andean people were devastated."

Some colonial officials in Lima knew that they would never be able to track down and destroy all of the mummies. The bodies were too well hidden and the Andeans would never give them up willingly. So as a further measure, the officials came up with another plan. They ordered the removal and resettlement of entire villages, thereby severing the ties between the people and any remaining mummy shrines and local gods. The scheme sounded foolproof, but it had one major flaw. There was nothing to stop inhabitants from creating new shrines with new mummies. So the Spanish clergy forced their reluctant parishioners to begin burying their dead as Christians did theirs in Europe—beneath church floors.

The descendants of the Inca hated to do this. They confided to local priests that they were tormented by the voices of their dead parents and grandparents, who called out to them piteously through the church floors. Unable to rest comfortably in their new tombs, the dead told them they felt like prisoners. They could no longer sit upright and move around as they had in their old shrines: they were pinned down in graves that felt like straightjackets.

In time, the plaintive voices of the dead began to fade in the Andes. The descendants of the Inca embraced Catholicism and prayed fervently, as the Spanish did, to the Incorruptibles. But in Chile, said Arriaza, they did not forget the ancient religion of the land. Nor did they shed their old beliefs about the dead. This more than anything else, he said, explained why the country remained so troubled after the rule of General Augusto Pinochet. During the general's regime, army officers arrested hundreds of Chilean activists and dissidents, who subsequently vanished without a trace. The executions had taken place decades ago, but Chileans were incapable of closing that chapter of their history. Pinochet's greatest wrong, said Arriaza, was not in arresting and murdering his opponents, as terrible as that was. It was in destroying and hiding the bodies, for this meant that Chileans could never bring the dead dissidents back into the world of the living.

And that was something the descendants of the Inca could never forgive nor forget.

SELF-PRESERVATION

⟋

A CERTAIN POETIC TRUTH LAY in what Arriaza said, and it seemed perfectly possible to me that these ancient ideas still stirred and fermented in Chile today. I had discovered long ago from my writing about archaeology that rituals for the dead are among the most conservative and enduring of all cultural traditions, changing only gradually over time. This makes much sense from a psychological point of view. Our relations with the dead are fraught with bewildering emotions—regret, sorrow, guilt, fear, longing, and hope—and mourners feel bound to do all they can to make things right at the end. For most, this entails falling back on familiar, time-honored formulas of solace, whatever those might be—vigils, eulogies, last rites, mummification, funerals, graveside partings, wakes. To depart from these too radically has long seemed a sign of disrespect to the dead, a kind of casual good riddance at parting.

So I didn't doubt that many Chileans still revere the dead and feel a deep psychic attachment to their bodies. Indeed, I had come to suspect something of the sort during the final morning of the Mummy Congress in Arica. After nearly a week in the confines of the congress hall, concentrating on an assembly line of papers delivered in two languges at a frenetic staccato pace, and after evenings spent socializing over bottles of Chilean cabernet with the strange crowd of mummy experts I had fallen in with, I was beginning to feel rather the worse for wear. I had been barely able to drag myself out of bed. I was certainly not alone; more than half the chairs in the congress hall for that last morning were empty. But as Chilean researcher Julia Cordova took to the podium and began warming to her subject, "The Fascination for Mummies," I felt my interest pique again.

Cordova had taken it upon herself to conduct a small survey at the nearby archaeological museum in San Miguel de Azapa, which houses, among other things, a splendid display of Chinchorro mummies. She wanted to find out what visitors thought about the mummies on exhibit, and people had kindly obliged her. Just over half of those she talked to ranked the ancient bodies as the most impressive part of the museum: three-quarters badly wanted to see more of the preserved bodies. But the thing that interested me most was a rather odd question Cordova had slipped into the survey: "Would *you* like to be mummified?" I was very curious about the results. Thirty-one percent of the respondents, it transpired, were all in favor of being mummified. They definitely wanted their bodies preserved. But the majority, 60 percent to be exact, demurred at the thought: they feared that future generations would put them on display in a museum.

Cordova's survey said a great deal about the fascination that many Chileans still feel for the preserved dead, but it occurred to me later that her results also perfectly captured a curious paradox about mummies I had noticed. We are, most of us at least, enthralled by the sight of ancient preserved bodies, with their gaunt faces, their fringe of eyelashes, their tresses and curls, their lustrous fingernails, and their bony leanness. We are enchanted by the immortality that they represent. Even so, most of us shrink from the thought of actually becoming one ourselves. We are repelled by the vision of the embalmer's cold loveless hands on our bodies. We shudder at the idea of being stripped, splayed, inspected, carved into, hollowed out, stuffed, chemically treated, and wrapped. Most of all, however, we fear the prospect of looking less than our best for eternity, serving as pathetic figures of fun for future generations.

These, of course, are all legitimate fears, quite enough to convince most that speedy putrefaction is far preferable to lingering, moth-eaten mummification. But in some parts of the world, people are unable to relinquish the idea of eternity so easily. To transcend death, they have embarked on a bizarre quest: to preserve and mummify their own bodies. In America and Europe, for example, a host of new industries has arisen to pander to these desires among aging baby boomers. As I began thinking about these rabid self-preservationists—it was impossible to ignore them—I became very curious. I wondered just how far human beings were prepared to go in their quest for immortality. How far was I prepared to go? In search of answers, I turned first to some of the world's most extreme self-preservationists: a select group of ancient Buddhist monks in Japan who had perfected the art of self-mummification.

~

IWATORO MORIMOTO WAS in failing health and said as much in the very first lines of his neatly typed letter. Felled just three months earlier by a major stroke, the venerable Japanese anatomist explained in flawless English that he was now paralyzed along one side of his body and that his heart could no longer be depended upon: it relied for its spark on the invisible circuitry of a pacemaker. For Morimoto, a man of great curiosity who had studied mummies from Egypt to Bolivia, this was a luckless fate. His life had begun shrinking into smaller and smaller circles. As a result, Morimoto had reluctantly decided to retire from his post at the Japanese Red Cross College of Nursing in Tokyo and had set aside his research on Japan's little-known Buddhist mummies.

Japan, let it be said straight off, is not a place where many specialists would bother looking for mummies. There are good reasons for this, the first being environment. In the north, the climate swings wildly between hot, sultry summers and bitter winters, with a few typhoons thrown in for good measure; in the south, conditions are subtropical. Neither seems terribly promising for natural preservation of a human cadaver. Then there are the Japanese themselves. By ancient tradition, they abhor dead bodies: They see corpses as impure, and this sense of repugnance runs deeper still among the country's many Buddhists. To them, according to Buddhist scholar Robert Sharf, a dead body is nothing more than "a lifeless lump of fetid flesh to be disposed of posthaste." To rid themselves of this rubbish in times past, families cremated or buried their dead; not to do so smacked of ignorance, for Buddhists saw the body as something inherently transient.

So Morimoto and his medical colleagues were much taken by surprise in 1961 when they learned of the chance discovery of six mummies of Buddhist priests hidden away in temples in the remote northwestern mountains of Japan. The news seemed too bizarre to credit, but it turned out to be absolutely true. Devout Buddhists had tended to the mummies for centuries, although they were not much to look at. Most of the bodies were mottled, blackened, and thin to the point of emaciation; they sat crumpled over in a lotus position, wearing the grotesque rictus of death. Holes gaped in the chests of some like great rips in a sere cloth. Others looked as ragged and torn as mangled toys. Yet all the same, dutiful priests had enshrined them in special halls in their gilded temples and guarded them carefully: only a small group of modern devotees knew anything about them. Television crews from Tokyo raced to the remote region to capture the images for an astonished public.

Japanese anthropologists, historians, folklorists, and religious scholars were entranced by these discoveries. So, too, were many medical people. They formed an official committee led by the late Kôsei Andô and set about ferreting out more of these ancient priests. Eventually they counted nearly two dozen throughout the country. Most of these priests had lived between the twelfth and the nineteenth centuries and many were followers of Shugen-dô, an antique form of Buddhism that blended elements of mountain worship, shamanism, Taoism, and magic. Those priests who devoted their lives to Shugen-dô retired from the world and made their homes for many years in lonely places with names like the Swamp of Wizards. There they lived lives of great asceticism. They crawled up to tiny shrines on sheer mountain pinnacles and immersed themselves for hours in cold waterfalls. They sat in rooms filled with the stinging smoke from burning peppers.

By such acts of self-denial, Morimoto learned, Shugen-dô masters obtained great powers for the good. These they often employed on their travels through the countryside in order to to protect others. Indeed, some legends described the magical ways in which these priests controlled nature itself, curbing plagues, droughts, earthquakes, and typhoons. The eighteenth-century master Tetsumon-kai, for example, was particularly renowned for his feats of healing. According to legend, Tetsumon-kai once ripped out his own left eye in order to earn enough divine merit to cure the sufferers of an infectious eye disease. On another memorable occasion, he reportedly lopped off his own genitals.

As old age approached, Tetsumon-kai and other great Shugen-dô ascetics began contemplating death. If they could transform, by dint of their immense self-discipline, the sickly transience of flesh into something immutable and eternal, they could perfect the self and become enlightened beings, Buddhas. So Tetsumon-kai and others set about mummifying themselves. For a thousand days or more, they abstained from eating the staples of their diet: rice, barley, soybeans, red beans, sesame seeds, millet, broomcorn, panic-grass seeds, buckwheat, and corn. They nibbled only at such things as the bark of pine trees or the meat of torreya nuts and sometimes they sipped at bowls of lacquer, a varnish made from tree resin. As they grew weaker, they endured all the torments of slow starvation: bone-weariness, melancholia, mental dullness, and endless cravings for food. When at last they were little more than skin and bone, they announced their readiness for death. Some asked to be buried alive in wooden caskets. Others died chanting in stone chambers underground. Only later did their disciples open these tombs. The ascetics, said legend, were untouched by decay. Their followers were practical men, however: they often salted or smoked the mummified bodies to further preserve them.

Morimoto and many of his medical colleagues were intrigued by these stories. They wondered how much truth lay in them. Had the Shugen-dô masters really succeeded in mummifying themselves or had their followers secretly practiced some unknown form of artificial preservation? The physicians decided to investigate. Like modern pilgrims, they toured the Buddhist shrines and, with the permission of the priests, undressed and studied the mummies. The stories of self-mummification, they soon discovered, were true. Only one of the Shugen-dô masters they found, the nineteenth-century abbot Tetsuryu-kai, had failed to mummify naturally in the tomb. Morimoto concluded that the mysterious diet of the ascetics had played a vital part in what had transpired. "By abstaining from five or ten cereals during three years or more while in life," he observed in *Acta Anatomica Nipponica*, a prominent Japanese medical journal, "the [priests'] body composition was altered to be strongly resistant to decomposition."

Just how human flesh could be so transformed by these methods has never been scientifically tested—perhaps because so few people today are willing to volunteer for experiments which would have them dining out for years on sparse salads of pine bark and torreya nuts washed down by bowls of lacquer. But as I mulled over Morimoto's papers and neatly typed letters, I realized that this fierce desire to transcend the ceaseless ticking of the clock and to escape the ruinous touch of time was not confined to an obscure cult of ancient Buddhist priests. It blazes intensely in modern North America and Europe. To ward off the first portents of decay—sagging skin, rippling cellulite, flabby stomachs, and drooping rears—millions of baby boomers have turned into ascetics, too, devoting themselves to the new cult of fitness and beauty.

Indeed, I am no stranger to this cult myself. Like many others of my generation, I hustle off daily to the local temple of sweat for my own regular ritual of self-denial. As I heave and hoist, crunch and curse, I watch my fellow devotees closely. Surrounded by mirrors and outfitted in form-fitting Tactel and Lycra, they grimace and wince as they push themselves to the brink of exhaustion. They pump iron, jump rope, pound rubber, spin wheels, crunch abs, squeeze glutes, tighten triceps until their weary muscles vibrate like tuning forks. On the weekends, they rise at dawn for fun runs, marathons, triathalons, and dragon-boat races; in their spare time, they mountain-bike, canoe, kayak, ski, snow-board, windsurf, and kickbox. In the locker room each day, they pirouette and preen in front of the full-length mirrors, checking for the slightest sign of decrepitude.

To stay motivated is no easy matter. But, like other devotees, they have found sources of inspiration. Indeed, they even have their own Incorruptibles. The most famous of these is undoubtedly Jane Fonda, whose exercise videos exact much admiration and whose motto, "Discipline is liberation," seems so apt. It isn't so much Fonda's workouts, *Lean Routine* and *Favorite Fat Burners*, that dazzle; these are thorough, but they are rather routine. Instead, what truly fascinates the fitness crowd is the spectacle of Fonda's uncanny youth. The actress was well into her fifties when she filmed *Favorite Fat Burners*. Decades past her *Barbarella* days, she appeared more svelte, toned, and youthful than many a twenty-year-old. No mere exercise regime seemed able to account for such superb physical condition. Self-preservationists shook their heads in awe: Fonda's flat stomach and lean thighs seemed proof that miracles could and did happen in the gym.

As age takes its toll, however, many devotees move on to other forms of self-preservation. They radically prune their diets. An intimate relationship exists, after all, between the natural process of growing older and the accumulation of fat. As American feminist Naomi Wolf has pointed out, postadolescent women naturally put on fat tissue, which is needed by the body to store sex hormones and maintain fertility. Cross-cultural studies reveal that the average middle-aged women is padded with nearly 38 percent body fat, a big jump from the 28.7 percent layering the body of a twenty-year-old. Such increases, observed Wolf in her book *The Beauty Myth*, have little to do with North America's penchant for batter-fried potatoes, Big Macs, Häagen-Dazs ice cream, and double-foam lattes. "They are norms characteristic of the female of the species."

Even so, few women watch the creeping advance of their scales with anything less than despair. Intent on staying willowy and young, many shun food with a sense of self-discipline that would do a Shugen-dô master proud. Moving relentlessly from one diet to another, from Pritikin to Dr. Atkins, and from Weight Watchers to The Zone, they sup for days at a time on cabbage soup and grapefruit and sip at carrot juice and vinegar. They boost their serotonin levels and balance their eicosanoids. They fret daily about their weight, commiserating in the locker room with their many dieting friends. "On any day," writes Wolf, "25 percent of women are on diets, with 50 percent finishing, breaking, or starting one."

To reach their ideal of thinness, many endure what Wolf has dubbed "self-inflicted semistarvation." A woman on the Hilton Head Metabolism Diet, one of North America's best-selling diets, dines on child-sized portions of protein and carbohydrates, consuming just 800 calories a day. This is far less than the 2,000 to 2,250 calories that a moderately active woman needs daily. On such spartan fare, dieters are consumed with hunger. They crave thick porterhouse steaks, bowls of buttery mashed potatoes, desserts of crème brûlée and custardy torte. Their thoughts are absorbed with food. Those as disciplined as a Shugen-dô master end up with gaunt, gawky, pubescent bodies. On occasion, they also end up fatally anorexic. What I find haunting is just how much these shrunken women resemble dessicated mummies.

For some of my generation, however, self-denial at the table and in the gym are only halfway measures. They venture further still, waging war on time and nature with the scalpel and the cosmetic surgeon's skill. Between 1990 and 1999 alone, the number of liposuctions performed in America skyrocketed by 800 percent. Tummy tucks soared higher still, at 1,280 percent. And these procedures by no means exhaust the austerities that baby boomers are willing to endure. Gritting their teeth, they undergo microabrasion, laser resurfacing, face-lifts, and ultrasound lypolysis. In 1999 alone, nearly 623,588 Americans—a population roughly the size of Milwaukee—submitted to botox treatments, the injection of a paralyzing toxin, botulinum, into facial muscles to temporarily erase furrows and frown lines.

Few cosmetic surgeons like to think of themselves as being in the mummification business. Their promotional materials stress the leading-edge research that they bring to bear on the anti-aging industry. But some enterpreneurs make no secret of what they are about. A few years ago, Christian Fischer, an expert on bog bodies and the director of Norway's Silkeborg Museum, received a peculiar phone call from an American businessman. He had an unusual question: he wanted to know who owned the bog where the best preserved of all Europe's ancient bog bodies, Tollund Man, had been discovered. As it turned out, the caller wanted to buy the rights to bottle the essence of this peat for a women's anti-aging cream. Fischer assumed the inquiry was little more than a prank. A few years later, however, an English colleague mailed him a leaflet she found tucked into a package of skin cream, the Essence of Time. The lotion's key ingredient was pulverized peat from England's Lindow bog, home of Lindow Man. The accompanying leaflet described the mummy's exceptional preservation, noting that the skin of Lindow Man was soft and flexible and his nails neatly manicured. The secret, claimed the copy writers, lay in the natural chemistry of the bog. "This peat contains the unique combination of high organic energy nutrients which were transferred to the skin of this man, keeping it young, soft and resilient for two and one half millennia."

Moreover, the dream of perfect preservation has led others to contemplate similar measures. During the early 1990s, the American film actress, Isabella Rossellini, the daughter of Ingrid Bergman and Italian director Roberto Rossellini, was riding high in her modeling career. She was the official face of the cosmetic firm Lancôme, appearing in all its major magazine, newspaper, and billboard ads. But shortly after celebrating her fortieth birthday, Rossellini received word that she was about to be fired: Lancôme no longer wanted her gracefully aging face to adorn their campaigns. Rossellini was crushed and angered by the news. A few weeks earlier, she had read an article about Sergei Debov, then the head of the Moscow Mausoleumists responsible for Lenin's body. She picked up her pen and wrote a letter to Lancôme, replying to her dismissal. "Dr. Debov," she observed archly, "may be of some help to us."

Rossellini was only trying to score a point, but others did not hesitate to embrace the preservative secrets of the mummies. During the late 1990s, spa enthusiasts in Scottsdale, Arizona, stretched their Visa limits for what one reviewer called "something mummifying" at the Camelback Inn. Once the campaign headquarters for American presidential hopeful Barry Goldwater, the fashionable resort boasted a well-known health spa. In 1998, it featured a ritual that would have sounded eerily familiar to any Egyptologist or mummy expert. Clients were first led into a dark room, where they were asked to disrobe and lie down on a towel-covered bed. A wrapper then appeared. Working slowly and methodically, she slowly draped their bodies in hot sheets of linen. Each piece of cloth was drenched in plant residues and oils: among the favorites were two arborial fragrances, eucalyptus and cloves. The cumulative effect, reported one reviewer, was a strange, soothing, otherworldly experience. "I fell into what seemed like semiconsciousness," she recalled later. "I loved it."

THOSE WHO ARE truly bent on self-preservation do not have to settle for such temporary measures, however. Real mummification is also available for a price in North America. In a pyramid-shaped building in Salt Lake City, Utah, Summum Mummification caters to the eternity-minded by blending ancient Egyptian lore with New Age mysticism and modern organic chemistry. Summum's founder, a licensed funeral director who goes by the name of Summum Bonum Amon Ra, but who likes to be called Corky, sees mummification as a kind of travel agency for the dead. Death, explains his company's Web site, is a confusing state for the newly expired. "You look for anything familiar that will help reduce your fears and the body you just left is the most familiar thing to you. Most people are buried or cremated and this places their spirit in less than favorable circumstances, leaving it to fend for itself. In mummification, the preserved body serves as a reference point for your soul, allowing communication of instructions that will help guide you to your new destination."

The staff at Summum are happy to pass on Ra's spiritual road map once they mummify your body. For a starting price of $60,000, Summum will fly your cadaver to its human mummification division in Boca Raton, Florida.

There, after washing your body with a sacramental wine in a "designated sanctuary," staff members will take out your viscera and inject your brain with a chemical preservative that will harden it. Then they will immerse your body and internal organs for up to a month in a secret chemical cocktail. When you are ready at last, Ra and his colleagues will haul you out; coat you with polyurethane and a mixture of glycerin, wine, and oils; wrap you in yards of linen gauze; and give you a few preservative coats of polyurethane or latex rubber and a final shellacking with fiberglass. You will then be slid into a cast-metal casket of your choice. One local talk-show host has ordered a coffin in the shape of a man holding a microphone.

If you want companionship, you can always take along a friend. Ra has already mummified his own dog Butch, a Doberman pinscher, and his tabby, Oscar. As he happily points out on his Web site the tradition of mummifying pets is a particularly time-honored one. Among the families of the ancient pharoahs, the young doted on their pets—hunting dogs, cats, gazelles, and monkeys. To preserve them forever, the Egyptian royals entrusted their pets' dead bodies to the embalmers, who coated the animals in resin and wrapped them in linen. Ra gladly offers to do much the same. For $14,000 and up, he and his colleagues will not only mummify your favorite hound or tabby Summum-style, they will also craft a bronze casket in the likeness of your pet. Obligingly, Ra includes detailed instructions for shipping a dead pet to Summum on his Web page. "Together with your beloved companion," he rhapsodizes, "Summum will lift you and set you into the hands of timelessness. Our mummification process makes it possible for you and your treasured pet to be together eternally."

Like many of his clients, Ra plans to be mummified himself; he hates to think of his own physical decay. "I spend a lot of time keeping my body in great shape," he told one interviewer. "I do aerobics, lift weights, and I'm proud of it." His wife, a bodybuilder, feels exactly the same way, as do many of their fitness-conscious clientele. But some Summum clients sign up for other reasons. A few Christian customers chose Summum because they wanted to put their best foot forward on Judgment Day, meeting their Maker in sterling condition. Others, the rich and famous mainly, view mummification as a mark of distinction. Ra won't divulge any names. "We did that a few years ago," he told me, "and our clients ended up in the tabloids. Their pictures were next to Boris Karloff's. We almost got sued." Summum is now trying hard to woo back the celebrities. Its plans call for a mountainside mausoleum that will enable great-great-grandchildren to ogle the sarcophagi of their ancestors through glass viewing windows.

Corky is not the only one willing to make you immortal, however. Engineers in the cryonics industry also have a game plan. They want to freeze your dead body so that it can be thawed and brought back to life—as soon as science figures out how to do it. In many respects, cryonics is an idea that the ancient Egyptians would have happily embraced: their greatest wish was to be preserved in such a way that their souls could once again inhabit their bodies. But exponents of cryonics aren't much interested in dead religions or the fusty past: their eyes are firmly fixed on the far horizons of the future and the rich possibilities of science. The father of human cryonic suspension, Robert Ettinger, first got the idea of this form of preservation from researchers' attempts in the 1940s to freeze frog sperm. If medicine could slip sperm into a state of suspended animation, then wake it gently back to life, why not other types of cells? And if that were possible, why not a whole body—a human one at that? Sci-fi writers in the 1960s and 1970s reveled in the idea. They swiftly peopled their novels and short stories with recycled humans.

Since then, cryonics has attracted its largest following from the Silicon Valley crowd, who are accustomed to forward thinking and rapid technological progress. In 1998, just over one-quarter of the more than four hundred signed clients for one of the world's largest cryonics organizations, Alcor Life Extension Foundation, in Scottsdale, Arizona, toiled in either the computer or engineering industries. Alcor prides itself on its scientific credentials. One of its founders, Fred Chamberlain, describes himself as a former NASA electro-optical engineer responsible for portions of the unmanned *Mariner, Venus-Mercury,* and *Voyager* missions into space.

Alcor takes an upbeat approach. Its staff members don't like using the word *dead* when they describe their clients: they prefer talking about "patients" and people who are "potentially alive." This optimism stems from something they call the "grace period," the length of time that human cells remain undamaged after the heart stops beating and the bloodstream stops toting oxygen and nutrients to the body's cells. Some thirty years ago, when physicians first developed cardiopulmonary resuscitation (CPR) to push oxygen manually through the lungs and blood through the circulatory system of someone in cardiac arrest, the grace period was about four minutes. Today, with the jump-start of hospital defibrillators, that has grown to about eight. Cooling the body extends the grace period much further: some people, particularly children who have drowned in cold water, have been known to survive virtually undamaged when resuscitated more than sixty minutes after their hearts stopped. These figures give cryonics supporters much hope for the future. "We believe," it says on the Alcor Web site, "that *so long as a person's brain cells and brain structure are properly preserved*, the person is still potentially alive, no matter how much time has passed without heartbeat or respiration. 'Death' is not the lack of heartbeat and breathing, even though it is still used in this archaic fashion. 'Death' is a state which cannot ever be reversed to restore life."

The only hitch is that science is not even close to finding a way to restore life Lazarus-like to a long-frozen human being. The problem is this: the human body consists of some 53 trillion microscopic cells; when these are frozen, the water within each begins to leak out. The minute droplets then freeze into jagged ice crystals that rip the delicate walls of neighboring cells like needles in a sea of balloons. Science currently has no way to mend 53 trillion cells. Cryonics supporters, however, seem unperturbed by this. They are fond of talking about the theories of Eric Drexler, the California guru of nanotechnology. Drexler envisions a world of bacteria-sized machines created by enzymelike assemblers, the engines of creation. By injecting huge armies of these invisible repair machines into a frozen body, Drexler and others hope to repair the trillions of rips and tears in the body's fabric.

All this optimism doesn't come cheap. To finance their own immortality, many clients take out special life insurance policies that pay out to the cryonics company of their choice. As with embalmers of every age, there is first-class cryonics, and then there is economy. At Alcor, some $120,000 to $130,000 will buy preservation of the entire body and all the trimmings; $50,000 will pay for conserving and storing the head only. People who take the budget route have to hope like hell that some medical researcher will not only happen upon a way to resuscitate the frozen dead but also devise methods for growing a new body from spare cells and gracefully grafting it onto the resuscitated cranium and brain. They also have to hope that Alcor outlives its founders by centuries, if not millennia, and that their insurance policies will be sufficient to pay for their long-term maintenance. A sense of humor certainly helps—animators for *The Simpsons* are fond of portraying clutters of bodyless heads in scenes of the future.

Alcor's clients also have to be prepared for some fairly drastic postmortem surgery. Upon receiving word of a client's impending death, the folks at Alcor promise to dispatch a CryoTransport team immediately to the scene. Once you are deemed clinically dead, they will begin administering drugs, packing you in ice, applying the automated equivalent of CPR, pumping out your blood, and injecting you with intravenous drugs designed to halt the process of cellular decay. Then you will be shipped off for major surgery in the Alcor headquarters in Scottsdale. Among other things, your head and chest will be shaved and your skull drilled with little holes to check for signs of swelling. Staff members will cut open your chest and saw your ribs apart. They will pump out all remaining blood with a bypass machine and replace it with chemicals designed to minimize damage to your tissues.

Clients who signed up for full-body preservation will then be enshrined in something that looks much like a giant stainless-steel Starbucks thermos. Instead of steaming java, it contains liquid nitrogen. People taking the budget route will have their heads placed in smaller canisters. In either case, their flesh will be chilled to minus 310 degrees Fahrenheit, at which point molecular motion reportedly dies almost to a standstill. According to the calculations of one science writer, decomposition requiring one second at body temperature will span thirty trillion years in that big chill.

If nothing else, such state-of-the-art medical technology promises to churn out hundreds of wondrously preserved mummies in the future. I confess I rather enjoy the image of entire warehouses stacked full of frozen Napster hackers, Yahoo programmers, and Apple engineers, complete almost down to their last DNA base pairs. But does Alcor's glorious vision of the future really mean that all these dot-com millionaires will be guaranteed their shots at eternity? It seems unlikely, for if the strange history of mummies shows us nothing else, it reveals just how much can go wrong when the dead are unable to lift a finger to defend themselves. Even the world's most devout mummifiers, the Egyptians, were prone to horrible foul-ups. They switched bodies, took out all the wrong organs, slapped on too much boiling resin, and slipped bodies into too little natron. They tied together already rotting limbs with the Egyptian equivalent of duct tape, then concealed their mistakes under yards of linen. Then the most unscrupulous spent their evenings plundering those they had embalmed just a few months earlier.

Eternity, moreover, lies at the whim of future generations, and who knows what they will make of all these twenty-first-century mummies? Five thousand years from now, when nameless treasure-seekers crawl down into the eerie darkness of a long-buried warehouse and stumble blindly like moles into rows of giant stainless-steel thermoses, now rusty and bent and toppled, who knows what will happen? Will these fearless adventurers pry off the lids and see long rows of ancient saints with delicate perfect hands and rosy cheeks? Will they, after offering up silent prayers, begin cutting out their hearts as sacred relics? Or will they size up this trove of ancient human flesh for its commercial potential and auction off its primeval DNA and untainted blood cells on some future version of eBay? Will they view these strange corpses as some quaint curiosity of ancient earth technology and cart them back as trophies to molder in their own galactic museums? Or will they disdain all this fleshy debris as just selfish clutter, yards of human bubble paper that should have been recycled long ago? And will they consign it to the nearest recycling bin?

Whatever they decide, there seems precious little chance that these rosy elders will sleep dreamless and undisturbed through the millennia. Mummies have always spoken to us on some deep primal level, and we are simply unable to leave them alone. We love them and we fear them, we aspire to be them and we dread that fate. But one thing is certain: we are powerless to resist their potent appeal. As long as humanity yearns for eternity, we will surely try to destroy our only material chance at it.

CODA

⁓

THE LABORS OF the world's mummy experts are clearly, unquestionably heroic. Confronted daily by our talent for destroying the ancient dead, they labor on nevertheless, preserving all they can of mummies. Few spare themselves in this grand quest. They empty their bank accounts and relinquish their holidays and retirement years, ignoring the bewildered looks of family and friends. They spend years sniffing out lost mummies in cobwebbed basements and filling filing cabinets with thick dossiers on missing bodies, hoping one day to encounter them in the catalogues of estate sales. They raise money to build entire new museums and acquire climate-controlled display cases. They examine mummies minutely. They calculate their height in life from the length of their femurs, and measure the thickness of their resin coatings, the width of their navels, and the eminence of their pubes. They debate earnestly among themselves the ethics of putting the ancient dead on display. They maintain coolly professional relationships with their subjects. They don latex gloves to conduct their examinations and refrain at all times from making personal jokes at the expense of the dead. They never talk lightly or unfeelingly about the mummies' ailments. Indeed, they often speak as if the mummies themselves can hear exactly what is being said.

By these daily acts of devotion, the world's mummy experts throw open the doors to lost worlds and lost times. They offer us proof, as clear as can be, that the distant past was not peopled with vague shadows and shades, but with men, women, and children who were very much like us. They show us that even the greatest kings and holiest saints were really human beings, people of flesh and blood and frailty. And they poignantly reveal, time and again, that even the most illustrious and legendary once suffered the common toll of humanity—disease, injury, and pain.

The scientists I first met at the Third World Congress on Mummy Studies, when all is said and done, are a most exceptional group of people. They are compassionate, considerate, and fiercely stubborn, lavishing the kind of devotion on the dead that most of us reserve for the living. They are some of the finest people I have met—bright, engaging, funny, exuberant, and full of life. I count it an honor to have made their acquaintance in Arica. I certainly look forward to seeing them again. And I have a good idea when and where that will be. The Mummy Congress organizers have already announced the host city for their next meeting: the tiny city of Nuuk, Greenland.

BIBLIOGRAPHY

Allen, T. H. 1996. The Silk Road's Lost World. *National Geographic*, March 1996, 44–51.

Allison, M. 1985. Chile's Ancient Mummies. *Natural History*, October 1985, 75–80.

American Academy of Cosmetic Surgery Conference, 2000. *Anti-Aging and Cosmetic Surgery Magazine* 3, 12.

Andrews, C. 1998. *Egyptian Mummies*. London: British Museum Press.

Arriaza, B. 1995. *Beyond Death: The Chinchorro Mummies of Ancient Chile*. Washington: Smithsonian Institution Press.

———. 1995. Chinchorro Mummies. *National Geographic*, March 1995, 68–89.

———. 1995. Chinchorro Bioarchaeology: Chronology and Mummy Seriation. *Latin American Antiquity* 6, 35–55.

———. 1998. Making the Dead Beautiful: Mummies as Art. *Archaeology*, online feature, 16 December 1998.

Asimov, I. 1963. *The Human Body*. New York: New American Library.

Aturaliya, S., Wallgren, J., and Aufderheide, A. 1995. Studies in Human Taphonomy I. An Experimental Animal Model. *Proceedings of the Ist World Congress on Mummy Studies 1992*. Tenerife: Museum Arqueologico Y Etnografico de Tenerife.

Aufderheide, A. C., and Rodriguez-Martin, C. 1998. *The Cambridge Encyclopedia of Human Paleopathology*. Cambridge: Cambridge University Press.

Balabanova, S. 1993. *Aber das Schnonste an ihr war ihr Haar, es war rot wie Gold*. Ulm, Germany: Universitätsverlag Ulm.

Balabanova, S., Parsche F., and Pirsig, W. 1992. Drugs in Cranial Hair of Pre-Columbian Peruvian Mummies. *Baessler-Archiv* 40, 87–92.

———. 1992. First Identification of Drugs in Egyptian Mummies. *Naturwissenschaften* 79, 358.

Balabanova, S., et al., 1992. Cocaine, Xanthine Derivates and Nicotine in Cranial Hair of a Pre-Columbian Peruvian Mummy. Paper read at the First World Congress on Mummy Studies in Tenerife, Canary Islands.

———. 1993. Was Nicotine Known in Ancient Egypt? *Homo* 44, 92–94.

———. 1996. Was Nicotine Used as a Stimulant Already in the VI Century A.D. from the Christian Sayala Population? *Journal of Paleopathology* 8 (1), 43–50.

———. 1997. Nicotine and Cotinine in Prehistoric and Recent Bones from Africa and Europe and the Origin of These Alkaloids, *Homo* 48, 72–77.

Barber, E. W. 1999. *The Mummies of Ürümchi*. New York: W. W. Norton and Company.

Barber, P. 1988. *Vampires, Burial and Death*. New Haven: Yale University Press.

Beaver, H. 1976. *The Science Fiction of Edgar Allan Poe*, London: Penguin.

Begona del Casal Aretxabaleta, M. 1995. La Droga en el Antiguo Egipto, *Estudios Egiptologicos* 2. Madrid: Asociacion Espanola de Egiptologia.

———. 1997. Alucingenos Para Viajar con los Dios, *Misterios de la Arqueologia* 1 (7) 33–37.

———. 1998. Los Conos de Unguentos, Estado de la Cuestion. *Boletin de la Asociacion Espanola de Egiptologia* 8, 220–228.

———. 1998. Plantas Para la Eternidad. Paper read at the Third World Congress on Mummy Studies, Arica, Chile, May 1998.

Bland, O. 1986. *The Royal Way of Death*. London: Constable.

Blumenbach, J. F. 1794. Observations on Some Egyptian Mummies Opened in London. *Philosophical Transactions of the Royal Society* 84, 175–95.

Breitman, R. 1991. *The Architect of Genocide: Himmler and the Final Solution*. New York: Alfred A. Knopf.

Brier, B. 1994. *Egyptian Mummies: Unraveling the Secrets of an Ancient Art*. New York: William Morrow.

———. 1998. *The Encyclopedia of Mummies*. New York: Facts on File, Inc.

———. 1999. Napoleon in Egypt. *Archaeology*, May/June 1999, 44–53.

Brier, B., and Wade, R. 1997. The Use of Natron in Human Mummification: A Modern Experience. *ZÄS* 124, 89–124.

———. 1999. Surgical Procedures During Ancient Egyptian Mummification. *ZÄS* 124, 89–96.

Budge, E. A. 1893. *The Mummy: A Handbook of Egyptian Funerary Archaeology*. Reprint. New York: Dover Publications, Inc.

Bull, D., and Lorimer, D. 1979. *Up the Nile: A Photographic Excursion: Egypt 1839–1898*. New York: Clarkson Potter, Inc.

Carter, C., and Mace, A. C. 1923. *The Discovery of the Tomb of Tutankhamen*. Reprint. New York: Dover Publications, Inc.

Cartmell, L. W., Aufderheide, A., and Weems, C. 1991. Cocaine Metabolites in Pre-Columbian Mummy Hair. *The Journal of the Oklahoma State Medical Association* 84 (1), 11–12.

Cartmell, L. W., et al. The Frequency and Antiquity of Prehistoric Coca-Leaf-Chewing Practices in Northern Chile: Radioimmumoassay of a Cocaine Metabolite in Human-Mummy Hair. *Latin American Antiquity* 2, 260–268.

Cartmell, L. W., Springfield, A., and Weems, C. 1995. Nicotine and Nicotine Metabolites in South American Pre-Columbian Mummy Hair. Paper read at the Second World Congress on Mummy Studies in Cartagena, Colombia.

Cartmell, L. W., and Weems, C. 1998. Overview of Hair Analysis for Drugs of Abuse and a Report of Hair Analysis for Cocaine and Nicotine from Dakhleh Oasis, Egypt. Paper read at Third World Congress on Mummy Studies in Arica, Chile.

Chagas' Disease Investigation, *Texas Preventable Disease News*, 4 August 1984.

Chriss, L. Drozd, S. 1999. The End of the Lines. *Men's Health*, October 1999, 94.

Cockburn, A., Cockburn, E., and Reyman, T. A. 1998. *Mummies, Disease and Ancient Cultures*. Cambridge: Cambridge University Press.

Cox, M. 1998. Grave Concerns: Death and Burial in England 1700 to 1850. CBA Research Report 113. London: Council for British Archaeology.

Cruz, J. C. 1977. *The Incorruptibles: A Study of the Incorruption of the Bodies of Various Catholic Saints and Beati*. Rockford, Illinois: Tan Books and Publishers, Inc.

Daly, N. 1994. That Obscure Object of Desire:Victorian Commodity Culture and Fictions of the Mummy. *Novel: A Forum on Fiction* 28, 24–51.

Dane, J. 1995. The Curse of the Mummy Paper. *Printing History* 17 (2), 18–25.

Dannenfeldt, K. H. 1985. Egyptian Mumia: The Sixteenth-Century Experience and Debate. *The Sixteenth-Century Journal* 16 (2), 163–180.

David, A. R. 1997. Disease in Egyptian Mummies: The Contribution of New Technologies. *The Lancet* 349, 1760–63.

————. 1998. *The Ancient Egyptians: Beliefs and Practices*. Brighton: Sussex Academic Press.

David, R., and Tapp, E. 1984. *Evidence Embalmed: Modern Medicine and the Mummies of Ancient Egypt*. Manchester: Manchester University Press.

David, A. R. and Tapp, E., eds. 1992. *The Mummy's Tale: The Scientific and Medical Investigation of Natsef-Amun, Priest in the Temple at Karnak*. New York: St. Martin's Press.

Davies, V., and Friedman, R. 1998. *Egypt*. London: British Museum Press.

Dawson, W. 1927. Making a Mummy. *Journal of Egyptian Archaeology* 13, 40–49.

Demieville, P. 1973. Momies d'Extreme-Orient. *Choix d'etudes Sinologiques (1921–1970)*. Leiden: Brill.

Dillehay, T., ed. *Tombs for the Living: Andean Mortuary Practices*. Washington, D.C.: Dunbarton Oaks Research Library and Collection.

Diodorus Siculus. 1985. *Diodorus on Egypt*. Translated by E. Murphy. Jefferson, North Carolina: McFarland & Company, Inc.

Dobbs, M. 1999. Kosovo: Six Hundred Years of Serb Defiance. *Moscow Times*, 31 March 1999, 9.

Dunand, F., and Lichtenberg, R. 1994. *Mummies: A Voyage Through Eternity*. New York: Harry N. Abrams.

El Mahdy, C. 1989. *Mummies, Myth and Magic*. London: Thames and Hudson.

Elerick, D. V. 1997. *Human Paleopathology and Related Subjects: An International Bibliography*. San Diego: San Diego Museum of Man.

Fatal American Trypanosomasis (Chagas' Disease) Texas, 1978. Photocopied report from Texas Department of Health.

Fischer, C., n.d. *Tollund Man and the Elling Woman*. Silkeborg: Silkeborg Museum.

Fornaciari, G. 1998. Renaissance Mummies in Italy. Lecture given at XXII Congress of the International Academy of Pathology, Nice, France.

Fornaciari, G., et al. 1989. Analysis of Pulmonary Tissue from a Natural Mummy of the XIII Century (Saint Zita, Lucca, Tuscany, Italy) by FT-IR Microspectroscopy. *Paleopathology Newsletter* 68, 5–7.

Found Two Cases of Chagas' Disease. n.d. *Texas Health Bulletin*.

Fowler, B. 2000. *Iceman*. New York: Random House.

Fulcheri, E. 1996. Mummies of Saints: A Particular Category of Italian Mummies. *Human Mummies: A Global Survey of Their Status and the Techniques of Conservation*. The Man in the Ice 3, 219–30.

Guhl F., et al. 1997. *Trypanosoma cruzi* DNA in Human Mummies. *The Lancet* 349, 1370.

———. 1999. Isolation of *Trypanosoma cruzi* DNA in 4000-Year-Old Mummified Human Tissue from Chile. *American Journal of Physical Anthropology* 108, 401–7.

Gabrielli, N., et al. 1996. Trattamenti Conservativi effettuati su Corpi di Santi e di Beati. Photocopy.

Germer, R. 1991. *Mumien: Zeugen des Pharaonreiches* (Zurich: Artemis and Winkler)

Glasschieb, H. S. *The March of Medicine: The Emergence and Triumph of Modern Medicine*. New York: G. P. Putnam's Sons.

Glob, P. V. 1965. *The Bog People: Iron Age Man Preserved*. Translated by R. Bruce-Mitford. London: Faber and Faber.

Gonzalez-Crussi, F. 1985. *Notes of an Anatomist*. San Diego: Harcourt Brace Jovanovich.

———. 1995. *Suspended Animation: Six Essays on the Preservation of Bodily Parts*. San Diego. Harcourt Brace Jovanovich.

Goodich, M. 1982. *Vita Perfecta: The Ideal of Sainthood in the Thirteenth Century*. Stuttgart, Germany: Anton Hiersemann.

Gould, S. J. 1996. *The Mismeasure of Man*. New York: W. W. Norton & Company.

Granville, A. B. 1825. *An Essay on Egyptian Mummies; with Observations on the Art of Embalming among the Ancient Egyptians*. Philosophical Transactions of the Royal Society of London 115, 269–319.

Greek Team Doubts Site Holds Alexander's Tomb. *New York Times*, 6 February 1995, A8.

Guillén, E. 1982. El Enigma de las Momias Incas. *Boletin de Lima*, 1982, 29–41.

Hadingham, E. 1994. The Mummies of Xinjiang, *Archaeology*, April 1994, 68–77.

Haggard, H. 1934. *The Doctor in History*. New York: Barnes & Noble.

Hamilton, R., ed. 1990. *Inca Religion and Customs by Father Bernabe Cobo*. Austin: University of Texas Press.

Herodotus. *The Histories*. Translated by G. Rawlinson. Reprinted 1998. London: J. M. Dent.

Hewett, D. 1997. This Mummy Is No Lady. *Maine Antique Digest*, 1997.

Holbert, R. D., et al. 1995. Chagas' Disease: A Case in South Mississippi. *Journal of the Mississippi Medical Association*, January 1995, 1–5.

Hori, I. 1962. Self-Mummified Buddhas in Japan: An Aspect of the Shugen-dô ("Mountain Asceticism") Sect. *History of Religions*, 1962, 222–42.

Ikram, S., and Dodson, A. 1998. *The Mummy in Ancient Egypt: Equipping the Dead for Eternity.* Cairo: The American University in Cairo Press.

Iserson, K. 1994. *Death to Dust: What Happens to Dead Bodies?* Tucson, Arizona: Galen Press, Ltd.

Jacobs, W. Toke Like an Egyptian. *Fortean Times* 117.

Jäger, U. 1998. The New Old Mummies from Eastern Central Asia: Ancestors of the Tocharian Knights Depicted on the Buddhist Wall-paintings of Kuchaand Turfan? *Sino-Platonic Papers* 84.

Kamberi, D. 1994. The Three-Thousand-Year-Old Charchan Man Preserved at Zaghunluq. *Sino-Platonic Papers* 44.

Katz, M., et al. 1982. *Parasitic Diseases.* Vienna: Springer-Verlag.

Kaye, L. 1994. Mummy Dearest: The Expensive Art of Preserving a Great Leader. *Far Eastern Economic Review*, 1 September 1994, 17.

Kean, L., and Bernstein, D. 1999. More than a Hair Off. *The Progressive*, May 1999.

Kipple, D., et al. 1998. Three Dimensional (3-D) Reconstruction Applied to Mummy Conservation and Display. Paper Read at the Third World Congress on Mummy Studies in Arica, Chile.

Kirsehnblatt-Gimblett, B. 1991. *Objects of Ethnography: The Poetics and Politics of Museum Display.* Washington, D.C.: Smithsonian Institute, 386–43.

Koch, E. 1998. *Neolithic Bog Pots from Zealand, Mon, Lolland and Falster.* Copenhagen: Det Kongelige Nordiske Oldskriftselfskab.

Leith, W. 2000. Isabella Rossellini. *National Post*, 7 October 2000, W6–W7.

Lenin for Sale, 1991. *Forbes*, 25 November 1991, 58–59.

Lepke, J. 1999. EN Rates Diet Books—Which to Choose, Which to Lose. *Environmental Nutrition*, January 1999, 2.

Levathes, L. 1987. Mysteries of the Bog. *National Geographic*, March 1987, 397–417.

Lombardi, G. 1999. Egyptian Mummies at Tulane University: An Anthropological Study. Master's thesis, Tulane University.

Lucas, A. 1914. The Question of the Use of Bitumen or Pitch by the Ancient Egyptians in Mummification. *Journal of Egyptian Archaeology* 1, 241–45.

———. 1914. The Use of Natron by the Ancient Egyptians in Mummification. *Journal of Egyptian Archaeology* 1, 119–23.

———. 1932. The Use of Natron in Mummification. *Journal of Egyptian Archaeology* 18, 125–40.

——. 1932. The Occurrence of Natron in Ancient Egypt. *Journal of Egyptian Archaeology* 18, 62–66.

Mair, V. H. Mummies of the Tarim Basin. *Archaeology*, March/April 1995, 28–35.

Mair, V. H., ed. 1998. *The Bronze Age and Early Iron Age Peoples of Eastern Central Asia*. Washington: Institute for the Study of Man, Inc.

——. A Collection of Papers on the Mummified Remains Found in the Tarim Basin. *Journal of Indo-European Studies* 23.

Mallory, J. P. and Mair, V. H. 2000. *The Tarim Mummies: Ancient China and the Mystery of the Earliest Peoples from the West*. London: Thames and Hudson.

Manniche, L. 1999. *An Ancient Egyptian Herbal*. London: British Museum Press.

Maples, W. R., and Browning, M. 1994. *Dead Men Do Tell Tales: The Strange and Fascinating Cases of a Forensic Anthropologist*. New York: Doubleday.

Meier, D. C., and Reinhard, K. J. 1998. Radiographic Assessment of Mummies for Museum Exhibit, Conservation and Research: A Case Study. Paper read at the Third World Congress on Mummy Studies in Arica, Chile.

McKinley, M. 1999. Earning a Halo. *National Post*, 24 April 1999, 17–19.

Merrillees, R. 1999. Opium for the Masses: How the Ancients Got High. *Archaeology Odyssey*, Winter 1999, 20–29.

Milei, J., et al. 1992. Does Chagas' Disease Exist as an Undiagnosed Form of Cardiomyopathy in the United States? *American Heart Journal* 123 (6), 1732–35.

Miller, S. 1999. *Finding Hope When a Child Dies*. New York: Simon & Schuster.

Moore, N. 1993. Drugs in Ancient Populations. *The Lancet* 341, 1157.

Morimoto, I. 1993. Buddhist Mummies in Japan. *Acta Anatomica Nipponica* 68, 381–98.

Nissenbaum, A. 1992. Molecular Archaeology: Organic Geochemistry of Egyptian Mummies. *Journal of Archaeological Science* 19, 1–6.

Nolli, G., et al. 1987. *Cardinale Josyf Slipyj: Relazioni sul trattemento conservativo eseguito sul suo corpo*. Rome: Editrice Elettrongraf.

——. 1987. *S. Chiara D'Assisi: Relazioni sul trattemento conservativo eseguito sui resti del suo corpo*. Rome: Editrice Elettrongraf.

Nott, J. C., and Gliddon, G. R. 1854. *Types of Mankind: Or Ethnological Researches, Based upon the Ancient Monuments, Paintings, Sculptures, and Crania of Races, and upon their Natural, Geographical, Philological and Biblical History*. London: Trübner & Co.

Parch, L. 1998. The Spa at Camelback Inn. *Home Arts*, May 1998.

Parsche F., Balabanova S., and Pirsig, W. Drugs in Ancient Populations. *The Lancet* 341, 503.

Pettigrew, T. 1834. *A History of Egyptian Mummies*. Reprint. Los Angeles: North American Archives.

Powledge, T., and Rose, M. 1996. The Great DNA Hunt. *Archaeology*, September/October 1996, 36–44.

Quigley, C. 1996. *The Corpse: A History*. Jefferson, North Carolina: McFarland & Company.

———. 1998. *Modern Mummies: The Preservation of the Human Body in the Twentieth Century*. Jefferson, North Carolina: McFarland & Company.

Ragon, M. 1983. *The Space of Death: A Study of Funerary Architecture, Decoration, and Urbanism*. Translated by A. Sheridan. Charlottesville: University Press of Virginia.

Rathje, W. L. 1999. Kosovo & the Archaeologists: Manipulating the Past to Change the Future. *Discovering Archaeology*, July/August 1999.

Reeves, N. 1990. *The Complete Tutankhamun*. Reprint. London: Thames and Hudson.

Reinhard, J. 1988. *The Nazca Lines: A New Perspective on Their Origin and Meaning*. Lima: Editorial Los Pinos.

———. 1992. Sacred Peaks of the Andes. *National Geographic*, March 1992, 84–112.

———. 1996. Peru's Ice Maidens: Unwrapping the Secrets. *National Geographic*, June 1996, 62–81.

———. 1997. Peruvian Mummies Revisited. *National Geographic*, January 1997, 36–43.

———. 1999. Frozen in Time. *National Geographic*, November 1999, 36–55.

Rivera, M. 1991. The Prehistory of Northern Chile. *Journal of World Prehistory* 5, 1–47.

Roberts, C., and Manchester, K. 1995. *The Archaeology of Disease*, Ithaca, New York: Cornell University Press.

Rose, A. 1999. No Surrender Is a Central Theme in Serb Folklore. *National Post*, 29 May 1999.

Rothhammer, F., et al. Chagas' Disease in Pre-Columbian South America. *American Journal of Physical Anthropology* 68, 495–98.

Rutherford, P. 1999. Immunocytochemistry and the Diagnosis of Schistosomiasis: Ancient and Modern. *Parasitology Today* 15, 390–91.

Ryabzev, V. 1997. Experiment That Lasted 73 Years. Translated by Natalia Dobrynin. *Technika Molodyozhy* 10, 18–26.

Sayed, A.M.A.H. 1977. Discovery of the Site of the 12th Dynasty Port at Wadi Gawasis on the Red Sea Shore. *Revue d'Egypt*.

———. 1978. The Recently Discovered Port on the Red Sea Shore. *Journal of Egyptian Archaeology* 64, 69–71.

———. 1983. New Light on the Recently Discovered Port on the Red Sea Shore. *Chronique d'Egypte* 58, 23–32.

Schmidt, G. D., and Roberts, L. S. 1989. *Foundations of Parasitology*. 4th ed. St. Louis: Times Mirror/Mosby College Publishing.

Sharf, R. H. 1992. The Idolization of Enlightenment: On the Mummification of Ch'an Masters in Medieval China. *History of Religions*, 1992.

Smith, E., and Dawson, W. 1925. *Egyptian Mummies*. New York: Dial Press.

Smith, G. E. 1915. *The Migrations of Early Culture: A Study of the Significance of the Geographical Distribution of the Practice of Mummification as Evidence of the Migrations of Peoples and the Spread of Certain Customs and Beliefs*. Manchester, England: Manchester University Press.

Spindler, K., 1994. *The Man in the Ice*. Toronto: Doubleday Canada Ltd.

Spindler, K., et al. 1996. *Human Mummies: A Global Survey of their Status and the Techniques of Conservation. The Man in the Ice*, vol 3. Vienna: Springer-Verlag.

Stanton, W. 1960. *The Leopard's Spots: Scientific Attitudes Toward Race in America 1815–59*. Chicago: University Press.

Steegmuller. F., ed. 1979. *Flaubert in Egypt*. Chicago: Academy Chicago, Ltd.

Sullivan T. D., et al. 1949. Incidence of *Trypanosoma cruzi*, Chagas', in Triatomoa (Hemipthera, Reduviidae) in Texas. *American Journal of Tropical Medicine* 29, 453–58.

Tanner, A. 1994. Lucky Stiff. *National Review*. 7 November 1994, 33–34.

Taylor, J. H. 1995. *Unwrapping a Mummy*. London: British Museum Press.

Team Claims to Find Tomb of Alexander in West Egypt. *New York Times*, 2 February 1995, A3.

Terribile Wiel Marin, V., Cappelletti. 1997. The Embalming Process of St. Gregorio Barbarigo. *Paleopathology Newsletter* 100, 5–7.

Tyldesley, J. 1999. *The Mummy: Unwrap the Ancient Secrets of the Mummies' Tombs*. Carlton Books.

Väisänen, L. Family Grief and Recovery Process When a Baby Dies. Ph.D. dissertation, University of Oulu, Finland.

van der Sanden, W. 1996. *Through Nature to Eternity*. Amsterdam: Batavaian Lion International.

———. 1996. Wetland Archaeology in the Province of Drenthe, the Netherlands. *Bog Bodies, Sacred Sites and Wetland Archaeology.* Proceedings of a conference held by WARP and the National Museum of Denmark, in conjunction with Silkeborg Museum, Jutland, September 1996, WARP Occasional Paper 12. Exeter, England: WARP (Wetland Archaeology Research Project).

Vauchez, A. 1997. *Sainthood in the Later Middle Ages.* Translated by J. Birrell. Cambridge: Cambridge University Press.

Verdery, K. 1999. *The Political Lives of Dead Bodies: Reburial and Postsocialist Change.* New York: Columbia University Press.

Wilson, M. E. 1995. Infectious Diseases: An Ecological Perspective. *British Medical Journal* 311, 1681–84.

Windshuttle, K. 1999. The Romance of Orientalism. *National Post,* 23 January 1999.

Wolf, N. 1991. *The Beauty Myth.* Toronto: Random House.

Woodcock, S. 1996. Body Color: The Misuse of Mummy. *The Conservator* 20, 87–94.

Woody, N. C., and Woody, H. B. 1974. Possible Chagas' Disease in the United States. *New England Journal of Medicine* 290, 749–50.

Xu, Y., n.d. *The Ancient Corpses in China.* Shanghai: Shanghai Scientific and Technological Education Publishing House.

Zbarsky, I., and Hutchinson, S. 1998. *Lenin's Embalmers.* London: The Harvill Press.

Zimmerman, M., Brier, B., and Wade, R. 1998. Brief Communication: Twentieth-Century Replication of an Egyptian Mummy: Implications for Paleopathology. *American Journal of Physical Anthropology* 107, 417–20.

Zwolak, J. 1999. A Tale of Two Mummies. *The Tulanian,* Spring 1999, 22–27.

———. 1999. A Tale of Two Mummies. *Inside Tulane,* 1 February 1999, 1.

ACKNOWLEDGMENTS

THE IDEA FOR this book emerged from a long, rather convoluted conversation I had three years ago with Polly Shulman, who was then at *Discover* magazine. I had just returned from the Mummy Congress, almost feverish with excitement over the wonderful stories I'd heard there, and as we talked, Polly glimpsed the germ of a book in my ramblings. Soon after, she mentioned the idea to one of her colleagues at Hyperion. I am exceedingly grateful to her.

I am also deeply in debt to Will Schwalbe at Hyperion, whose canny insights, probing questions, and judicious eye have so helped in guiding and shaping this book. I feel extremely fortunate to have worked with such a superb editor. I also want to extend my gratitude to Anne McDermid, a true force of nature and a wonderful literary agent who has been unstinting in her efforts on my behalf.

Sincere thanks also go to Wayne Grady and his colleagues at *Equinox* magazine, who dispatched me and photographer Peter Bennett to Egypt to cover the research at Dahkleh, and to Natalia Dobrynin, who was such good company in Moscow and graciously smoothed the waters there.

I also want to extend my deep gratitude to the many mummy experts who so generously gave of their time and helped me with this book. In addition to all those I describe or profile in these pages, there were many, many more researchers who patiently answered my letters and e-mails, guided me about on extended mummy tours, and, in ways too numerous to mention, immensely improved the quality of this book. I would particularly like to thank Salima Ikram, Eve Cockburn, Peter Lewin, Renate Germer, Gayle Gibson, Robert Sharf, Pia Bennike, Harco Willems, Maarten Raven, Otto Appenzeller, Renée Friedman, Bernard Faure, Wolfgang Pirsig, Olaf Kaper, Ronn Wade, Teodoro Hampe-Martinez, Trish Biers, Rose Tyson, María Begona del Casal Aretxabaleta, Niels Lynnerup, Gino Fornaciari, Wang Binghua, Xu Yongqing, Joanna Mountain, Richard Neave, Dieter Kessler, Diane Flores, Tony Mills, and El Molto.

Both Guido Lombardi and Pat Horne deserve special gratitude for all the digging up of obscure quotes and for repeatedly pointing me in the right direction in my research. And I would very much like to thank all the scientists who were kind enough to read through various portions of the text and correct my factual errors. This book has benefited enormously from their labors. The final responsibility for mistakes and omissions rests firmly, however, with the author.

Finally, I'd like to extend my heartfelt thanks to those who listened almost daily to my tales of the dead and to my moans about the difficulties of doing their stories justice: John Masters, Andrew Nikiforuk, Alex Pringle, and Kathleen Hodgson. Thanks are also due to Wendy Falconer and Mac McKinna, who generously shared their digs and their bountiful knowledge of London with me. Most of all, however, I'd like to extend my deepest gratitude to my husband, Geoff Lakeman, who listened to the most appalling stories of death and decay over the dinner table each night, then spiced them with his wit and humor. He now knows far more about mummies than he ever wanted to.

INDEX